The Saved
and the
Spurned

The Saved
and the
Spurned

NORTHERN IRELAND, VIENNA AND
THE HOLOCAUST

NOEL RUSSELL

NEW ISLAND

THE SAVED AND THE SPURNED
First published in 2024 by
New Island Books
Glenshesk House
10 Richview Office Park
Clonskeagh
Dublin D14 V8C4
Republic of Ireland

www.newisland.ie

Print ISBN: 978-1-84840-939-2
eBook ISBN: 978-1-83594-000-6

British Library Cataloguing in Publication Data. A CIP catalogue record for this book is available from the British Library.

Typeset by JVR Creative India
Edited by Seán Farrell
Cover design by New Island Books
Cover image: Alamy. Jews forced to scrub the pavement, Austria, 1938.
Printed by Opolgraf Printing House, Poland, opolgraf.com.pl

New Island Books is a member of Publishing Ireland.

10 9 8 7 6 5 4 3 2 1

For Mary

To those who came, and those who could not come

They're begging us, you see, in their wordless way,
to do something, to speak on their behalf
or at least not to close the door again.
Lost people of Treblinka and Pompeii!
'Save us, save us,' they seem to say,
'let the god not abandon us
who have come so far in darkness and in pain.
We too had our lives to live.
You with your light meter and relaxed itinerary,
let not our naive labours have been in vain!'

Derek Mahon, 'A Disused Shed in Co. Wexford'

CONTENTS

ABBREVIATIONS

AJDC	American Joint Distribution Committee
BCGR	Belfast Committee for German Refugees
BHC	Belfast Hebrew Community
BJRC	Belfast Jewish Refugee Committee
BDM	Bund Deutscher Mädel
CBF	Central British Fund for the Relief of German Jewry
CGJ	Council for German Jewry
COJE	Central Office for Jewish Emigration (Zentralstelle für Jüdische Auswanderung)
CZA	Central Zionist Archives
DÖW	Dokumentationsarchiv des Österreichischen Widerstandes (Documentation Archive of Austrian Resistance)
GJAC	German Jewish Aid Committee
IKG	Israelitische Kultusgemeinde (Jewish Community Organisation)
NIDA	New Industries (Development) Act, passed by Northern Ireland government in 1937
NSDAP	Nationalsozialistische Deutsche Arbeiterpartei (National Socialist German Workers' Party), the Nazis
PRONI	Public Record Office of Northern Ireland
SA	(Sturmabteilung) Paramilitary organisation linked to the Nazi Party, also known as stormtroopers or Brownshirts
SD	(Sicherheitsdienst) Security branch of the SS, Nazi intelligence agency and one of the key bodies responsible for the Holocaust

| SS | (Schutzstaffel) Nazi party organisation charged with planning and carrying out the so-called Final Solution, the extermination of Jews in the Holocaust |
| UDC | Ulster Development Council |

Acknowledgements

This book could not have been written without the generous help of a considerable number of people. I am especially grateful to a number of Holocaust survivors and their descendants who shared memories, family histories, memoirs and photographs. Their encouragement and advice throughout the research and writing has been inspiring. I would like to thank those who gave me interviews about their individual experiences or those of their families. Their stories are at the heart of the book. They include Ronnie and Shoshana Appleton, Michael Black, the late George Bloch, Lord Alf Dubs, Mel Goldberger, the late Walter Kammerling and his wife Herta, Billy Kohner and the late Ruth Kohner, Eric Langhammer, Vivienne Magee, Paul Sochor, George Szanto, Vivienne Vermes, Charlie Warmington, David and Siobhan Weiniger and Richard Weiniger.

Several descendants of those who played key roles in helping refugees enter Northern Ireland were most supportive, with interviews, family histories and answers to questions, including Dr Owen Finnegan, Dr Michelle Fink and Dr Tom McNeill. My research has also been helped by the work of other researchers and historians. I first became aware of this story after reading an article by the late Dr Eamon Phoenix in the Irish News. That started me on my quest to find out more about this little-known chapter in our history.

The following authors and scholars generously shared their knowledge and research, and patiently answered several queries: Dr Gordon McCoy, on the 7,000 Gibraltar evacuees, including 250 Jews, who came to Northern Ireland in 1944, another barely-known episode; Dr John Privilege and Dr Pamela Linden Aveyard, authors, respectively, of an important article on Stormont's New Industries Act and a pioneering doctoral thesis, 'Jewish identity and community in Belfast, 1920–1948'; Professor Gisela Holfter, leading expert on Irish-German Exile studies; Chris Hagan on east Down's important Jewish exiles; Ian Bartlett, the late David Bigger, Ken McCormack, Professor Emerita Carol Rittner and Philippa Robinson on the history of Derry's Jewish community; Dr Trevor McCavery, on the Ards factories of Alfred Neumann and Zoltan and Anny Lewinter-Frankl; Sean Beattie, on Donegal's Jewish connections.

When I started my research, two people immediately offered their support. Mel Goldberger told me about his father Otto's escape from a Nazi detention centre in Vienna and gave me Otto's memoir. Dr Sidney Katzen has been a constant help. A remarkable researcher, he has devoted many hours to tracing the family histories of several of the key figures in this book. His assistance has been invaluable, and this book has benefited greatly from his investigative talents.

Two fellow journalists, and friends, Charlie Warmington and Franziska Meinhardt, shared their family stories, and were 'hearers and hearteners of the work' throughout its long gestation.

The book has greatly benefited from my agent Jonathan Williams' encouragement and expert editorial nous, the support and guidance of my publisher, Djinn von Noorden, Mariel Deegan, managing director of New Island Books, and Seán Farrell's astute editing.

My research has been helped by the contributions of a large number of people. Several have given detailed interviews, while many others have offered advice, guidance on sources and assistance in the form of memoirs, photographs and other material. I can only list them briefly here but their contribution has been invaluable and I am indebted to them all: Gloria Apfel; Ronnie and Shoshana Appleton; Eva Arnott; Dr Pamela Linden Aveyard; Dr Sandra Baillie; Dr Brian Barton; Ian Beattie; Rachel Beniso; David Bigger; Michael Black; George Bloch; Nicholas Bloch; Sir Ken Bloomfield; Professor Emerita Charmian Brinson; Olga Cairns; Arthur Chapman; Ross Chapman; Dr Eóin Clarke; Julia Crampton; Yanky Fachler; Sonja Frank; Alan Franklin; Dr Owen Finnegan; Dr Winfried Garschka; Joseph Ghirardello; Paul Gilmore; Joe Gingell; Katrina Goldstone; John G. Gordon; Richard Gordon; Bronwen Haire; Dr Maurice Hayes; Roddy Hegarty; Daliah Hindler; Professor Gisela Holfter; Dr Steven Jaffé; Barry Kafka; Walter and Herta Kammerling; Marie-Claude Klein; Billy Kohner; Ruth Kohner; Eric

Langhammer; Mark Langhammer; Shirley Lennon; Dr Leon Litvack; Vivienne Magee; Dr Trevor McCavery: Ken McCormack; Dr Gordon McCoy; Fr Thomas McGlynn; Dr Finbarr McLoughlin; Lynn McNally; Gerry McNamee; Philip Newman; Dr Máirtín Ó Catháin;; Professor Pól Ó Dochartaigh; Robin O'Neill; Quentin Oliver; Trevor Parkhill; Mr Robert Ramsey; Professor Emerita Carol Rittner; Philippa Robinson; Stuart Rosenblatt; Jo Scott; Professor Karl Sigmund; Paul Sochor; Dr Damian Smyth; Philip Spain; Charlie Warmington; Dr Robert Tobin; John Trew; Vivienne Vermes; Dr Colin Walker; Dr David and Denise Warm; Richard Weiniger; David and Siobhan Weiniger; Dr Brigitte Ungar-Klein; Dr Fionnuala Carson Williams.

I am grateful to the staffs of the following libraries and archives: the Public Record Office of Northern |Ireland (PRONI); Queen's University Belfast; Trinity College Dublin; the Linen Hall Library, Belfast; Belfast Central Library; Derry Central Library; the Cardinal Tomás Ó Fiaich Memorial Library, Armagh; the Irish Quaker Historical Library, Dublin; the Wiener Library, London; the Library of Society of Friends, London; the National Archives, Kew; Documentationsarchiv des Österreichischen Widerstandes (Documentation Archive of the Austrian Resistance, DÖW), Vienna; Österreichische Nationalbibliothek (Austrian National Library), Vienna; Wiener Stadt und Landesarchiv (WStLA, Municipal and State Archives), Vienna; Niederösterreichische Landesarchiv und Landesbibliothek, St Pölten; the Central Zionist Archives, Jerusalem.

Thanks are due to the Arts Council of Northern Ireland, the Esme Mitchell Trust and the Anglo-Austrian Society for grants towards the completion and publication of this work.

'A Disused Shed in Co. Wexford' by Derek Mahon from The Poems: 1961–2020 (2021) is reproduced by kind permission of the author's estate and the Gallery Press. www.gallerypress.com

For any errors or omissions in the work, I alone am responsible, and apologise for them.

The person to whom this book is dedicated, my wife, Mary Kelly, has encouraged my work from the start, raised my spirits when they flagged, and inspired me to complete it. She read various drafts of the text, suggested many improvements, and sacrificed much while I worked on it. Her unflagging belief in the project has been vital to my finishing it. Our children, Michael, Daniel, and Lucy, have been enthusiastic supporters throughout the journey, and their generous backing helped shorten the road.

Introduction

In August 1938 a two-paragraph news item appeared in the only Jewish newspaper the Nazis allowed to operate in Vienna. It said that the Northern Ireland government had supported an Austrian Jew who was employing Viennese refugees in an Ulster factory, and was prepared to consider applications from employers and skilled workers who could train local people.

Immediately hundreds of letters from Viennese Jews started to arrive at the Ministry of Commerce headquarters in Belfast. A small number of civil servants had the job of appraising the applications; they rejected most of them. The applicants were simply told they had been refused or did not receive a reply. A number of employers and their families and some skilled workers were admitted. It is impossible to give exact figures, but a reasonable estimate is that up to 100 were granted entry under the scheme. Several of these employers created significant employment, particularly after World War II broke out in September 1939, and in many cases for several decades afterwards. In March 2008 the *Irish News,* in its daily column 'On This Day', reported a speech by Dr Conrad Hoffman, an American Presbyterian minister, in Belfast in May 1939. He told an audience at the YMCA about the persecution of the Jews in Germany and appealed for a more generous response to refugees seeking to come to the United Kingdom.

In a note below the column, the historian Eamon Phoenix gave details of Jews in Vienna who had applied to come to Northern Ireland in 1938. They included a woman whose son was already in a concentration camp, a distiller, and a jazz band. Hundreds had written letters asking to be admitted. Almost all had been refused. The policy of both the northern and southern Irish governments had not been generous. It had to be presumed that some of those who had applied had been killed in the Holocaust.

This shocked me. I had never heard about this story, nor about the probable deaths of persecuted Jews who had tried in vain to escape to Northern Ireland. I knew of the farm at Millisle, County Down, where Jewish children (up to the age of seventeen) from German-occupied Europe who arrived in the UK through the Kindertransport scheme were taken from July 1939 onwards, and where some stayed for a time after the war. In Northern Ireland people who are aware of the farm are rightly proud of it. But few have heard of the letters written by hundreds of Jews to the Ministry of Commerce in Belfast.

I decided to find out more. I read the letters, which are filed in the Public Record Office of Northern Ireland (PRONI). Then I began to contact some of the few surviving refugees who were lucky enough to be admitted to Northern Ireland. In 2009 I was working as a senior producer at BBC Northern Ireland in Belfast, and submitted a programme proposal about the story. The idea was not commissioned. I had other work commitments and had to postpone my research.

In June 2016, after leaving the BBC, I returned to the files. I read around 300 applications naming more than 700 men, women and children, nearly all from Vienna, but including fewer than fifty from Germany, Czechoslovakia, France, Switzerland and Hungary. The letters came from people in every walk of life – textile and clothing manufacturers, seamstresses, tailors, leather workers, engineers, doctors, lawyers, chemists, dress designers, musicians, photographers and fancy goods makers. The vast majority were highly qualified or skilled men and women. Many applied for themselves, their spouses and children, and several employers mentioned key workers. Some couples or single people applied just for themselves. Occasionally, applicants asked to bring ageing parents with them. Behind the people named in the letters were hundreds, if not thousands, of unnamed employees, relatives and colleagues.

The Viennese Jews who applied had heard of a scheme passed by the Northern Ireland government in December 1937. The New Industries (Development) Act was intended to reduce the state's chronic high unemployment, which then stood at more than 100,000.

It was aimed at creating jobs, not helping persecuted Jews in Europe, but the Stormont government was open to applications from foreign employers and skilled workers. Its primary purpose was to recruit employers or highly skilled trainers who could provide work for local people, not offer a rescue service to the victims of Nazi terror.

On 12 March 1938 the German army invaded Austria in the Anschluss (annexation). Immediately, thousands of Austrian Nazi anti-Semites took part in a vicious campaign against the country's Jewish population of 185,000, of whom 170,000 lived in Vienna.[1] Across Austria, they attacked Jews on the streets, in their homes and workplaces, and robbed them of money, possessions and property. So destructive was this 'wild', unofficial terror that even the SS was forced to threaten legal action against its fellow Nazis unless it stopped. The Nazi dictatorship immediately began official persecution, arresting thousands of Jews, political opponents and officials connected with the government led by Chancellor Kurt von Schuschnigg. They evicted Vienna's Jews from their homes, sacked them from their jobs and confiscated their businesses. All this was aimed at forcing Jews to emigrate while filling the coffers of the Hitler regime.

The PRONI letters are a precious record of the Viennese Jewish community, once one of the most creative and talented in the world, on the edge of catastrophe. In total, 65,000 Austrian Jews were murdered in the Holocaust. The vast majority of them were from Vienna, which in 1938 had the third largest Jewish population in Europe after Warsaw and Budapest, larger even than Berlin's. The Jews of Vienna produced outstanding contributions to European science, mathematics, philosophy, literature, economics, psychology, music, painting, sculpture and architecture. It was the city of Freud, Mahler and Schiele, among so many others. Jewish businessmen and skilled workers had also played a significant role in building up the Austrian economy.

But along with its cultural achievement, it was also a breeding ground for an anti-Semitism so virulent that the measures developed there in a few months in 1938, the so-called 'Vienna Model', became the blueprint for Nazi persecution and ultimately for Nazi genocide throughout occupied Europe. Of the people named in the letters, and refused entry by the Northern Ireland Ministry of Commerce, at least 125 Viennese, men, women and children were murdered in the extermination camps and ghettos of eastern Europe, and the concentration camps of Germany and Austria.

The letters give us a privileged access to that community as its members tried to escape the intense persecution it experienced. In them we hear the voices of a people under siege, forced out of their jobs and homes, liable to humiliation, violent attack, arbitrary arrest and imprisonment, pauperised, penalised in every sphere of their existence by hundreds of anti-Semitic measures, and fearful of their future. The letters contain details common to any CV, such as qualifications and work experience, from highly skilled professionals offering to create jobs for local people and seeking entry visas. They also provide us with rare personal records of hundreds of individuals and families, and their hopes and dreams of a new life. Many of them had been made destitute, and relied on Jewish soup kitchens for survival. The writers for the most part adopt a practical, respectful and business-like tone, but on rare occasions they express their desperation and plead for assistance.

The applications link Northern Ireland to Vienna and the Holocaust in a tangible way. They illuminate the plight of the entire Jewish community in Nazi-controlled Vienna on the eve of World War II, and Northern Ireland's response to the challenge of helping this beleaguered population. A small number of Northern Irish people did outstanding work in lobbying for refugees to be admitted and helping those who came. I have tried to record their role too.

Almost all those who came and those who helped have died. This book tries to tell the story of those admitted to Northern Ireland and what I could find out about those who were excluded. The majority of those rejected survived by finding other paths of emigration. Some went to France and the Low Countries, to Palestine, to North and South America, and to Australia. Several were captured by the Nazis in western Europe and murdered in the death camps. But we know most about the small numbers of people allowed in, who rebuilt their shattered lives in Northern Ireland. Where possible, I have spoken to them or their descendants. Several of those admitted left family members behind in Vienna, most often elderly parents, hoping to have them admitted to Northern Ireland. A lucky few succeeded, but many failed. Their parents and many of their closest relatives were murdered. Soberingly, these victims are now part of Northern Ireland's history too.

1

'PERISH JUDAH!'

In February 1938 the German Chancellor Adolf Hitler ordered his Austrian counterpart Kurt von Schuschnigg to Berchtesgaden in the Bavarian Alps. Historian Tim Bouverie captured the scene: 'There he subjected him to a diatribe on Austrian iniquities before forcing him, under threat of immediate invasion, to lift the ban on Austrian National Socialists and accept two Austrian Nazis, Arthur Seyss-Inquart and Edmund Glaise-Horstenau, into his government. The threat of *Anschluss* was clear …'[1]

Shocked and humiliated, on Wednesday, 9 March 1938 Schuschnigg announced a plebiscite for the following Sunday. He was confident of a strong 'Yes' vote in favour of Austrian independence. Next day, Vienna was awash with patriotic fervour, with demonstrators marching through every district shouting their loyalty. But on the Friday evening, Schuschnigg broadcast that the German government had ordered President Wilhelm Miklas to cancel the referendum, replace him with a Nazi chancellor and obey their choice of ministers in the Austrian government. They were giving way to brute force, Schuschnigg said. Hitler was fearful that he would lose the plebiscite, and the Nazi Arthur Seyss-Inquart took over as Chancellor. That night, moviegoers went to the cinema with the streets full of Austrian flags and pro-Schuschnigg slogans, and came out to find them already replaced with red, black and white swastika flags. German troops, tanks and artillery crossed the border at 5.00 a.m. and were given a rapturous welcome when they reached Vienna later that day.

They entered a city that had seen 'an enormous and comparatively rapid growth' of the Jewish population, from 6,217 in 1857 to 175,318 in 1910, which had 'aroused strong anti-Semitic sentiments among the local population. In no time at all the Jew had

1

become the proverbial scapegoat for the many faults of the "sick man of Europe", and anti-Semitic journals sprang up like mushrooms.'[2] Anti-Semitism increased when many small Jewish employers were forced into bankruptcy by the country's economic crisis and had to pay off their non-Jewish employees:

> The situation was further aggravated by the very high proportion of Jews in many trades and professions … The preponderance of Jews in vital fields of the economy, such as exports and tourism, and the influence of Jewish capital (Dr Desider Friedmann, the President of the Jewish community in Vienna, was on a mission abroad by the Federal Chancellor, Dr Kurt Schuschnigg, a few weeks before the Anschluss in an attempt to save the Austrian currency) made the Jew, in public opinion, responsible for the continuous economic crisis.[3]

The Austrian National Socialist Workers' Party had grown in strength since the early 1930s. It had been banned in 1933 by the Austrian government, and Nazis had assassinated the country's Chancellor, Engelbert Dollfuss, in a failed coup the following year. The left-wing Social Democrats staged an uprising in February 1934, but it was crushed and the party banned. Hitler increased pressure on Austria, and in July 1936 Schuschnigg concluded an agreement with the German Reich. 'The Austrian government undertook to suppress all anti-Nazi propaganda, to grant amnesty to Nazis in prison, to include the "national" minister Edmund Glaise-Horstenau in the government, thereby stepping up its discrimination against the Jews.'[4] Austria's Jews backed Schnuschnigg against Hitler, desperately hoping with other democratically minded sections of the community for the survival of Austrian independence.

As soon as German troops crossed the border, Austrian Nazis arrested thousands of members of the opposition parties, trade unionists, and of course Jews. The SS and the SA (Sturmabteilung, stormtroopers, the Nazi party's paramilitary wing) raided homes and dragged people off to makeshift prisons and concentration camps. Everything changed immediately for the city's Jewish population.

'Perish Judah!'

George Clare, aged seventeen, a Jew who became a writer,[5] described in his autobiography listening to Schuschnigg's broadcast with his family in Vienna:

> They played the national anthem. After the last few bars of Haydn's tune, we all sat in utter silence for a few moments. Then, before any of us had had a chance to say anything, the sounds of hundreds of men shouting at the top of their voices could be heard. Still indistinct, still distant, it sounded threatening none the less. Those raucous voices grew louder, were coming closer.
>
> I rushed to the window and looked out into Nußdorfer Strasse. It was still quite empty ... Then the first lorry came into sight. It was packed with shouting, screaming men. A huge swastika flag fluttered over their heads. Most of them had swastika armlets on their sleeves, some wore S.A. caps, some even steel helmets.
>
> Now we could hear clearly what they were shouting: '*Ein Volk, ein Reich, ein Führer!*' [One people, one empire, one leader] they were chanting in chorus, followed by '*Ju-da verrecke! Ju-da verr-rrecke!*' ('Per-rish Judah!') In English this sounds softer, less threatening, but in German, coming from a thousand throats, screaming it out in the full fury of their hate, as lorry after lorry with frenzied Nazis passed below our window, it is a sound one can never forget ...
>
> I was still looking out into Nußdorfer Strasse when I suddenly heard a muffled shout from right below our window. I craned my neck and saw an Austrian policeman, a swastika brassard already over his dark green uniform sleeve, his truncheon in his fist, lashing out with berserk fury at a man writhing at his feet.
>
> I immediately recognised that policeman. I had known him all my life. I had seen him on traffic duty at the nearby crossroads, had chatted with him when we occasionally met in the shops around the corner, had seen him give Father a polite salute in the street ... Within minutes of Schuschnigg's farewell, that policeman, yesterday's protector, had been

3

transformed into tomorrow's persecutor and tormentor. That was more terrifying even than the frenzied *'Ju-da verr-recke!'* Nothing could have driven home more clearly what had happened on this one day than this single incident ... We did not know what was yet to come, but we all knew that our life in Austria and a family history linked so closely with that country for so long, were over.[6]

Family friends of the Clares, the Ornsteins, had listened to Schuschnigg's speech with them. The words that Selma Ornstein spoke to her friend Stella Klaar, George's mother, stayed with him for the rest of his life: 'Tell me, Stella, what on earth did we talk about before? Maids, children, dresses, food? What world did we think we were living in?'[7] George Clare, his mother and a small number of other Viennese Jews made it to Ireland thanks to co-operation between the Irish government and Austrian employers there.

Anti-Semitic violence and pillage got underway immediately. Gangs of looters stole property, while Jewish shopkeepers watched powerlessly or were taken to Vienna's police stations, barracks or makeshift holding centres. The Nazis immediately set about a campaign of repression against anyone deemed to be an opponent or critic, arresting trade unionists, civil servants, bank officials, and political leaders of all persuasions. In the months following November 1938 Alfred Wiener and his colleagues at the Jewish Central Information Office in Amsterdam collected over 350 contemporary testimonies and reports of the pogroms in Austria and Germany that year.[8] An anonymous sixteen-year-old youth gave an account of his experience in the days following the Anschluss in Vienna:

Nowhere was safe for life as a Jew any more, since even a five-year-old boy had a knife 20 cm long, with which he threatened 'Saujuden' [Sow Jews] or was allowed to or should [*sic*] injure them.

I myself attended a Realgymnasium [grammar school] where the majority of pupils were Aryan. After Hitler invaded, the Aryan pupils beat the Jewish ones so severely that the Nazi director of our establishment felt obliged to issue the following instruction: 'Aryan pupils in future will not be aggressive towards Jewish pupils in the school building, since the fate of these people is being determined outside the school.'

I would like to point out that this directive naturally had not the slightest effect on the 'German-Aryan' pupils equipped with revolvers, knives, boots, brown and white shirts: they continued to come to lessons in the same garb and clearly showed that the Nazis were there now.

Another eyewitness reported how public humiliation and vicious attacks on Jews started immediately the Nazis took over:

The operations were applied with great vehemence directly after the Anschluss – one was continually asked on the street whether one was Aryan, and on replying in the negative [one was] taken away and involved in so-called Reibekolonnen [rubbing columns] for washing off slogans from the road embankments etc., which stemmed from the Schuschnigg vote. No consideration was given for women's clothing, they too had to kneel on the street and wash with very caustic bleach – an acquaintance of my wife sustained such a serious injury to her knee from it that the flesh on the bones came off and after three months the wound is still clearly visible ... Some of my acquaintances who are absolutely reliable, amongst them a young man of twenty-five, had their mouths smeared with shoe cream and ink poured in their mouths. Lorries are continually driven past cafés and take Jews away in large numbers, using them for 'Reiben' or shoe-cleaning or some such work.

Fourteen- to fifteen-year-old armed Hitlerjugend [Hitler Youth] members entered clothes shops and commandeered suits. Riot squads incessantly trundled through the streets, rarely intervening to help Jews. The Vienna SA behaved worst of all, whereas the German military were comparatively restrained and to some extent disapproved of the Vienna SA's approach.

In April, above all on Saturdays, Reibekolonnen of Jews were formed and marches organised on which signboards had to be worn by Jews, with the inscription 'Only a pig buys from Jews' and by Catholics with the inscription 'Jesuitisches Schwein' [Jesuit pig]. In this way so-called carnival processions were organised, which moved through the main avenue of the Prater [a large Viennese park] and ended with the Jews having to amuse crowds by dancing, jumping and crawling in groups.

The regime quickly started to deprive Vienna's Jews of their homes and livelihoods. Many businesses had already been unofficially looted and their owners attacked by anti-Semites immediately after the Anschluss. So bad were these unauthorised 'wild' thefts, that on 4 April Josef Bürckel, the Reich Commissioner for Austria, halted 'further arbitrary confiscations of Jewish property in order to prevent any more damage to the Austrian economy and to help restore Austria's trade, which had been hurt by an international boycott of its products'.[9] Bürckel did take proceedings against a tiny number of the Austrian Nazi 'commissars' who had stolen Jewish property without instructions from their superiors. Despite threats of action against those involved in such unauthorised confiscations, from Reinhard Heydrich, deputy leader of the SS, they were still going on in late April 1938. The official persecution of Jews increased. Bruce Pauley, a leading historian of Austrian anti-Semitism, has written:

> Jews were also excluded from most areas of public entertainment and to some extent even public transportation by the early summer of 1938; similar rules were not imposed on German Jews until November. The number of coffeehouses and restaurants that would not serve Jews grew from day to day. All the public baths and swimming pools were closed to Jews. Park benches all over the city had the words 'Juden verboten' [Jews forbidden] stencilled on them. Jews were not admitted to theatre performances, concerts, or the opera. Numerous cinemas had notices saying that Jewish patronage was not wanted. Sometimes Jews were ejected from a motion picture theatre in the middle of a performance if Gentiles complained about them.[10]

The Gestapo and SA arrested Jews talking on the street, took them to police stations and interrogated them separately, the slightest difference in their stories leading to their arrest. Herbert Rosenkranz, the greatest chronicler of Austrian Jewry in World War II, described the hate-filled atmosphere: 'SA men prevented "Aryans" from buying from Jewish shops, which had to be marked as such by their owners. Anyone who did patronise a Jewish shop was paraded through the streets with a placard, reading "This Aryan swine buys from Jewish shops", much to the delight of non-Jewish Viennese shopkeepers.'[11]

Jewish religious figures were particularly vulnerable to attack, as historian Doron Rabinovici noted: 'Torah scrolls in synagogues were burnt. Orthodox Jews were dragged through the streets and their beards shaved off, to the delight of onlookers. The victims were fair game for anyone to give vent to their passionate hatred, envy or personal dissatisfaction or bad mood. The Viennese anti-Semites were able to indulge in this witch-hunt with jeering cynicism.'[12]

On Sunday, 13 March, the day after Nazi troops entered Vienna, the SS and SA arrested 150 Jewish bankers and businessmen. The offices of Zionist organisations were vandalised, robbed and shut down. That night, 'armed SA men and civilian plunderers roamed the streets, looting Jewish synagogue offices and taking action without authority against Jewish functionaries'.[13] All Jewish newspapers were closed down.

On 15 March 1938 Adolf Hitler told a delirious crowd of up to 250,000 Austrians in Heldenplatz (Heroes' Square) in Vienna: 'Today I report to history Austria's return to the German Reich.' He had fulfilled his threat in *Mein Kampf* that he would unite Austria with Germany, by any means possible and by force if necessary.[14] Leo Lauterbach visited Vienna as an emissary of the Executive of the World Zionist Organisation and reported on the effects of the intimidation campaign on Vienna's Jews: 'It revealed to them that they did not merely inhabit a fool's paradise but hell itself. No one acquainted with the average Viennese of those times would have believed it possible that they could sink to such levels.'[15]

The Nazis quickly announced that Austrian men aged over twenty were eligible to vote in a plebiscite on Austrian unification with Germany on a date to be decided. Jews were barred from voting.[16] On Friday, 18 March the Nazi authorities entered the offices of the Israelitische Kultusgemeinde (IKG, the Jewish community organisation), beside the main synagogue in Seitenstettengasse in central Vienna, and plundered the building. That same day, Adolf Eichmann, a Second Lieutenant in the Sicherheitsdienst (SD, the security branch of the SS) arrived in Vienna from Berlin. The fate of the city's 170,000 Jews was soon primarily in his hands.

Adolf Eichmann was born in Solingen, an industrial town in the Rhineland, in 1906 and had been brought to Linz in Austria at the age of eight. His father, Adolf Karl, had gone ahead the year before as commercial manager for the Linz Tramway and Electricity Company. His mother, Maria, followed with her eldest son Adolf and her four other children. The family were committed Protestants living in a largely Catholic city of 100,000 people. Eichmann's mother died in 1916 and his father, an elder in the Evangelical church, quickly married Maria Zawrel, whom he had met at a church meeting, and who was also a devout Protestant. She was from a prosperous family well-connected in Viennese circles. Some of her relatives had married into equally well-to-do Jewish families.[17]

Adolf Eichmann performed poorly in both the secondary schools he attended, and left without any formal educational qualifications. His father managed to find him work with a mining company, then as a salesman with the Austrian Tech company. But at the age of nineteen, using his family's Jewish connections, he obtained a position as a travelling salesman for the Vacuum Oil Company. He was good at his job, organising oil deliveries across Upper Austria, but his Jewish employers paid him off in 1933, according to one account, because he was a member of the Nationalsozialistische Deutsche Arbeiterpartei (National Socialist German Workers' Party, the Nazis).[18] However, Eichmann's biographer David Cesarani argued persuasively that his Nazi views had nothing to do with his sacking. Business was slack and single employees were paid off first. He was given a generous dividend, left amicably and sought to join the German branch of the company.[19]

Soon his career as a salesman was left behind. He had joined the Austrian Nazi party and SS in 1932. At some stage in the 1930s, his father followed him into the party. He was soon moved to Department

II 112, at the Reichssicherheitshauptamt (Reich Security Head Office) in Berlin, where he became departmental head of Zionist affairs. He visited British-occupied Egypt in 1937, and tried and failed to go to Palestine, though he later falsely maintained he had visited there. When he became a powerful SS figure in Vienna, he even told its Jewish leaders he had been born in Palestine. He had picked up a few words of Yiddish and Hebrew, could quote from Viennese academic Adolf Böhm's authoritative *History of Zionism*, and now positioned himself as an expert on Jewish affairs. He was determined to gain promotion quickly, at the expense of Austria's Jewish community.

Known to posterity as the balding, bespectacled, nervous 'man in the glass booth' of his trial in Jerusalem in 1961, in Vienna he cut a very different figure. 'And then came Eichmann, like a young god; he was very good-looking, tall, dark, radiant in those days. The pictures of him today bear no resemblance to how he used to be', said a survivor, Adolf Brunner.[20]

Eichmann came from Berlin on 16 March with a list of prominent Austrian Jews who were to be arrested, particularly the leaders of assimilationist organisations such as the B'nai Brith. On 18 March, he took part in the raid on the IKG premises. He directed the removal of documents, membership lists and 'evidence' of 'subversive' activities, such as Jewish support for the legally constituted Austrian government. Two huge removal vans took this material to SD headquarters in Berlin, where it was sifted: 'More arrests and imprisonments flowed from their research. Jews were subsequently killed in concentration camps on the strength of "evidence" from Eichmann's Sonderkommando (special unit)'.[21]

The SD under Eichmann found receipts for the IKG's contribution to the Schuschnigg referendum campaign, and arrested the leaders of the Jewish community in the building, including the IKG president Desider Friedmann, vice-presidents Josef Ticho and Robert Stricker, and administrative director Dr Josef Löwenherz. Many religious leaders, whether member of the ruling Zionist grouping or the opposition Union (assimilationists), were also taken into custody. The Nazis found paperwork confirming a Jewish contribution of 500,000 Reichsmarks to the Schuschnigg referendum fund, and forced them to pay an equivalent sum 'in compensation'.[22] But while the SS plundered the building, three senior welfare workers at the IKG, at great risk, managed to save the money itself and used it to help Jews unofficially. They met with members of the community in cafés and at the Jewish Rothschild hospital, and arranged assistance for those most in need.[23]

Welfare workers also set up a Jewish self-help service, which now offered the only assistance available for thousands of Jews who had lost everything. The American Joint Distribution Committee (AJDC, the 'Joint') and the British Council for German Jews were among the organisations that supported the Jews of Vienna with subsidies. In Leopoldstadt, the main Jewish district, eight free kitchens were set up with financial aid from overseas:

> Poor relief had to be extended to all those who, after the Nazis came to power, no longer had accommodation or income. Now there were 8,000 people instead of 800 previously who had to be fed. Free meals were distributed eight times a day. The SA and Bund Deutscher Mädel (League of German Girls, BDM) took delight in disrupting the distribution. They upturned the tureens on the street and stole food.[24]

Eichmann called a meeting of eighty representatives of the city's Jewish organisations in late March 1938. A Holocaust survivor, Yehuda Brott, formerly Weissbrod, recalled: 'Eichmann sat at a desk in the large room of the Palestine Office. The room was completely empty; I remember Eichmann sitting there at the end of the room, like when people were summoned by Mussolini. There were no chairs and everyone had to give their reports standing up. I gave my report and was dismissed.'[25]

Eichmann was unashamedly anti-Semitic in his behaviour. He ordered Jewish leaders to stay at least three steps away from him, and refused for 'ideological reasons' to shake hands with Jewish representatives or even Zionist emissaries. 'He berated, threatened and taunted the Jews.'[26] He enjoyed humiliating senior members of the Viennese Jewish community, particularly Dr Josef Löwenherz; he kept him standing for hours, while offering a representative of the Graz Jewish community a chair. On one occasion he slapped Löwenherz, an academic and lawyer twenty years his senior, in the face.

In April 1938 Eichmann had Löwenherz, still in custody, brought to him at Rossauer Lände police prison. He told him to prepare a plan to enable 20,000 Jews without means to emigrate from Austria within a year and had him released. A week later, Löwenherz gave Eichmann a thirty-page draft report. Eichmann rejected it and told him Jewish functionaries in prison were not to be included. A second draft was also rejected and modified. On 28 April, Eichmann told Löwenherz and Dr Alois Rothenberg, of the Palestine Office – responsible for community affairs – that the IKG offices would open on 2 May 1938.

On 1 April the Nazis had sent the first train to Dachau concentration camp, carrying 150 'Prominents' – former leading politicians, government officials, and military and police officers. It included 61 Jewish prisoners, among them well-known community leaders, political and cultural figures, and employers. Eichmann boasted to his superior Herbert Hagen in Berlin: 'I'm in total control here. They don't dare take a step without checking with me first. That's how it should be since it guarantees better ways of keeping them on their toes … At least I lit a fire under those gentlemen, believe you me!'[27] He shared details with Hagen of his plan to accelerate the expulsion of 20,000 Jews within a year. Far more would be forced out within months, much to Eichmann's delight.[28]

Eichmann was also proud of his new role as censor of the *Zionistische Rundschau*, the Jewish weekly: 'In a way, it will become "my" paper.'[29] The Nazi authorities had closed down the city's eight Jewish-owned newspapers immediately after the Anschluss, but opened this periodical in May 1938 to help deal with the chaos created by their anti-Semitic measures. They insisted on a new title, the *Zionistische Rundschau*, instead of the old *Judische Rundschau*, a blunt statement of Nazi intent to drive out the country's Jewish population.

With a circulation of about 30,000 in Vienna, the weekly was avidly read by the city's Jewish community. The paper was both a Nazi-controlled propaganda sheet to encourage Jews to emigrate and a community newspaper. It carried features and photographs of smiling pioneers working the land in Palestine, news reports on visas and emigration, and a weekly Hebrew lesson. Soon its classified advertising carried growing lists of men and women desperately seeking marriage partners, who might aid their emigration. Of course, no mention of the intense and brutal persecution of the Jewish community was allowed. Leo Lauterbach was one of the first to realise that Vienna was now a laboratory for methods to expel Jews as quickly and as profitably as possible. He made a chilling prediction:

> A clear policy with regard to the Jewish problem in Austria has neither been announced in public, nor was it conveyed to us in the few interviews we succeeded in having. One cannot, however, avoid the impression that this policy will be essentially different from that adopted in Germany and that it may aim at a complete annihilation of Austrian Jewry. To all appearances, it is intended to eliminate them from economic life, to deprive them of all their financial resources, and to compel them either to starve or to leave the country without means, at the expense of the great Jewish organizations abroad and with the help of such countries as may be willing to receive them.[30]

Within weeks of the Anschluss, tens of thousands of the city's Jews had lost their jobs, and in many cases their homes, and were penniless. The Nazi persecution of Jews benefited Aryan Vienna. With German spending on armaments in Austrian industry, unemployment was reduced from 536,000 to 416,000 within two months. White-collar workers, many of them Social Democrats dismissed by the Dollfuss-Schuschnigg regime, replaced Jewish state officials on 15 March 1938. Jewish judges were sacked two days later. Lawyers were obliged to wear the swastika, and cases involving Jews were often decided in advance by statements in red ink on the papers saying, 'The defendant is a Jew!' On 31 March Jewish lawyers and patent agents were 'provisionally' prohibited from practising their professions.[31]

On 16 March 1938 the text of the referendum question, now set for 10 April 1938, was published, and reported in the Northern Ireland press. Voters would be asked: 'Do you acknowledge Adolf Hitler as our Führer and acknowledge the reunion of Austria with the German Reich, which was effected on 13 March 1938?' Even the wording was a lie. Austria had never been 'united' with Germany. That afternoon, there was an immediate response from Viennese Nazi supporters:

Jubilant crowds invaded the Jewish quarter in the Leopoldstrasse, where families were hauled from their homes and ordered to get down on their knees to scrub from the pavements the printed slogans such as 'Hail Schuschnigg', which were part of the plebiscite campaign. Later in the day, the S.S. Police [Black Guards], arrived to supervise this proceeding.[32]

The *Belfast Telegraph* ran reports by G. E. R. Gedye, the *Daily Telegraph's* expert correspondent in Vienna. He reported that notices such as 'Jews not wanted here' had appeared in restaurants and bars. The cleaning of the pavements caused large crowds to assemble and jeer at the Jews, shouting, 'Who has found work for the Jews? Adolf Hitler!' In the Austrian passport offices, six notices had appeared since 14 March, with the ominous words 'All Frontiers are Closed to the Jews'. The paper reported 'Frantic efforts of Jews to get across Czechoslovakia', with Nazi sources stating that stormtroopers were exercising 'strict control'. It said that all over Vienna big Jewish cafés, shops and hotels were being seized. Gedye noted that one Berlin Nazi had expressed astonishment at the speed with which anti-Semitic measures were being introduced, far quicker than in his city.[33]

On 27 March the Austrian bishops, led by Cardinal Theodor Innitzer, Archbishop of Vienna, in a declaration read in all churches, called on the faithful to vote for unification with Germany:

We joyfully recognise that the National Socialist movement has done and is doing great things for the German Reich and people both in the matters of social and economic policy, and particularly for the poorest classes of the people. We are also convinced that the danger of the all-destroying Godless Bolshevism has been averted by the effects of the National Socialist movement ... It is naturally the national duty of us Bishops on the day of the Plebiscite to declare ourselves for the German Reich, and we also expect all believing Christians to realise what they owe to their people.[34]

The German Official News Agency warmly welcomed the bishops' statement: 'The whole German people learns of this declaration with joy and sincere satisfaction. It should have the effect of opening a new chapter for it proves that at this eventful time for the whole German people the Catholic church also wishes to find its place in the new State.'[35] Four years after Austrian Nazis murdered the Austrian Catholic Chancellor Engelbert Dollfuss in an attempted coup, and less than three weeks after the Germans had invaded Austria, the Church's leaders were now endorsing the dictatorship. Innitzer's stance took many in Austria by surprise. He had been friendly towards the Jewish community, but he had greeted Hitler with the Nazi salute on his first meeting with him on the day after he arrived in Vienna. The Vatican was displeased, and he was called to Rome and criticised for his behaviour.

The head of the main Lutheran denomination, Dr Robert Mauer, also published a greeting to the Führer, welcoming him to Austrian soil in the name of more than 330,000 Protestants in Austria: 'After an oppression which revived the worst times of the Counter-Reformation, you come, after five years of the direst need, as a rescuer of all Germans without distinction of faith. God bless your path through this German country, your homeland!'[36] Bells were ordered to be rung in Protestant churches to celebrate the new order.

After a month of terror and the crushing of democratic opposition, 99.7 per cent of the Austrians who voted backed the Anschluss. But the intense persecution had one unexpected result, as George Clare wrote:

> The paradox of Vienna's volcanic outburst of popular anti-Semitism was that it saved thousands of Jewish lives. The 'lousy anti-Semitism' of the Germans led many German Jews to believe that they could go on living in their beloved Germany, while the 'first-class anti-Semitism' of the Austrians left no Jew in any doubt that he had to get out of the country as quickly as possible.[37]

2

'BABY-COFFINS WERE COMING OUT OF EVERY STREET'

Northern Ireland in the 1930s was a place of chronic high unemployment, stark inequality, and sectarian discrimination. Slum housing and poor health services afflicted working-class areas of both the Catholic and Protestant communities. The 'hungry Thirties' was a period of prolonged economic depression, only briefly mitigated by temporary booms in production in key industries such as shipbuilding. In February 1938, 29.5 per cent of insured industrial workers were unemployed, the highest figure in the United Kingdom.[1]

A Methodist Church survey found that 76 per cent of 705 households were living below the poverty line in one area of Belfast in the winter of 1937/38. Poverty, inadequate health care and bad housing were a lethal combination. In 1938 Belfast had the highest rate of infant mortality compared to six British cities, ninety-six per one thousand, as against fifty-nine in Sheffield. Belfast woman Anne Boyle recalled: 'There was so much infant mortality that it seemed as if every week blue baby-coffins were coming out of every street. I had three brothers and a sister dead before they were two years old, out of eleven of us.'[2]

The Northern Ireland government had little success in overcoming its persistently high unemployment in the 1930s. It passed a New Industries Act in 1932, offering incentives to new and existing businesses, but only seven new companies employing 6,000 people were set up between 1932 and 1937.[3] The British government introduced a similar scheme in 1934, the Special Areas Act, covering the worst jobless areas, but it was not a success. So, the Special Areas commissioners were from 1936 onward willing to consider foreign industrialists, and sent representatives to Europe to persuade them to relocate. British consular staff in Germany and Austria made it known that they would grant residence permits and entry visas with minimal delay to those willing to set up business in Special Areas.

There was, however, no question of Northern Ireland benefiting from the Special Areas Act. It was the only region of the United Kingdom to have its own devolved government, which was responsible for economic policy and industrial development. Under the 1932 Stormont Act, it could offer only free sites and local rate rebates, while industrialists in Britain would have better access to raw materials and the huge London market. Neither could it offer new businesses a monopoly and protection against outside competition, unlike the Irish Free State government. So the Stormont government passed the New Industries (Development) Act in December 1937, with inducements similar to those in Britain – grants and loans for new and existing businesses, as well as training subsidies and relief from local rates and income taxes.

MPs at Stormont welcomed the new Act, though Harry Midgley, the Labour member for Dock in Belfast, warned about southerners taking advantage of it to 'steal' jobs from Ulster workers. The Northern Ireland government, however, was still at a disadvantage compared to the British government. It could not conclude trade agreements with foreign governments, nor recruit refugee industrialists in Europe, as the Special Areas bodies were doing. Instead, Stormont lobbied the Home Office to have its consular officials abroad bring Northern Ireland to the attention of businessmen. By June 1938 Northern Ireland's Ministry of Commerce officials were frustrated because they could not even obtain the Home Office questionnaires used to assess business proposals from foreign industrialists.[4]

But the Ministry of Commerce in Belfast did not rely solely on the Home Office to sell Northern Ireland to refugee businessmen. In November 1937 it set up the Ulster Development Council (UDC) under the chairmanship of Sir Roland Nugent, Northern Ireland senator and former director of the Federation of British Industries. Its role was to publicise the attractions of Northern Ireland for industrialists thinking of setting up new businesses. It also offered advice on whether a business proposal deserved support under the New Industries Act.

The Ministry of Commerce was responsible for recruiting employers, including foreign business owners, and evaluating their proposals before making recommendations to the Ministry of Home Affairs. The British government retained control over the admission of foreigners, but Stormont's Ministry of Home Affairs could apply for visas and residence permits for them to the Home Office in London. These were usually granted. An advisory committee of civil servants and local industrialists was set up to help the Ministry of Commerce. It was soon playing a central role in deciding which business proposals to support, and which foreigners to allow into Northern Ireland.

Events in Vienna quickly influenced developments in Northern Ireland. The Nazi measures to force Jews out of jobs and housing made thousands of Vienna's Jews desperate to escape. This huge talent pool included experienced Jewish factory and small-business owners, and highly qualified professionals, such as engineers and technicians, as well as thousands of skilled workers, many of them women, from Vienna's large clothing industry. But just as the Nazis in Vienna made life impossible for its Jewish citizens, Britain made it harder for them to come.

German and Austrian passport-holders had been able to enter Britain without a visa since 1927, and the British cabinet decided not to impose visa restrictions after the Nazis came to power in Germany in 1933. Restricting Jewish immigration then would have meant reintroducing a visa requirement for all German citizens. Instead, refugees with German passports continued to be processed on arrival at British ports. It would have been easy to terminate the agreement with Germany, but the Germans could have retaliated and imposed visas on British travellers, which would have been inconvenient and expensive for applicants and tedious for officials.[5]

In March 1938, as a Jewish exodus from Austria seemed likely, the Home Office was considering reintroducing visas for both Germans and Austrians. Ten thousand Jewish refugees were then in Britain and the numbers of Austrian Jews arriving increased after the Anschluss. A few days later, the Council for German Jewry (CGJ), running out of money, informed the Home Office that it could support only Jews already in the United Kingdom, but not new arrivals. On 1 April, the Home Secretary, Sir Samuel Hoare, told a

Jewish delegation that visas would be reintroduced. The last thing they wanted 'as a nation, was a Jewish problem'.[6] Otto Schiff, the Jewish delegation leader, agreed.

The Home Office Aliens Department tightened up the rules for Austrian immigrants even before the visa requirement started. Refugees had to register immediately with the police, could not accept work, and would be admitted only on a three-month time limit. The Home Office said 'that sympathy would be shown to refugees but that a policy of indiscriminate admissions was not possible'.[7] No public guidance was given on which applications would be granted. In the words of historian Louise London, the Home Office felt 'no obligation to admit more than a select few persecuted Jews from the continent'.[8]

Austrian passport holders needed visas to enter Britain after 2 May 1938, and German passport holders after 21 May. The Foreign Office enlisted the German Jewish Aid Committee to deal with queries for assistance or advice. The Aliens Department of the Home Office sought the aid of the Co-ordinating Committee, an umbrella organisation of the main refugee organisations. This distanced civil servants from the dire circumstances of Jews seeking admission.[9]

In Vienna, the Society of Friends helped thousands of Jews fill in visa application forms. The IKG, the only significant Jewish organisation allowed to operate by the Nazis, also became involved in helping Jews apply to come to Britain as domestic servants. But the introduction of visas slowed up decision-making, and within six months 10,000 applicants were awaiting judgement.[10] Sir Warren Fisher, the permanent secretary of the Treasury, submitted a line for ministerial approval:

> The principal element is of course the Jews, who are exposed to unspeakable horrors. It is clear that however much we may sympathise, we cannot provide a solution of this terrible problem (which is not confined to Germany) ... I think we shd [sic] be well advised from every point of view – if not for reasons of humanity – to keep open minds (without avowing it) & be on the look-out for the opportunity of intelligent assistance. (This of course won't help the majority of these poor people.)[11]

The Chancellor of the Exchequer, Sir John Simon, initialled these suggestions without comment. Eighteen months after Nazi persecution in Austria began, the British government had severely tightened its rules on admission, and refused to create funds for often destitute refugees.[12] The sole exceptions, where refugees were offered financial help, was the British Special Areas scheme and the Northern Ireland government's New Industries Act. The 11,000 German and Austrian refugees admitted to Britian between 1933 and 1938 had created 15,000 jobs, boosting rather than weakening the economy.[13]

While the Nazi terror in Vienna increased from March 1938 onwards, the ability of Jewish aid bodies in Britain to help weakened. The British government set up several expert committees to advise the Home Office about admitting refugees in professional occupations. Only 50 out of 1,000 Austrian doctors were admitted on the insistence of a Medical Advisory Committee composed of doctors and refugee organisation representatives. The Home Office sought to let in 500 but 'felt unable to override the doctors' opposition'.[14] The refusal rate for domestic servants was much lower at 15 per cent, a clear sign of the large number of staff still employed by wealthier families.

The refugee organisations in London were nearly broke, and the Home Secretary, Sir Samuel Hoare, appealed to the cabinet for more funds. The aim was to improve the chances to emigrate from the United Kingdom, not 'expanding the chances of escape from Nazi territory'.[15] The British government agreed to match private funds provided other governments made a contribution. The offer was withdrawn in October 1939. The US government hindered re-emigration by refusing to relax entry controls for refugees in the United Kingdom seeking transit to the United States.

In German and Austrian passport offices, Jewish people queued endlessly. 'Between May 1938 and the end of January 1939, some 50,000 visas were granted to refugees, many covering more than one person. Of those 13,500 had been granted in Vienna and 34,000 in Berlin. Refugees received five-sixths of all visas granted at these posts.'[16]

In Vienna, 100 visas were granted daily and 200 people a day interviewed. A returned Home Office official worried that it would be disastrous if the Gestapo tried to 'unload the wrong type of emigrant' – Austrian Jews of eastern European origin.[17] While this former civil servant fretted about how disastrous it would be if the 'wrong type' made it to the United Kingdom, in Vienna the SS had no such qualms. They wanted every Jew out of Austria, the poorer and more humiliated the better, and stepped up their repression mercilessly.

In November 1938 Britain agreed to admit unsupported children aged seventeen or under from Nazi-occupied territory in a Kindertransport (Children's Transport) rescue scheme funded by non-governmental bodies as well as charitable donors. Sponsors of the children had to guarantee the £50 for re-emigration agreed under the plan, which was initially envisaged as a temporary measure. Between December 1938 and August 1939 Britain admitted 9,354 predominantly Jewish children, but when the Second World War broke out in September 1939 all transports ceased. Of these children, 100 or so were brought to the farm at Millisle, County Down. The Belfast and Derry Jewish communities had put up the money. Overall, 60,000–70,000 Jewish refugees were present in the United Kingdom when war broke out in September 1939, though the Central British Fund for the Relief of German Jewry (CBF) had files on 600,000–700,000 cases.[18]

3
'A DAILY BARBARISM'

Immediately after the Nazi invasion, the pressure on Jewish organisations in Vienna increased enormously. Eichmann interrogated the president of the IKG, Dr Desider Friedmann, several times in the Rossauer Lände police prison, where the Austrian Chancellor Kurt von Schuschnigg and many prominent politicians and civic leaders were also held. Prisoners, many of them Jews, were assaulted, and several were tortured there. Chaos had followed the suppression of the city's Jewish welfare organisations, and Eichmann set about allowing selected bodies to operate under his dictatorial control. His strategy was simple: force the Jews out by making life unbearable. Hans Safrian described the consequences:

> When the Kultusgemeinde reopened in early May under the direction of Dr Josef Löwenherz, its newly created department for emigration was confronted by a flood of people seeking advice and help for leaving Austria. Tens of thousands of emigration forms were distributed; approximately 45,000 completed forms supposedly were returned shortly thereafter. Thousands of people had been robbed of their jobs, incomes, savings and property: they needed assistance for their very survival. On account of the soaring expenses for 'emigration aid' and charitable measures, coupled with a simultaneous reduction of income, the Kultusgemeinde soon found itself in dire financial straits. The needed funds could be raised only with the help of international Jewish aid organisations. For this reason, Dr Löwenherz, with Eichmann's permission, contacted representatives of the [US] Joint Distribution Committee.[1]

21

The Irish writer Hubert Butler started working at a Society of Friends centre in central Vienna some months after the Anschluss. He filled in hundreds of emigration application forms for Jewish applicants. He described the poisonous atmosphere of Vienna in the summer of 1938:

> What would we have done if some instinct had told us of Auschwitz? Why was I the only non-Quaker there? ... I think now it was obtuse of us not to have anticipated Auschwitz. I had walked along the Praterstrasse to the Prater, the great Viennese Park where bands played and stalls sold ice-cream and coffee. The street must have had a great many Jewish shopkeepers in it, because all the way down there were broken windows in front of looted shops with VERHOLUNG NACH DACHAU ('Gone for a rest-cure to Dachau') scrawled over the surviving panes, and the air was full of the mindless hatred which war, that fosters all our basest passions, would inevitably make murderous.[2]

Butler also witnessed the suffering caused by the 'tremendous drive' for Nazi Aryanisation of blocks of flats and private homes. On one day, four people came who had been given notice to quit their flats by 1 August 1938, and had nowhere to go. 'They might get taken in by a Jewish landlord, but what are they do to do with their furniture? Aryans who take Jewish lodgers in also are liable to lose their flats.'[3]

When Jewish emissaries from British-ruled Palestine asked Adolf Eichmann to help the illegal migration of Jews, he permitted the use of a farm at Kagran, a suburb of Vienna, with training facilities for prospective young emigrants. He even expelled a group of nuns from a convent to provide the training camp for young Jews. The Friends' centre put Butler in charge of the Kagran Gruppe. He described the scene at the Kagran farm:

> The group worked under the supervision of armed guards from the Gestapo who relished watching middle-aged Jews, many of them once rich, sedentary businessmen, cutting trees, digging irrigation trenches, making a road; men who had never before held a shovel in their hands. They worked

all the summer, while Emma Cadbury, Mary Campbell and I tried desperately to get entry permits for them to Peru, Bolivia, Rhodesia, Colombia, Canada.[4]

Within the first three weeks of the reopening of the IKG office, there were 20,000 registrations for emigration, involving between 40,000 and 50,000 people. Its Emigration Department interviewed 3,000 people daily, with the help of retired professionals who set up special departments for particular occupations.

By personal negotiations in Vienna, Berlin, Paris and London, Löwenherz secured grants of $100,000 in June and $210,000 in September from the 'Joint Fund' in Paris, on condition that the Nazi authorities paid the same amount out of confiscated Jewish property, to which Eichmann agreed. 'In addition, every emigrant from Austria had to pay 25 per cent of his property to the State as a tax for being allowed to leave the Reich.'[5]

On 20 May 1938 the Nuremberg racial laws were introduced in Austria, removing Reich citizenship and the right to vote or enter the public service from Austrian Jews and 'Jewish mongrels' (individuals with three Jewish grandparents, and the offspring of mixed marriages who had two Jewish grandparents). Viennese Jews seeking to emigrate had to find numerous documents all over the city, queuing for hours outside offices while running the risk of physical assault by anti-Semites, who operated without fear of arrest. Then they had to pay 'taxes', including rates and telephone bills, down to the last penny, before they could be considered for an exit visa.

Following Gestapo raids in Germany against the 'work shy' in April 1938, the Nazis in Austria launched a major action in May specifically targeted against Jews described as 'asocial', 'criminal', or otherwise 'disagreeable'. The SS and Austrian police raided parks, squares and restaurants and arrested Jews. This added impetus to migration, which reached a peak in August with 9,729 emigrants. Nikolaus Wachsmann, the leading historian of the Nazi concentration camps, described what happened to those arrested:

The sufferings of these Austrian Jews began well before they reached Dachau. Unusually, the trains from Vienna were guarded by SS men from Dachau, not by police officials, and the men with the Death's Head on their uniforms battered their victims during the gruelling journey. Several Jewish prisoners were dead by the time the transports arrived at a new track inside the Dachau complex, where the trains were greeted by a baying SS mob, who kicked and punched the survivors with rifle butts until they panicked and ran towards the camp, protecting their heads. The new arrivals were chased along the way by the frenzied guards, who were cheered by off-duty colleagues watching from their quarters; left behind on the road were the hats, scarves, clothes and shoes of the Jewish men. So excessive was the violence – SS officers estimated that on one transport, around seventy per cent of the prisoners had been assaulted, some suffering deep stab wounds – that representatives from the state's attorney's office came to the camp to investigate, but to no avail.[6]

The brutality was so savage on one transport that twelve Jews died before they reached Dachau. Several hundred more Austrian Jews also arrived on mixed transports to Dachau. 'Between 1,600 and 1,700 Jews on the "blacklist" were arrested in two days in Vienna and sent to Dachau on May 30.'[7] Jewish prisoners were crammed into several barracks in a new compound there. Five thousand Jews were deported to Dachau between 2 May and 20 June 1938.[8] The SS Deputy Leader, Reinhard Heydrich, halted the mass arrests because of adverse foreign publicity and the majority of the detained were released within a year, on the strict condition that they emigrate.

The campaign of terror against Vienna's Jews also led to a large increase in Jewish suicides in the city. These had begun immediately after the Anschluss pogrom. The suicide numbers rose from 5 in January 1938 and 4 in February 1938 to 91 in March 1938, 73 in April and 70 in May 1938. On both 17 and 18 March, 22 Jews committed suicide in the city. Other opponents of the regime also took their lives, but Jewish suicides rose most dramatically. The dead included several of the city's most prominent Jewish professionals, and in some cases their wives. Egon Friedell, an eminent Jewish writer and actor, threw himself from the window of his apartment when he heard the noise of jackboots approaching his door. On 12 April 1938 the *Jewish Telegraph* agency reported the suicides of several prominent Viennese Jews, and the death in Dachau of Will Kurtz, an athlete and boxer, the third Jew to have perished there.[9]

The *Jewish Chronicle* feared that some Jewish suicides were in fact murders, committed for 'personal' reasons. In one case, the Viennese authorities refused to arrest or take legal action against a Nazi who had shot dead his sister's Jewish fiancé, because he had acted from 'racially understandable' motives. A nineteen-year-old Austrian student persuaded his Jewish lover, a minor, to assist in the murder of her forty-five-year-old mother, who was strongly against the relationship. While the girl occupied the woman in conversation, he shot her once in the head, and then again because the first bullet had not killed her. He chose 10 April, the date of the Nazi referendum, as the day of the murder to make it appear more plausible that a Jewish woman would take her own life out of desperation. The killer wanted the mother's considerable property. The murder came to light only when the young girl confessed two years later, after her lover had left her and gone to Germany. The criminal police were interested in the killing only as 'a racial disgrace'.[10]

By the end of the Nazi occupation in 1945, some 1,200 Viennese Jews had died by their own hand, and many others had attempted suicide and failed, but suffered often serious injuries. An unknown number of Austrian Jews forced out of the country also committed suicide.

Within weeks of the Anschluss, the housing crisis became acute. Löwenherz protested to Eichmann about the mass evictions, but was undermined by a court verdict in favour of a German tenant who had left his rented flat because there was a Jew in the same building. Christians rarely dared to take in Jews, while others demanded payments in advance for several months. The Nazi Party requisitioned Jewish flats, and municipal offices refused either to allocate them to Jews, or to see homeless Jewish applicants. Many Jewish families no longer had money to feed themselves.

Daily rations distributed by the soup kitchens increased from 700 in February to 12,000 in July. A special kitchen was opened for intellectuals, and 7,500 food parcels were sent to people who were ashamed to queue up publicly for meals. Artists were supported with 15–20 Reichsmarks a month. Jewish patients had to be removed from municipal hospitals, while, at the same time, Jewish welfare, educational and other institutions were requisitioned. In September alone an invalid home, a nursery and a Jewish school building were occupied, and Eichmann replied cynically to the complaining Löwenherz that 'Aryans' also had to suffer from requisitions.[11]

In the summer of 1938 the Nazi authorities stepped up their anti-Semitic repression. On 19 July Eichmann forced Löwenherz to sign a secret declaration that he was resigning from the library and archives of the community, which were later transported to Berlin. On 23 July they introduced a law requiring all Jews over fifteen to queue, often for nights on end, for identity cards with their fingerprints and photographs, as if they were criminals. On 15 August a virulently anti-Semitic exhibition, 'The Eternal Jew', opened in Vienna and attracted 350,000 visitors in three months. It had already had 412,300 visitors, or over 5,000 per day, when it ran in Munich from November 1937 to January 1938. A German secret police report claimed that it helped to promote a sharp rise in anti-Semitic feelings, and in some cases violence against the Jewish community.[12]

The ultimate economic aim of this 'Aryanisation' of Austrian society – a euphemism for the plundering and persecution of its Jewish community – was to fund the rearmament of the German armed forces for the war Hitler was planning. Reichskommissar Josef Bürckel closed down 80 per cent of Austria's 26,000 Jewish-owned businesses, allowing only the largest and most productive enterprises to operate. These had to be managed by Reich Germans. The Nazi leadership in Berlin considered these policies a great success, and at the end of April 1938 ordered that 'Aryanisation Instructions' be speeded up throughout the entire Reich. Administrative methods developed in Austria also became models for both the 'old Reich' and the newly conquered territories. A Jewish enterprise could be Aryanised only if such an act did not harm the general interest of the German economy. The principles Bürckel developed for taxing Aryanised property were also later used in the German Reich.[13]

These Aryanisations were brutally effective. By May 1939 only 6 per cent of Vienna's Jews were still in work, compared to 30 per cent in Berlin. Segregation also raced ahead quicker in Vienna, where Jewish pupils and teachers were separated and Jewish professionals banned from having Gentile clients.

The Jewish community was divided politically between Unionists (assimilationists) and Zionists, who controlled the IKG executive. Both groups were committed to social welfare. The numbers of young Polish Jews illegally crossing into Austria en route to western Europe or Palestine increased when Hitler's Germany blocked their entry. Penniless, they were helped by the Jewish community, as were young German Jewish refugees. Several thousand Jewish professionals also found themselves quickly without work. They were rarely given any warning or severance pay. As Bruce Pauley notes: 'Among those dismissed were all state and municipal employees (what few there were), including 183 public school teachers, and employees of banks, insurances companies, theatres and concert halls. Meanwhile, private Jewish businesses, large and small, were either confiscated outright or their owners were paid only a small fraction of the property's true value.'[14]

This huge pool of unemployed professionals faced a second handicap. Their qualifications and talents were not highly sought after abroad at this time of global recession. A manual trade improved the chances of emigration, particularly to South America. The IKG opened an Advisory Department for Professional Retraining, and within one year 24,025 people had graduated from 1,600 two-month courses in approximately 100 trades, including the metal and leather industries, clothing, food and chemical manufacture, cosmetics and medical care, handicrafts and decoration, domestic service and catering, and agriculture.[15]

The vast majority of the trainees were adults, apart from 1,700 agriculture students, who were Youth Aliyah members, committed to going to Palestine. The courses were so successful that they were soon imitated by other countries, and they also 'instilled thousands with confidence and satisfaction in their manual work'.[16]

The scheme extended beyond courses. In March 1938 former Jewish soldiers acquired expensive machinery and set up a labour camp in Stadtlau, near Vienna, specialising in farm work. It numbered 500, including wives and children. But the efforts of these Viennese Jews to improve their skills in order to better their chances of emigrating were often blocked by the Gestapo.

The hopes of the Jewish community were raised by the Inter-Governmental Evian Conference on the refugee problem in France in July 1938, convened by US President Roosevelt. Dr Josef Löwenherz and two other leading members of the Vienna Jewish community attended as observers, and spoke with the heads of the principal delegations among the thirty-two states, including Lord Winterton of Britain. Hubert Butler also attended as an observer for the Society of Friends.

But the conference did little to help the Jews of Austria or Germany. The principal French delegate, Henry Bérenger, opened it by proclaiming that France had already done much to solve the refugee problem and could do no more. Myron Taylor, the US chair of the conference, did not allow a single German or Austrian Jew to explain their plight.[17]

The only positive result was the creation on 13 July 1938 of the Inter-Governmental Committee for Refugees. Like the League of Nations High Commission for Refugees, it had no funds and no powers, though it had a broader remit which encompassed the Jews of Austria and eastern Europe. George Rublee, an American who was appointed its head, was authorised to negotiate with the Germans to allow Jews to emigrate and to cajole other countries into letting them in.

Only the Swiss border was open at that time. Some Austrian Jews continued to cross that border as tourists, by 'discovering' hitherto unknown Jewish relatives abroad who invited them for a visit. This escape route was kept secret, because, had it become widely known, a sudden increase in 'tourists' would have alerted Swiss officials. But that single avenue of escape was quickly closed:

> On October 5, a death blow was struck at Jewish emigration when German passports held by Jews were declared void, unless they were marked with a red 'J' (Jew). This measure was demanded by Dr Heinrich Rothmund, the chief of the Swiss Federal Police, who wanted to prevent an immense influx of Viennese Jews 'for whom Switzerland ... has as little use ... as Germany'. Rothmund threatened the termination of the Swiss-German visa agreement unless the passports of German Jews 'clearly indicate' that the bearer is Jewish. To ensure that Rothmund's demand was met, the Swiss Minister was ready to sacrifice the rights of Swiss Jewish citizens. The disastrous effect of the red 'J' was immediately felt not only on the Swiss frontier but also on other borders which were closed to the marked 'tourists'.[18]

The British delegation was not much more helpful. Whitehall feared that allowing in more refugees would encourage Poland and Romania, already anti-Semitic, to force out more Jews.

Hubert Butler was disillusioned: 'Vague gestures of goodwill were made. I talked to the two delegates from Ireland, or rather from the Irish Embassies in Paris and Berne. One remarked, "Didn't we suffer like this in the Penal Days and nobody came to our help."'[19] When Butler returned to Vienna, he visited all the embassies to try to obtain visas for Jewish people seeking to emigrate. A kindly official at the Mexican embassy told him he would sign an entry visa for anyone who asked. Even though it might not gain them admission to Mexico, it would help them escape Austria. 'So many applicants arrived that he had to get his wife and family in to help him.'[20]

Butler noted one incident as typical of many of the obstacles and disappointments would-be emigrants faced. The Bolivian embassy was one of the most crowded in Vienna because its government was reputedly offering land to agriculturalists on favourable terms, and needed engineers and craftsmen. Most applicants were rejected, but in the autumn of 1938 a group of 200 were told to prepare immediately for the journey. They quickly sold all their possessions for whatever money they could get, keeping only the bare necessities and what they could carry with them. 'A few days before the boat was due to sail, they were informed that there had been a misunderstanding between the Gestapo and the Bolivian consulate. No visas would be given for Bolivia and the expedition could not set off. The 200 settlers, now without homes or property, had to wander round the streets looking for hospitality from their friends.'[21]

Nazi Germany gloated over the conference's failure to persuade states to open their borders to Jewish refugees. They mocked expressions of sympathy for the plight of the Jews from countries that refused to offer them a haven. The conference's weak response to the crisis encouraged the Nazi campaign to force out the Jews of Austria and Germany. Despite this, the three Jewish delegates from Vienna returned from Evian hopeful, a sign of how desperate the community was to grasp at any straw.

In the summer of 1938 IKG officials suggested to Eichmann that a Central Office for Jewish Emigration (COJE, Zentralstelle für Jüdische Auswanderung) be set up to streamline the tortuous process.

The Nazi authorities gave the go-ahead on 20 August with Eichmann as its effective head. Eichmann, ambitious as ever, claimed ownership of the proposals and soon boasted to his superiors about the numbers he was driving out. The process may have been streamlined but it was brutal, and Jews were systematically mistreated. Those 'willing to emigrate' had to queue from the previous night to prepare for the opening of the office at 7:30 a.m. One who experienced the process gave a vivid description:

> On the right side ordinary Jews were lined up, on the left the 'Dachauer', those who had returned from Dachau, in wrinkled clothes and easy to recognise because of their shorn heads. Their turn came first, not because they had suffered more than the others but because they had tight 'deadlines' and were supposed to 'disappear' as soon as possible. SS men drove them across the street at a run and led them inside.[22]

Inside, Jews had to queue up again to obtain the vital documents they needed. But woe betide anyone who approached the counters and their Aryan personnel with anything incorrect in their papers. The slightest omission, no matter how trivial, would lead to a rejection and dismissal, and the whole stressful, dangerous and time-consuming business would start again.

4
'THE MAKINGS OF A REAL ULSTERMAN'

On 26 August 1938 a two-paragraph news item appeared in Vienna's *Zionistische Rundschau* headlined 'Jewish artisans for Northern Ireland'. It was, as one refugee, Paul Grünwald, leader of a group of Jewish refugees in Switzerland, described it in a letter to the Ministry of Commerce, 'like a sign from destiny'.[1]

The news report said 'Ireland' was ready to support immigrants from Central Europe as much as possible, if they were capable of starting up new enterprises in Northern Ireland, or of improving already existing ones to reduce unemployment. It said the Northern Ireland government had shown a willingness to support an 'Austrian Jew' in setting up an artisan cottage industry:

> They allowed him to bring over seven foremen from Austria to Belfast to train 70 women and girls. It is hoped that in this way 600–700 jobs will be created. During the training period, the Northern Ireland government will grant a subsidy of 10 shillings per worker to support the new enterprise. Applications for the registration of start-ups should be sent to the Northern Ireland Ministry of Commerce, which will examine them in a careful but supportive manner.[2]

The writer reminded readers that 'more than 200 years ago, Northern Ireland offered refuge for French Huguenots who laid the foundation for the world-famous Ulster Linen industry'.

But who was this Austrian Jew? He was Alfred Neumann, aged fifty-six, an export agent and member of a prosperous Viennese family. His father Josef had come to Vienna from Hungary. Alfred's younger brother Julius had a successful career as an export agent, establishing business contacts throughout Europe, Turkey, India and the Far East. Julius was also an important campaigner on behalf of Jewish communities in the Middle East in some of the most dangerous conflicts in twentieth-century history, and was a significant figure in British Jewry. He had settled in London in 1924, and was granted British citizenship on 1 July 1931.[3]

Alfred Neumann set up in London early in 1936, but kept his Vienna apartment in a large building at Rossauer Lände 33, close to the huge police prison on the banks of the Danube Canal, where many of the most prominent Jewish detainees were held after the Anschluss. By the spring of 1938 he had established important contacts with Northern Ireland's Jewish community and had been appointed to the Ministry of Commerce advisory committee, which appraised applications under the New Industries (Development) Act.

Neumann was not mentioned by name in the *Zionistische Rundschau* article in August 1938, but a small number of letters from Viennese applicants to Northern Ireland name him.[4] The Stormont scheme and his role in it was by this time known to Jewish authorities in Vienna, and Viennese Jews living in Northern Ireland had no doubt alerted relatives and friends to it. When the news item appeared in the community's only newspaper, it immediately raised hopes of emigration.

On 25 May 1938 the Ministry of Commerce became very enthusiastic about an Alfred Neumann plan to create jobs in Northern Ireland. Its advisory committee said the Ministry of Finance was prepared to authorise the payment of special grants to 'Dr Neumann' to train workers and it decided to recommend an annual subsidy to cover the rent of any premises and an allowance towards income tax, both payable for the first five years.[5] Over a period of two years, 480 workers were to be trained, the maximum cost to the exchequer being £4,316.

Once the advisory committee backed his plan, Neumann moved quickly. On 8 August 1938 he opened the firm in Newtownards, County Down, to much fanfare. There was extensive coverage in the local daily and weekly press. *The Northern Whig* reported that seven trainers had been brought out of Vienna and were now training local people who would work at home.

The town laid on a civic reception for the Viennese team. Sir Roland Nugent, chairman of the Ulster Development Council, said there were markets all over the world, particularly in America, eagerly awaiting Ulster's newest products. Extensive orders were awaiting execution as the recruits became proficient. Gloves, belts, handbags and crochet-work, based on leather and fabric, were to be the products of the industry. Sixty workers at a time would be trained, for two to three months, and training would begin the next day at the Court Square premises. Plans envisaged a total of several hundred workers to be trained within a period of two years, but, like all good plans, they were growing and he understood that wider possibilities were already in prospect.

Alfred Neumann thanked all concerned for the 'great' civic welcome. He wanted to help out some of his own people who found their country had been changed for them, and wanted it also to do a service for Britain, where he had been living for two and a half years, during which time he had learned 'to love this country always deeper and deeper for her freedom, her liberty, and her democracy. And I want it also to show that aliens and refugees shall not be taken as a burden, but that they can bring a lot of good for the country which gives them a new home.'

With this wonderful, heartfelt civic welcome, the key workers would feel truly at home there, he said. 'I want only to say for human reasons that a daily barbarism, for which there is no example in the whole of history, has made it impossible for my key workers, like a hundred thousand others, to make a living in their country.' That day was proof that they would be cornerstones of a new kind of industry, with far-reaching benefits for 'this people, which has helped us to become again free human beings'.

W. D. Scott, Permanent Secretary to the Ministry of Commerce, said he had watched with the keenest interest the grit and determination with which Mr Neumann had tackled and overcome well-nigh insuperable difficulties. Mr Neumann had in fact demonstrated that he had 'the makings of a real Ulsterman'.

He said James Stewart, secretary of the Ulster Development Council, who negotiated for new industries, believed that other businesses would develop similar work. One firm specialising in carpet-making was employing, on a purely experimental basis, eighty workers in County Fermanagh. He looked forward to the time when work in constant and abiding quantity would be available for the great majority of the home workers in Northern Ireland. Another industrialist was carrying through a series of experiments in several counties.

The *Northern Whig* also reported on 9 August that Alfred Neumann and six Jewish trainers were met at Euston station in London en route to Belfast and that a young woman, a Miss Lerner, had escaped just in time. Six workers, not seven, had managed to get out of Vienna. Miss Lerner, in an interview with the *Newtownards Chronicle*, brought home the dangerous reality of life for Jews in Austria. She had almost been arrested on the day they left, but managed to get away. A man in the group was not so lucky. The Nazi authorities in Vienna detained him and he did not make it out.[6]

But that merited only a mention in the local weekly paper. This was a good news story. On a sunny Wednesday in Newtownards, five elegantly dressed Jewish women and one man posed for the camera with Alfred Neumann and James Stewart. It seemed like a happy day for all concerned. The Jewish workers were starting a new life. They had left families and friends behind in Vienna, and their fate doubtless weighed heavily on their minds. But they had escaped Nazi terror, and hoped that their loved ones might soon be able to follow them.

The refugees were seeking to join a Northern Irish Jewish community of around 1,450.[7] Jewish migration to Northern Ireland began in the mid-nineteenth century, when a small number of German Jewish merchants settled and exported Irish linen to Europe, North America and other markets. The families' names included Jaffe, Loewenthal, Boas, Betzold and Portheim. Gustav Wolff, a co-founder of the world-famous Belfast shipyard Harland and Wolff, also settled in the North.[8]

The Jaffe family was particularly significant. Daniel Joseph Jaffe prospered, and his son, Sir Otto Jaffe, was twice Lord Mayor of the city, but his family was forced to leave Belfast in 1916 because of anti-German hostility. In the last decade of the nineteenth century and the first decade of the twentieth, the number of Jews increased to nearly a thousand with the arrival of refugees from eastern Europe who were fleeing poverty and persecution. Most of this second wave of Jewish immigration came from Lithuania, but there was also a minority of Polish Jews. The settlers also included glaziers, cabinet-makers and tailors. Several of these émigrés became successful business families, including the Goorwitchs, Berwitzes, Steinbergs, Solomons and Blacks.

Many of the new arrivals lived in north Belfast, in the streets which linked the Old Lodge and Crumlin Roads. At first, they established prayer rooms in private houses and formed breakaway congregations from the established community on Great Victoria Street. In 1904, the community united under one roof when Sir Otto and Lady Jaffe built a new synagogue at Annesley Street, off Carlisle Circus (replaced as the Belfast synagogue in 1964 by an award-winning building at Somerton Road). The Jaffe family also built a school on the Cliftonville Road, which by their stipulation was open to Protestant and Catholic as well as Jewish children. In the 1890s small Hebrew congregations were also established in Lurgan and Derry. Rabbi Jacob Shachter had presided over the community since 1926, and was an energetic leader, with a reputation as a scholar and public speaker. The community was generally well-regarded and respected.

There was little overt fascist activity in Northern Ireland, though individual political figures did voice sympathy for Nazism. 'In February 1938, for example, the Belfast branch of The Link, an Anglo-German association, met in the Grand Central Hotel and its secretary, Belfast Unionist Alderman James Duff, spoke in glowing terms of Adolf Hitler, and the goals of Nazism.'[9] In April 1938 the *Belfast Telegraph* serialised parts of a book, *Ourselves and Germany*, by Charles Tempest-Stewart, 7th Marquis of Londonderry, former Air Minister in Neville Chamberlain's Westminster government, calling for greater understanding of the Reich on the part of Western governments. Rabbi Shachter raised his concerns with the British Board of Deputies about The Link, and it agreed that it was 'nothing else but a Nazi organisation', while Lord Londonderry's book showed he was 'ignorant, as everybody seems to be'.[10]

Soon the leadership of the local Jewish community found itself in the closest contact with the persecuted Jews of Vienna. Apart from the PRONI letters responding to the *Zionistische Rundschau* news item, more than 550 letters from Jews in Nazi-occupied Europe also reached the Belfast Jewish Refugee Committee (BJRC). They were mainly written between March 1938 and August 1939 and addressed to the community's rabbi, Jacob Shachter:

> Most came from Vienna, Berlin and Prague, with some letters written in Paris, as well as neutral Antwerp and Switzerland. Refugees who managed to enter Britain wrote on behalf of relatives and friends, and local non-Jewish individuals also made representation on behalf of Jewish people they had met while on vacation or through work … The BJRC President, and Vice President sought out guarantors, made enquiries on behalf of applicants to government departments, and corresponded exclusively with the GJAC [German Jewish Aid Committee, which organised the admission of refugees to Britain, and their support] over what course of action was available.[11]

The BJRC also compiled a list of more than 160 Jewish refugees, whom they regarded as the most urgent cases or those it could most likely help. But attempts to update the list 'appear to have been abandoned as the volume of correspondence increased'.[12] The Jewish community in Belfast was now receiving almost daily reminders of the Nazi persecution of the Jews in Vienna.

5
'PLEASE HELP A DESPAIRED FAMILY'

The hundreds of refugee applications from Viennese Jews were appraised quickly by a small number of civil servants, helped by an advisory committee which included Alfred Neumann and local business figures. The words 'Regret' or 'No reply' are written on the majority of letters by the civil servants. These were notes to junior civil servants or typists instructing them to send, or not to send, a standard letter of rejection.[1] Alfred Neumann wrote to some applicants himself and a small number of his letters would themselves become the subject of embittered correspondence from their Jewish recipients.

The constant stream of letters came from Jewish men and women of every imaginable profession. The first to write were often those whose loved ones were in the most direct danger. Alfred Bermann, aged sixty-four, from Liechtenstrasse 64, wrote in English for an entry permit for his son Otto, aged twenty-nine, who had been imprisoned for six months in a concentration camp. Otto Bermann must have been among the thousands arrested immediately after the Anschluss. 'I beg you very much to be so kind to procure him a post anywhere and to render it possible for him to obtain the permission, for this would be the only possibility to get him free', his father wrote. Otto was very tall, of unblemished character, from a respectable merchant family in Vienna and perfectly healthy. He had several years' experience working at home and abroad as a weaver, and was very skilful and diligent.

'The unhappy old parents of this young man beg you very much to be so kind to grant their request and are waiting for your kind answer,' Alfred wrote. The letter included a photo of Alfred, but a civil servant has simply written, 'No reply'.[2]

A significant number of the applicants were female, both employers and skilled artisans, reflecting the thousands of Jewish women working in the Viennese textile and clothing industry. Vienna in the 1930s was one of the centres of European fashion manufacture and even boasted its own signature product, the 'Vienna style' of dress-making.

Hedwig Neufeld, aged thirty-eight, from Czerningasse 9, Vienna, wrote to Sir Roland Nugent, president of the Ulster Economic Council, on 31 August 1938, saying that she had read reports of 'Mr A. Neumann's action' and 'so felt encouraged to submit you a similar proposal'.

Hedwig had trained and employed many home-workers, finishing up the articles herself. She held a diploma from the 'famous Vienna Graphic Institute' and was an artistic photographer. Her principal customers had been in France, Sweden and the USA, though since the Anschluss 'my customers would not buy any more from Vienna, having become a German town. But they would willingly buy should I be able to make delivery from another country. The demand is still increasing.' German regulations forbade capital transfer abroad, so she had to look for an investor who would be interested in transferring her operations to Ulster.

'I should be able to coach up home workers in your country, as I have done in Vienna,' she said, requesting Sir Roland's 'kind patronage'. Her husband, Dr Heinrich Neufeld, had lost his job as head clerk of the biggest Austrian bank. He spoke and wrote English, French and German fluently. She had a son Erich, aged ten, and a daughter Anny, aged two. All four were refused entry.[3]

Dr Wilhelm Schieber, aged sixty-three, born in Gurahumora, Romania, of Laimgrubengasse 3, a highly qualified chemist, wrote on 26 August 1938 for permits for himself and his wife Sofia, aged fifty-five, his secretary. She was a 'wonderful teacher' of cooking and spoke English, French, Italian and German:

I could work for the best of my new fatherland and be worthy the permission. We, my wife and I, are not common people ... After losing a really significant fortune, I am forced to leave Vienna in some time, only of this purpose, being Jew. I can say it ... we are of the best of Jewish people, this sort of men, which are the spiritual promoter of all progress. Modest and working with brain and hand at least 8–10 hours the day. Excuse me this explication. I am able to erect innumerable industries of different manner. From the smallest one, till the greatest factory.

The Ministry of Commerce wrote to Dr Schieber, and he replied on 19 September 1938 asking if he could open an office to give advice and labour to some hundred men, and what sum of money he needed to take. He was refused entry.[4]

Fanny Bäck, aged fifty-three and single, had a millinery company and also produced knitwear and leather goods. With support, she could open a workshop or lead one already operating. She had a gift for organisation and could employ many working women. She was 'absolutely sound, ready to do any work' and spoke English 'rather well'. She signed off her typed letter with a beautiful copperplate signature. Her application, too, was refused.[5]

Otto Kisch, aged forty-nine, applied for visas for himself, his wife Hertha, aged forty-two, and daughter Vera, aged eight, from Fechtergasse 19, Vienna. He said he had worked in the shoe and slipper trade for thirty years and could found a slipper factory or work for one. 'The famous Vienna fashion and style no doubt also appreciated in your country will certainly prove an asset and give a new impulse to your markets.' His wife was 'an excellent household manager and an expert in culinary art, [and] would also be capable and ready to establish a cooking school, a confectioner's shop or the like'. They would be very happy to settle down in Belfast. They were refused.[6]

Hedwig Swoboda, aged forty-two, who had her own tie-making business, applied for visas for herself, her daughter Helene, aged eighteen, and craftsman Otto Urbach, aged forty-four, formerly of Deinhardtsteingasse 11, and his unnamed seven-year-old child. Writing in German, she offered to set up a similar business and could produce goods for both home and overseas markets. She was an expert in all aspects of the work and could teach home workers quickly on sewing machines. Like many of the applicants, she added that she had had her own business for several years but on account of the 'Jewish laws' had had to liquidate it. Unusually among the applicants, she was divorced; she described her daughter Helene as 'her right hand', who could fully represent her. Otto was a very skilled worker and knew the international market. Their application was rejected.[7]

Though most applicants were middle-aged, many with families, some young people wrote seeking entry. One of the most striking letters came from Helene Gutter, aged twenty, who lived at Darwingasse 4 in the second district of Vienna. She had attended the Academy of Fine Arts in Vienna, graduated with distinction from grammar school, and sought permission to come to work in Ireland: 'I am ready to accept every job I could find, and to accept every condition of work. I hope that you appreciate my qualities and knowledge and that you understand my distressed situation. Please try to help me and to obtain entrance into Ireland for me'. She was perfectly healthy, single and in her beautiful handwriting said she was 'waiting for their kind answer'. She mentions no one else, apart from her dead father. She was not admitted.[8]

Grete Schubert and Dr Aladar Tausig, of Favoritenstrasse 52, wanted to set up a knitwear factory. They were 'about to interest a wealthy personality living abroad, so that with Ministry of Commerce assistance they can build up operations without credit'. They wanted to bring over Grete's father, Alfred Schubert, aged seventy-two, and the wife and son of Dr Tausig, Franziska and Otto Tausig. A pencil note says '(1) too old (2) already catered for'.[9]

Elsa Abeles, aged fifty, and her husband Samuel, aged sixty-two, of Neustiftgasse 32–34, who made winter sports articles, wrote to say their refusal had 'perplexed us, because we have put all our hope in this project, but we won't give up our hope'. They had described in an earlier letter the difficulty of exporting money from Vienna. 'Perhaps it would be possible that if the Ministry of Commerce recommend our position to the authorities here, we could sooner get the allowance to take some money with us.' She asks how much capital was necessary to make it possible for them to establish in Northern Ireland.

'In the meantime we have got in a desperate situation as the authorities here have deprived all Jewish factories in our trade of the allowance of work. What that means, you will certainly understand and also comprehend, that we must try to find a new existence in a short time.' She asked the Ministry of Commerce to inform them as soon as possible, so that they could take the necessary steps to bring some money and machines out with them, and progress their request for the Home Office permit in London, which would certainly take a long time. In pencil on the letters 'Regret' is written.[10]

Some of the applicants made it clear that they had access to capital, hoping this would help their petition. Stella Fuchs, aged thirty-eight, and Josef Rostholder, aged forty, of Ventorgasse 12, wanted to set up a furrier business and asked the Ministry of Commerce to recommend a firm and to support their application. They were experienced furriers and could bring out furniture and machines but no money. 'Luckily we have well-to-do friends in a foreign country who will help us financially.' A note states, 'Big Firm, might be worth encouraging, 5 queries of persons to whom employment could be given with here'. They were refused entry.[11]

Gertrude Chat, aged fifty-two, wrote on 26 August 1938 requesting permits for herself, her husband Arthur and her daughter Edith, aged seventeen. Gertrude was a producer of nightwear and had employed thirty workers in Vienna in the past. She promised to employ between ten and twelve seamstresses if admitted to Northern Ireland. She was married, Jewish, and the daughter of a lawyer, from Graz. Her daughter Edith had graduated from the Technical School for dress-making and outfitting in Vienna. Edith was her assistant in the factory and she wanted to take her with her in order to make the workers acquainted with the Chats' work. A note on the letter in pencil states 'smaller firm but with good ideas' while another, later, note in red ink says 'not coming'.

The Chats' wedding photograph appears on the website of the Documentation Archive of Austrian Resistance (DÖW, Dokumentationsarchiv des Österreichischen Widerstandes), an extremely rare occurrence. Gertrude is dressed in a white high-necked blouse, skirt and hat with chiffon, and looks to camera; Arthur, older, in suit, winged collar and bow tie, looks admiringly at her as they hold hands. The photo was taken in the Moser studio in the spa town of Bad Aussee in Styria, said to be the geographical centre of Austria, and a honeymoon attraction.[12]

Heinrich Kantor, aged sixty-two, and his wife Fanny, aged forty-five, ran a jam- and chocolate-making business in the prosperous Josefstadter Strasse; he wrote to say he could get the capital for a factory from a friend in England. 'Of course I would employ only Irishmen as my workers,' he wrote. They were refused entry.[13]

Gisela Kompert, aged forty-eight, of Grimmgasse 3, and her husband Camillo, aged fifty-six, ran a woodwork manufacturing business and sought permits for themselves and their son Paul, aged eighteen. She said she could get access to 40,000 Reichsmarks of her own money and 10,000 Reichsmarks from her co-workers. 'Regret' is written on their letter.[14]

Fritzi Kohn, a ceramicist/technical manager of Windhabergasse 24a, aged twenty-nine, Joseph Kohn, a ceramicist, aged forty-two, Dr William Victor Spitz, aged forty, a furnace expert/art ceramicist, and Mrs Martha Spitz, aged thirty-three, a worker in applied arts, sought to come. 'We lost our means of livelihood in Germany, we beg you to grant us permission to enter North Ireland,' Fritzi Kohn said.

A second letter said that relatives in Switzerland would fund them with £120 and they would need money from the Ministry of Commerce only if the business was made bigger. A civil servant noted that 'Mr NM [Neumann] will write for a report on this man'. But 'No reply' is written on the letter.[15]

Julius Frankl, aged fifty-nine, a businessman living at Badhausgasse 18–20, wrote in German on 14 September 1938. He had set up a factory in 1908 for female home workers and employed many hundreds of women all over Austria between 1908 and 1924, knitting pearl handbags. He made lots of foreign currency for his homeland through the export of these bags. He lost his business through 'the inflation', but taught his home workers embroidery knitting. He had an industry giving workers a wage and bread until the German troops entered Vienna in March 1938. Since the employees were mainly Jews and a majority had fled, the industry was now in decline. Frankl had two firms in Brussels, but it was hard to set up institutions there as he had to leave the most valuable funds behind. 'However, I would like to humbly request you to consider that without exception all Jews and Catholics related to Jews, through pitiless elimination from the workforce and dispossession of property, find every further hope of continued activity impossible, even when it is a case of the most honourable and economically important people.' He said he would not do local people out of jobs. He could set up his business in Northern Ireland and wanted to bring his wife, three children and two employees with him. 'Regret' is written on his letter.[16]

Two sisters, Olga and Melanie Porges, aged fifty-six and sixty-two, of Wipplingerstrasse 12, who had their own knitwear shop, offered employment for a 'sound number' of workers in Northern Ireland. They were assured of $350 by a brother-in-law in New York and a friend in Buenos Aires. 'We were both born in Vienna and belong to a Viennese family, whose various members held esteemed positions. But as non-Aryans we fall to the very strict rules of this country.' They received the standard 'Regret' letter.[17]

Josefine Spielmann of Lowengasse 32, aged thirty-six, had her own firm employing women workers and female apprentices in knitting and art work, and her husband Benno, aged thirty-nine, was a joiner. Her friend Henny Feideck was going to Ireland in late October 1938 on a work permit and she hoped that they could get ones for themselves and their son Saul, aged eleven. She asked if Northern Ireland needed applied arts workers. They were refused.[18]

While some applicants were rejected because their plans were too big, or duplicated existing businesses, others were rejected as too small. In many cases no reason for rejection is given. Johanna Stein-Brand, aged fifty-one, of Barnabitengasse 7a, a dressmaker from Czechoslovakia, and her husband Nikolaus Michael Stein, aged fifty-seven, born in Yugoslavia, applied for permits. She had once employed between fifteen and nineteen workmen and two apprentices, and later four workmen and one apprentice. She could instruct apprentices and produce ready-made jersey dresses for export. (These were knitted items, often made from wool, used in dresses and underwear and widely produced in Vienna's large clothing industry.) Her husband had had a restaurant and wanted to establish one for 'dietary food'. Both their parents were dead. 'Both we are blameless', she added, meaning they had no criminal convictions.

She replied to a Ministry of Commerce letter and submitted proposals. She needed no financial assistance as long as she did not employ more than ten workmen. Her workshop was valued at

£100–130, but there was a 30-mark limit to what she could take out. She had sufficient work but wanted to emigrate because she was a Jew. 'My richness is my artistic creation in Viennese taste and charm. This can nobody take me as long as our good God keeps me healthy.' A note on their letters states, 'Too small'.[19]

Some applicants had heard about Alfred Neumann's factory in Newtownards, though the location was not mentioned by name in the *Zionistische Rundschau* article. Friederike Klein, aged sixty, a widow, applied for herself and her daughter Grete, aged thirty-two, saying she had heard about a knitting industry at 'Nutanmarus' (Newtownards, perhaps showing that the Ards factory became known by word of mouth), 'floated by a number of Viennese emigrants'. She wanted to know the chance of settling there as she was an expert in this field. She was looking after her mother. 'No reply' was written on her letter.[20]

Louise Nussbaum, aged thirty-nine, of Schönbrunnerstrasse 249, applied for herself and her mother Ida, aged sixty-three. She had her own knitwear factory employing more than thirty workers and wanted to set up a similar factory in Northern Ireland, which would employ a number of women. She too was refused entry.[21]

The letters also give a sense of the cosmopolitan nature of the city and its rich pool of Jewish manufacturing talent. Since 1920, Fritz Jökl, aged sixty-six, of Bernbrunngasse 29, married with two sons, had developed the largest factory making bed feathers and downs in Austria. He wished to set up in Northern Ireland. He expected a promising market abroad because he had already started an export business to foreign countries. He was refused, and died in Vienna on 10 January 1940 in unknown circumstances.[22]

Two brothers, Wilhelm and Leopold Wohlfeiler, wrote from Vienna on 7 September 1938, saying they were general printers with factories in three countries in Europe, each employing more than sixty people. They could quickly set up a factory employing a great number of people, and could teach them. Their elder brother Emmanuel, aged fifty-four, had died at the hands of the Nazis just over two weeks before they wrote, but they gave no further details. The DÖW website notes only that he died on 20 August. They were refused entry.[23]

Ernst Mautner, aged fifty-one, of Kaulbachstrasse 35, had a coloured paper and gold leaf factory and four houses in the city and wanted to set up in Northern Ireland with his wife and son Fritz, aged seventeen. If that was impossible, he sought permission to land there. 'I and my family, we are blameless, we had never a punishment and were never active in political relations.' He was recommended by Alfred Neumann and wrote again asking about factory space and tax relief, and offered his machines and three houses in Vienna and one in Italy as security. A note at bottom of this letter said 'follow up' but one at the top said 'No reply'.[24]

Stefan Guttmann, aged forty-seven, of Wehrgasse 25, applied for permits for himself, his wife Stella, aged forty-five, and their son. He said he had been a qualified blacksmith and master welder, his wife was a specialist in wood objects and his son had been forced to give up his Gymnasium (grammar school) and learn car mechanics.[25] 'My existence having been destroyed only for the reason I am not Arian [sic], I am searching abroad a new home with the purpose to be still more laborious.' They were refused entry.

Hans Nussbaum, aged thirty-two, had his own joinery works employing at least thirty workmen, and he said he was sure to increase that number in Ireland. He was an Aryan who had married a Jew. 'No reply' was written on his letter.[26]

Even Jewish owners of firms manufacturing goods which were not produced in Northern Ireland found it difficult to win backing from the Ministry of Commerce. Wilhelm Goldberger, aged fifty-three, and Otto Schulmann owned a pen and pencil factory at Tuchlauben 17, employing twenty people. They were refused entry.[27]

Employers and skilled trainers who had experience with the IKG had their applications carefully assessed but in the end few were admitted. Siegfried Wiener, aged fifty-three, of Seegasse 6, sought permits for himself and his wife Rosa, also aged fifty-three. He had owned his own knitwear business and asked to be admitted as an expert craftsman. His wife was also a specialist in that business. He was working as a course leader in the IKG in the knitwear trade. As a Jew, he had no possibility of making a living in Vienna. He would be very grateful. He was refused.[28]

Several applicants from Vienna were accepted by the Ministry of Commerce, often on Alfred Neumann's recommendation, but did not escape from Vienna. Among them was Arthur Holzer, aged thirty-five, from Paulanergasse 4, a producer of hand-woven rugs and carpets for which waste material was used. He sought a permit to enter and set up a factory in Northern Ireland for himself, his wife and one child, and perhaps one other trained person and one or two handlooms. The workers could be trained on the spot and hand looms could be found everywhere. He sent a second note saying he would not need any foreign aid as he would be helped to live and to set up a plant by relatives and friends in Holland. 'I have got their strict engagement on this behalf.'

A note in pencil states: 'makes carpets for works materials. Would be very useful. Recommended,' and a note in green ink on 19 September says 'written' and is initialled 'AN', indicating that Alfred Neumann had replied to Arthur Holzer. Whatever the content of his letter, Arthur, his wife Cäcilie, aged thirty-three, and daughter Erika, aged seven, could not get away from Vienna.[29]

Several other applicants recommended by Alfred Neumann were also unable to escape. One was Max Neumann (no relation), aged fifty-six, of Novaragasse 40, a leather goods manufacturer for twenty-five years in Vienna. He sought a permit for himself and his wife Dobe, aged fifty-five. He was leader on an IKG course for producing leather goods for potential emigrants and he had 'succeeded highly'. He needed only tools, not a great factory; goods such as belts, brooches and artificial flowers could easily be produced in a home industry. A note stated 'good. Written', initialled again by AN, but another note said 'not coming'.[30]

Dorothea Schorr, aged forty-six, who wrote from Dreihuf-eisengasse, employed more than 100 female home-workers, who 'were all very well paid'. She produced hand-knitted and hand-crocheted garments, blouses, dresses and overcoats. Her husband David was a professor at a commercial high school. Alfred Neumann wrote to her, and her idea is noted as 'good' on her letter, but 'not coming' is written in red ink. It is possible that either Neumann or the Ministry of Commerce civil servants received word from the Schorrs that the Nazis in Vienna would not grant them an exit visa.[31]

Sigmund Singer, of Gumpendorfer Strasse 25, had owned a workshop for ready-made embroideries, employing between twenty and fifty girls. 'Now I am intended to transfer my activity to foreign countries as owing to my Jewish origin, I have no possibility any more to continue my work in Austria.' A note says 'v g [very good], written 20.9.38, G and N later.' Alfred Neumann had responded, and was interested in bringing Singer over to work for the firm of Gilfillan and Neumann in Derry. (Neumann became a director of this firm, which received Ministry of Commerce support and started trading in November 1938.) Again, he was unable to get out of Vienna.[32]

On 3 September 1938 Ignatz Weiss, of Mariahilfer Strasse 32, one of the main shopping streets in Vienna, sought to transfer his clothing manufacturing business abroad and wanted a permit to set it up in Northern Ireland. He had employed hundreds of workers for more than twenty-five years, making dresses, blouses and dressing gowns in the Viennese style, 'famous throughout the world'. If admitted, he would give a chance of earning their livelihood to 'as many workmen and workwomen as possible'. A note on their letter states 'written to 8/9/38 A Neumann'. Weiss did not make it to Northern Ireland.[33]

The leader of the Swedish mission in Vienna, Göte Hedenquist, of Seegasse 16, a Protestant clergyman, sent a covering letter to the Ministry of Commerce with ten pages of letters from industrialists and company managers seeking entry to Northern Ireland. It is likely these were Jewish business-owners, though it is also possible that they were among the small number of Viennese Protestants who applied. They would be able to establish, direct and develop industries, could bring out machinery, 'as well as their expert capacities, and eventually also their own ideas and licences'. They had commercial connections, but could not take out their own funds into foreign countries because of regulations in Vienna. There was only a 'very small choice among our members'. He asked about the contribution of 'ready money', or cash, on the part of their members. Civil servants noted the possibilities against each application: among them were tinned food (doubtful), electric heating cushions (possible), repair of electrical goods (saturated); lingerie (no opening here), glass manufacture (interesting). A note on the top of the letters states, 'No reply'.[34]

Bernhard Rosenbaum, aged fifty-six, a designer of swimwear, sought permits for himself, Adele Rosenbaum, a cutter, and Hedwig Hausmann, aged sixty-five, a colourist, all working at Glasergasse 16. 'We do not wish to fail offering our sincere assurance that neither of us would ever tire in showing deep gratitude by always doing and giving our best for the benefit of the country, generously enabling us to use our working capabilities'. The three were refused.[35]

Berthold Kohn owned a weaving company in Vienna, and as a Jew 'compelled to transfer my residence to another place', sought permits for himself and two assistants to set up a factory in Northern Ireland. These were Hans Kraus, aged twenty-eight, of Ingenhausz 4, and Emil Eckstein, aged fifty-seven, of Reisnerstrasse 16. They were not admitted, and no note was written on their application.[36]

A few of the letter writers had managed to get into Switzerland but were still seeking escape. Paul Grünwald, in a hand-written letter in German, wrote from Dietisberg in the district of Basel on behalf of twenty Jewish emigrants working in an agricultural community. They could not practise their trade in Switzerland and were relying on Jewish welfare. 'This joyful news was to us like a sign from destiny', he wrote about the NIDA scheme. 'Regret' is written in pencil on top of the letter. Paul Grünwald is not listed in the DÖW website in Vienna. There is a good chance therefore that he and his twenty fellow Jewish emigrants survived.[37]

The letters are usually written in a neutral tone, but occasionally the writers plead. Nelly Gaspar, aged forty, of Czerningasse 12, wrote on 3 November 1938, seeking permits for herself, her husband Simon, aged fifty-seven, and daughter Ruth, aged fifteen. She was a glove maker, her husband a leather worker, and her daughter a trainee milliner, who could do 'all sorts of homework'. 'Please help a despaired family that it can work and so go on living. I remain yours very gratefully and beg you to answer soon and well.' A civil servant has written 'Regret'.[38]

While the refusals far outnumbered the acceptances, the applications continued to arrive. Hope continued to outweigh despair.

6
'A GOOD DEED FOR HUMANITY'

While hundreds of Vienna's Jews applied for visas to Northern Ireland, with little chance of success, groups of highly committed local activists were determined to help them come. Even before the Stormont government passed the New Industries (Development) Act in December 1937, a number of Ulster men and women had seen the Nazi dictatorship in action in Germany. Several of them had been visiting there for years, and had links with opposition groups.

In the spring of 1938, the BJRC was set up by the Jewish community in Belfast. It sought to influence government policy, speak for individuals seeking entry and provide aid and, where possible, work to refugees. It set up a hostel on Cliftonpark Avenue in north Belfast for the new arrivals. It was soon joined by a second group of largely Christian activists, the Belfast Committee for German Refugees (BCGR). An important group of activists was also formed in Derry. These voluntary groups included some of the most distinguished intellectuals and progressive campaigners of their generation.

The BCGR was launched with joint funding from the Christian churches, including Presbyterians, Anglicans, Catholics, Methodists and Quakers. Its small executive committee was rich in talent. Its chairman was the Rev. Ernest Davey, a distinguished scholar and later Moderator of the Presbyterian Church in Ireland; its joint secretaries were Margaret 'Peggy' Loewenthal, the daughter of one of Ireland's most important Jewish linen manufacturers and later an important figure in European refugee work, and the Rev. Alan R. Booth, a Belfast Methodist minister. Other members included Norah Douglas[1] and Margaret 'Peggy' McNeill, both Quaker activists, and Dr Eileen Hickey, a Catholic, the first woman to hold the post of clinical

49

examiner in medicine in Queen's University and later an independent MP at Stormont. In Derry, Professor Thomas Finnegan, a classics don at Magee College, and his wife Agnes, both left-wing pacifists, also played a key role in helping bring refugees to the city.

Professor Ernest Davey at Union Theological College in Belfast was widely regarded as 'the most brilliant scholar ever to hold a chair in an Irish Presbyterian theological college'.[2] In 1927 he was accused of heresy by fundamentalist members of his own church because of his liberal theological views, but was exonerated by a large majority. He became highly active in refugee work in the late 1930s. His daughter recalled coming down to breakfast to find strangers, tired and confused, in the kitchen. Their father had just met them off the Liverpool boat after their highly stressful journey.

Margaret 'Peggy' Loewenthal, aged twenty-five, quickly became a prime mover on the committee. She was the youngest of four daughters of an integrated German Jewish merchant family. Her paternal grandfather, Julius Loewenthal, came from Hamburg to Belfast to become a partner in and later the owner of Moore and Weinberg, linen merchants, and a major employer. His eldest son, John McCaldin Loewenthal, Peggy's father, was brought up a Presbyterian but became a free thinker. When Queen's University awarded him an honorary degree in 1940, he was described as having a connection 'with almost every progressive movement in the city'.[3]

Peggy was told about the plight of German refugees arriving in Britain in 1937 by her sister Helen, who was in London, and who suggested that the people of Northern Ireland should help.[4] According to her own memoir, *From Belfast to Belsen and Beyond: My Journey though the Upheavals of Twentieth Century Europe*, Peggy arranged a meeting of old girls of her former school, Richmond Lodge in Belfast, at her home in Lennoxvale Lodge on the affluent Malone Road. They decided to form a support group.

'Our committee did its best in getting people out on work permits, domestic permits etc and children were taken in by private families and a few individual guarantees,'[5] Peggy wrote in her memoir. The Jewish community, in contrast, signed 'endless guarantees regardless, just in order to get people out. Unfortunately, I do not think that any of us at that time had any idea of the horrors that were going on in Germany and Austria.' The Jewish community in Belfast opened the refugee Settlement Farm at Millisle where 300 Kindertransport children stayed during and after the war, some of the 10,000 allowed into the United Kingdom without their parents.

The committee was soon so busy that it employed a paid secretary, herself a refugee with a son aged seven. Peggy had a car and also frequently met the 'anxious and weary travellers' as they got off the Liverpool boat, and took them home for breakfast. Among those she helped was a Dr Kurt Sachs, a Viennese psychiatrist. He was mortified one day when Peggy innocently gave him his small weekly allowance on the street; another was Joseph Frey, who graduated from Queen's University, Belfast in 1946, and later became a lecturer in German there.

The committee had an 'excellent relationship with the Northern Ireland government, Home Office and police,' according to Peggy, and they were able to educate those in authority about Judaism.[6] They formed a close friendship with an RUC District Inspector, Bill Moffatt, who was highly sympathetic to the plight of refugees. 'It was often said that Peggy has the police in her pocket, ask her to get your permit', she said of herself.

In Derry, a group of socialists and progressives, as well as a handful of the city's employers, played a vital role in bringing in Jewish workers from Vienna. Some of them came to the attention of the RUC, who mistakenly, and in one case farcically, smelt a Republican plot behind the refugee work and acted accordingly.

The key figures in the Derry group were a couple who had first-hand knowledge of the situation in Germany.[7] Thomas Finnegan was a young professor of classics at Magee College and a progressive Presbyterian. His wife Agnes was a descendant of a radical United Irishman from Maghera in County Derry, Robert Stewart, who took part in the unsuccessful Irish rebellion in 1798, and managed to escape to America afterwards.

The Finnegans had by the early 1930s established a weekly discussion group, which met in the attic of their spacious home at 6 College Avenue in the leafy Northland Road area of Derry. It included two schoolteachers, dock labourers, trade unionists, and an unemployed blacksmith. They thrashed out ideas to combat the city's unemployment, poverty and sectarian discrimination in jobs and housing. Because of gerrymandering in local elections, Derry, with an overwhelmingly Catholic majority, always returned a Unionist-controlled corporation. Few new houses were built. Since the vast majority on the waiting lists were Catholic, this confined the nationalist majority to areas such as the Bogside, where families were crowded into slums.

Thomas Finnegan, born in 1906, was the son of John Maxwell Finnegan, scientist, entrepreneur, teacher and Academic Secretary at Queen's University, Belfast. John Finnegan had employed a governess who had taught the young Thomas German; he loved Germany and its literature, had frequently visited it as a young man and kept up many contacts there. Agnes Finnegan had spent six months there to learn something of the culture 'he knew and loved'.[8]

In a memoir written towards the end of her life, Agnes described a visit to Berlin they made in 1937 with a small group to investigate the 'tense situation of Hitler's growing power in confrontation with the movement against Nazism'. They stayed at the Kaiserhof Hotel, where Hitler was supposed to come every afternoon for tea, 'but the manager whispered to us secretly, "Do not think that we all agree …". We were wined and dined by the British ambassador, a polite and charming fellow, seemingly unaware of the volcanic pressures building up around him.'[9] This was Sir Nevile Henderson, a convinced appeaser.

They also met Alfred Rosenberg, the leading racist 'social philosopher' of the Nazi Party. 'He had absolute faith that the Aryan Germans were the Herrenvolk, the master race; they had inherited the strength and literalism of the Vikings and were the chosen people, therefore it was proper to eliminate all others!'[10] Rosenberg was hanged for war crimes and crimes against humanity at Nuremberg in 1946.

Thomas and Agnes Finnegan were among those who met resisters secretly in the evenings. Many were relatives of those detained in concentration camps, key figures in the Protestant anti-Nazi movement. The Finnegans were deeply impressed, Agnes recalled in her memoir:

> We talked with members and leaders of the Confessional Church, with the parents and children of men and women who were suffering and dying in the concentration camps

– tortured because they would not submit to the call for violence or who were simply of another race. We found desperate courage and determination with the faith that the spirit of man would prevail over wickedness. They felt that they had no choice but to believe that all men are one – neither Jew nor Greek, bond nor free.[11]

One meeting particularly shocked Agnes. A brother and sister came to see them at the hotel. He had been a young medical student she had met before she married Thomas, idealistic and keen to devote his life to healing 'the broken people' in the slums of Berlin. Now he appeared in full black SS uniform and made a 'rapid and incoherent' speech about loyalty to the leader. His sister, also a doctor, wept as he spoke, grief-stricken by the change in him. He was lost, she said.

On one of the visits, Thomas secretly went to visit an opponent of the regime in a German city. He knocked on his door, which was flung open by German soldiers. Shocked, he made an excuse that he had the wrong address, and left. Back in Derry, Thomas was asked by the YMCA to run work camps for unemployed men, and he and Agnes were among the founders of a local Labour Party, 'a mild, middle-of-the-road affair', but one avenue of political action. Agnes stood unsuccessfully in a municipal election, and publicised the dire housing conditions in the area. But the Finnegans' campaigning attracted the attention of the Royal Ulster Constabulary.[12]

One day, one of the attic group, a schoolmaster, arrived at their home, anxious and with urgent news. He had been playing poker in a pub when two policemen arrived, sat near him and purposely talked loudly enough for him to hear. The Finnegans were to be prosecuted, the schoolmaster said, though some 'peelers' liked Thomas. 'They know you're fair after the way you used to referee their hockey matches for them,' the schoolmaster said. So he wanted to tip them off about a scheduled raid at their home, 'just in case you'd anything to hide'.[13]

Earlier that day, a journalist friend called Hugh had arrived, looking nervous. Two detectives had called the previous night at his offices, had gone through the newspaper files and picked out any references to Thomas. Hugh said: 'They are going to have it in for you both and no mistake and they weren't satisfied for they found very little, so they will be up here before long – I know them.' He stood up to go. 'I had to give you warning.'

Before long, three policemen arrived and searched the house. Then a squad of police arrived with Thomas – they had taken him out of a lecture room at Magee College. 'I hoped that his students watching the event realized what he was prepared so serenely to suffer for the sake of truth – perhaps just one of them did understand it,' wrote Agnes.

The police searched the house and left with a 'rich haul' of what they thought were subversive Gaelic manuscripts, as well as bundles of old copies of the *New Statesman*. The treasonable Gaelic documents were in fact lecture notes in Greek for a course that Thomas was preparing. They found a small surveyor's plan of a site the Finnegans were thinking of buying in County Donegal, which could be used as a holiday home for workers. But the police thought that might be military intelligence that Thomas would sell to the enemy. They also 'pounced eagerly' on a letter in German, which they sent on to a local German teacher to translate. She told the Finnegans all about it. It was a letter from a distraught mother, a refugee from Nazi terror 'who had begged Tom as a governor of the grammar school to get her son into the school'. The Finnegans had already bought the boy his books and his uniform ready for his 'venture into British education'.

On a second raid, the police arrived in two armoured cars. No one was at home, so Thomas was taken out of Magee College, where he was lecturing on Plato's *Republic*. They accused him of running a secret society in the dark of his attic. Again, they confiscated a load of his teaching materials.[14] Infuriated, Thomas went to the central police station in Derry, and demanded to know from the District Inspector why his lectures were being disturbed and his home raided. They talked, but there was a gulf between them. Finally, the District Inspector said: 'And supposing the Nazis landed in Derry, as well they might in the central naval base – what would your position be then, I'd like to know?' Tom replied, 'You as head of the police would have to co-operate with the invaders in order to keep some semblance of law and order – I would be in a concentration camp.'[15]

As president of Magee College, Thomas would be invited to dinner on special occasions, such as the sitting of the High Court Assizes in Derry. Once, he made his way across the River Foyle on a night of heavy snow to dine with a judge, a man he knew and respected. The only other guest was the District Inspector. They had a pleasant evening and the DI drove him home. It was the last they saw of each other.[16] Thomas's pacifism also brought him into conflict with their local minister, who preached a sermon rousing the congregation 'to hate the Germans – "those wicked people"':

> Tom wrote to him pointing out that there were thousands of German dissidents in concentration camps to whom we had given little or no support and could not he as a Christian leader convince his flock that violence would never bring justice and peace and goodwill – as was the message of his Lord. The message was naturally not a popular one at a time when truth had been the first casualty so he was gradually edged out of any position of trust – he was not like Jeremiah or Steven [sic] actually stoned.[17]

Thomas published pacifist and anti-imperialist pamphlets in the 1930s and sponsored several Viennese Jewish refugees to come to Derry. Among them were Ludwig and Loni Schenkel, a couple from Vienna. The Finnegans gave Loni a job as a housekeeper, but she was actually a house guest and a qualified chemist. Thomas's son Owen, the youngest of five children, who became a consultant at the Causeway Hospital, Coleraine, has vivid memories of the Schenkels:

> Ludwig and Loni met at our house in Derry, married and had a very happy relationship. He became a successful businessman and a close friend of my parents, who also befriended Robert and Ellie Sekules, who had a much less successful factory on Spencer Road. Ludwig arrived in Derry with only a camera. A highly cultured man, he took thousands of photographs, many in Donegal, and was an expert on plants especially cacti. Ludwig had a very successful factory making canvas kit bags during the war and afterwards made travel bags. He also took photos all year round and sold them as Christmas cards.

The Schenkels didn't speak about their experiences in Vienna. Ludwig was very knowledgeable about world events, and not in the slightest bit bitter, a very generous man. Loni was lovely, vivacious, generous … they made a great partnership.[18]

Owen believes lack of knowledge about what was happening in Austria – despite coverage in newspapers and on the radio – had a bearing on people's attitudes:

There was a difference between refugees fleeing German atrocities and Germans inflicting the atrocities. I don't think the people realised the difference between the two and therefore it was sometimes interpreted that the refugees were supporting Germany. I think there was a lot of ignorance about the situation at that time.

My father didn't go out and run the gauntlet in dangerous underground movements to bring people here. He was in the background giving the support, the sponsorship, and other resources when they arrived. He gave financial help, using whatever influence he had with contacts, helping them to get employment. The sense was that the official channels were useless and more obstructive. To survive the official channels you were doing well; it was the unofficial lines that provided practical help.

Some of his colleagues knew what was going on, but by and large it was ignorance and probably not wanting to know the details. And of course that was always the big excuse, that we didn't know what was going on at that time. But he and my mother, and others, did know. It was his view that the authorities could have done more to help people. He gave that impression. He wasn't a person who would have lauded his own achievement. He probably would have regarded this as just the normal thing that anybody should have done.

Father was a very courageous and a very modest man. He was an academic and didn't quite always grasp the practicalities of life. He always thought the best of people and was therefore shocked when they treated him or other people badly. Mother was the practical one and was actually much more talkative and would say things. She kept in touch with a Jewish family who miraculously survived the war in Berlin; they were 'terribly deprived'. I am proud of them both.[19]

7

'MR NEUMANN'S SCHEME'

After the successful media launch of his Newtownards factory, Alfred Neumann returned to London on the night of 9 August 1938 to try to arrange for the migration of more Viennese Jews, including some of his wife's relatives. The six instructors he had brought over immediately began training locals. Initially, the firm took on forty workers, who were to be trained within two months, and would then work at home. All seemed set for a success story.

Neumann continued to travel back and forth between London and Belfast, and played a leading role in bringing in small numbers of Viennese Jews to work, lobbying civil servants on their behalf in October and November 1938. As a key member of the Ministry of Commerce advisory committee, Neumann was involved in evaluating the hundreds of visa and work applications from Vienna. So important was he that one senior civil servant referred to it as 'Mr Neumann's scheme'.[1]

He wrote to several applicants, and it was here that some conflict arose. Among the PRONI files are a small number of letters of complaint about Alfred Neumann. On 4 October 1938, Edmund Fehl, an engineer living at Porzellangasse 45, Vienna, protested to the Ministry of Commerce about his treatment by Neumann, and by the latter's rejection of his application.[2]

Fehl detailed his correspondence with Neumann, who had asked for 'full submission under his orders':

Today I have received the answer by Mr Alfred Neumann. The refusal he has written me has touched the very essence of the matter, but he was full of the very lowest expressions, and I may say, that never in my life I have read such a letter, nor I have received such a letter at any time. I can't imagine for what a purpose he has written me such an insolent letter and has insulted me, but in no case, I will believe, that it should be the intention of the Ministry that such an answer should be given to me.

Fehl then asked the Ministry of Commerce to read the correspondence to judge it for themselves, and to discuss his application directly with him.

A similar outraged letter, in German, arrived from Joseph Schechter, of Grünentorgasse 19/15, on 29 October 1938. Schechter, aged thirty, had first written to the Ministry requesting entry permits for himself, his wife May, aged twenty-nine, and their one-year-old son, Hans.

Neumann asked Schechter to send him some of his products so that he could see if they would be in competition with local articles. Furthermore, he didn't understand how Schechter could write that he had no money, for 'someone who had no competition must own at least a couple of houses':

> You must excuse the fact that I used your own words to you, but here one has to go into things in detail and when one writes that he would not be in competition, one assumes that he owns a large income on account of his monopoly, for to me that would be the evidence that the article is good, if it brings in good profit. Everything else is just stuff and nonsense (as my grandfather said).

Neumann added: 'The money you have there can be changed into something else, though of course legally. So, I await your reply about the property you have there.'

Schechter complained to the Ministry of Commerce about the 'insults and meannesses', and included a copy of Neumann's letter to let them make up their own mind Letters with such suspicious content, far from being issued using the Ministry's reputation, were something to be ashamed of, he said. He asked them to let Neumann know that he would not be insulted by him again. The Ministry, however, rejected both Fehl's and Schechter's applications.

Neumann was also busy on behalf of young Jews with civil servants in Belfast. He lobbied H. J. Campbell, staff officer at the Ministry of Home Affairs, for entry permits for seven Austrians, five children and two guardians, under the protection of the Belfast Jewish community. One of them, Vicki Raab, aged fifteen, had used Neumann's address at Rossauer Lände in Vienna when applying.[3]

Campbell told Neumann the Home Office entirely controlled admissions and Neumann produced signed guarantees from members of the Belfast Jewish community undertaking to be responsible for the refugees. The five Viennese children would be housed at 62 Cliftonpark Avenue, Belfast, which the Jewish community would rent. Seven other Viennese children who had already received permits would be installed there too.

The German Jewish Aid Committee in London also wrote to the Home Office seeking visas as quickly as possible for four Viennese children the Belfast Jewish community had agreed to bring over and support. The RUC investigated which members of the Jewish community were undertaking responsibility for the children. It reported that a BJRC had been elected, which included as chairman Abraham Coppel, honorary secretary Maurice Coppel, and Rabbi Jacob Shachter. More children who came would be housed with members of the Jewish community. H. J. Campbell noted that there was no objection to the children coming.[4]

Individual Jewish refugees who made their way to Ireland, north or south, without the required visa, found the authorities much less accommodating. One case involving a Jewish refugee, a 'Polish Romeo searching for his Irish Juliet,' gained national prominence, and showed the obstacles they faced once caught up in the law.[5]

Leon Apfelbaum, aged twenty-six, a Polish knitting machinist, mechanic and designer, came to Belfast from Dublin on 19 October 1938 to look for an Irish woman he had fallen in love with in London. Apfelbaum had arrived at Dover on 19 February 1937, having travelled from Warsaw on a Polish passport, which expired the following month. He had been granted a registration certificate on 15 May 1937, but was not allowed to establish himself or get a job. He worked clandestinely in London, but fell ill and was a patient at the London Jewish Hospital between March and June 1938, where he met an Irish nurse. She returned to Ireland, and he came to Bray, County Wicklow, on 17 September 1938 to find her, without success. His hospital stay had drained his resources, an RUC report to the Ministry of Home affairs said.

Apfelbaum worked for a time in a Dublin warehouse but his employers had to dismiss him since he could not receive a work permit. He travelled to Belfast, where he called at the Aliens' Registration Office, saying he had no money and wanted some means to take him to London. On 21 October 1938 he reported his arrival on a temporary visit, saying he was lodging at Carrick House men's hostel. He was arrested on 24 October when found wandering the streets without means of subsistence, and was remanded in custody for a week.

Apfelbaum told police he had no friends in Belfast and refused to ask for assistance from the Belfast Jewish Board of Guardians, stating that 'he had been eliminated from that body'. He then asked if he committed an offence would the police arrest him and send him back to London. He appeared in court again on 26 October 1938 and his solicitor said 'a number of good Samaritans' had come to his aid. Mr J. H. Campbell, Resident Magistrate, granted bail and an adjournment and said he considered 'the young man had had extremely hard luck'.

The RUC informed the Metropolitan Police and the Garda Síochána, sent fingerprints and photographs, and asked the Resident Magistrate to recommend to the Ministry of Home Affairs that Apfelbaum be deported. On 3 November 1938 David Gilfillan and Neumann wrote to Apfelbaum offering him a job, if he could obtain a work permit. His solicitor wrote to the Minister of Labour, John F. Gordon, seeking permission for him to work in Northern Ireland.

On 6 December 1938 the *Daily Express*, under the headline 'Leon Still Seeks His Lost Love', reported that he was still searching for the Irish nurse he had fallen for in London. The reporter said he met him strolling around Belfast watching the faces of the passersby. Apfelbaum said: 'Sometimes I stay in and read but I spend the time chiefly strolling around. I can do nothing until my case is finished. Some people must know the nurse's address. Perhaps they cannot tell me.' The Home Office informed the Ministry of Home Affairs that Apfelbaum should be charged with wandering without ostensible means of subsistence and the magistrate be asked to recommend a deportation order.

On 20 December 1938 the *Belfast News Letter* reported that Apfelbaum had not appeared in court the day before and his whereabouts were unknown. Police said they had traced Apfelbaum to Liverpool, but next day the RUC informed the Ministry of Home Affairs that Apfelbaum was now in St Kevin's Hospital, Dublin. Two days later, the *Northern Whig* reported that Apfelbaum had been jailed for a month in Dublin for failing to comply with a deportation order. He was sent to Mountjoy Gaol to give the Polish consul in London time to look into his case. On 4 February 1939, the *Daily Mail* reported that 'Romeo is to be extradited by the Polish authorities.'

Leon Apfelbaum's fate is unknown. It is possible he was among the estimated five million Polish citizens killed during the war, perhaps as much as seventeen per cent of the population, including up to three million Polish Jews murdered in the Holocaust.

While the local and national press occupied itself with this 'colourful' human interest story, in Vienna tragedy on a huge scale was unfolding.

8
'A BIG SETTLING OF
ACCOUNTS WITH THE JEWS'

On the night of 9 November 1938, Radio Vienna broadcast news of the death of a German diplomat, Ernst vom Rath, who had been shot two days earlier in Paris by a seventeen-year-old Polish Jewish refugee, Herschel Grynszpan. His family had been among thousands of stateless Polish Jews deported from Germany but refused entry to Poland. Vom Rath's death was the pretext for a planned pogrom against Jews throughout Germany and Austria. In Vienna, the SS, the SA, the Hitler Youth, and gangs of Nazi Party members launched a savage onslaught on the city's Jewish population. They attacked and murdered Jewish people, wrecked and looted houses, shops and businesses, bombed and set alight the city's synagogues and prayer rooms, and dragged men from their homes to police stations, makeshift holding centres and concentration camps. The Austrian historian Doron Rabinovici described the terror:

> The offices of the *Israelitische Kultusgemeinde* were also ransacked. Several hundred officials were arrested. The food kitchens were demolished, the food mixed with glass and the soup poured away.
>
> The arrest and mistreatment of large numbers of woman was something new. In Brigittenau [a district of Vienna], 200 women were forced to dance naked in a basement. A Jewish woman who refused was tied to a table and her fellow victims were made to spit in her face.

Twenty-seven persons were beaten to death in Vienna alone. A total of 6,547 Jews were arrested and 3,700 of them deported to Dachau. One of the deportees claimed that after his experiences of detention in Vienna, the deportation to Dachau concentration camp was 'almost like a holiday'.[1]

The violence quickly became known as Kristallnacht, or the Night of Broken Glass, though Reichspogrom better captures its official, sanctioned character. That night and for several days after Nazi thugs attacked Jews wherever they could find them – on the streets, on trams, in their homes. Many were forced to paint racist slogans on shops owned by Jews, as leering Viennese relished their humiliation. Others were taken away to clean toilets in Nazi barracks.

The SS Deputy Leader Reinhard Heydrich had ordered police and firemen in the Reich not to intervene in the arson attacks, except when neighbouring buildings were in danger. In Vienna, firemen stood by as forty-two of the city's synagogues and prayer houses were burned down or blown up. Only the city's main synagogue, the Stadttempel in Seitenstettengasse, was saved.

In towns, villages and cities across the Reich, Jews were paraded through the streets, sometimes past jeering mobs, in other places in silence. Soon some of their neighbours would be queuing at auctions to get their hands on any furniture or goods that had not been looted, at knockdown prices. Anyone who criticised the attacks was liable to be threatened, assaulted or arrested. Most acquiesced in the pogrom, through fear, indifference or support for the perpetrators, though some Germans and Austrians offered shelter and support to the terrorised Jews, at serious risk to their own safety.

The official death toll was ninety-one people murdered, but some historians estimate that hundreds more died from ill-treatment in concentration camps. Altogether, 1,400 synagogues and prayer rooms were destroyed, 7,000 shops and businesses damaged, and 30,000 men arrested and sent to concentration camps. Only those detainees who promised to emigrate within three weeks, leaving behind their property, were released in the following weeks and months. The Anschluss violence and the November pogrom received wide coverage in the Northern Irish daily newspapers, with G. E. R. Gedye's excellent reporting for the *Daily Telegraph*, carried by arrangement with the *Belfast Telegraph*, in particular conveying the horror.[2] *The Irish News* and *News Letter* also published regular accounts, and editorials took a strong line against the persecution, though individual papers reflected the particular concerns of their readers. The *News Letter* argued that the Jewish refugee problem was an international one and should not fall on the British Empire alone, while *The Irish News* raised 'the kind of persecution that might befall Catholics in Austria'.[3]

Eyewitness accounts given by Jewish refugees to the Jewish Central Information Office in Amsterdam set up by Dr Alfred Wiener, a German Jew, describe the violence and ill-treatment Vienna's Jews endured during Kristallnacht:

Another detainee described how he was among 200 men loaded into a cattle truck and forced to stand for five days and nights without food and water in a journey to Dachau. They were forced to stare continuously into a strong light on the truck roof, and anyone who bent his head was beaten. The truck was shot at if there was the slightest sound. A number of prisoners died before they reached the camp. On arrival they were forced to exercise for hours. If they complained of thirst, coffee was thrown on the stone floor for them to lick up. Jews were also held in the 'race crimes' section, where each prisoner was kicked in the stomach five times with a spiked shoe for each 'crime' committed. Many men died there. Another torture was to hoist the prisoners off the ground with a rope tied to their legs, and to drop them onto their heads. Many were 'smashed to pieces' on the floor. Prisoners were also ordered to lie on the floor in rows, ordered to open their mouths wide, and guards urinated into them. There were 'many indescribable variants' of this policy.

Other punishments 'for small things' included twenty lashes with a spiked stick, administered by twenty different guards so that each stroke was given by 'a tireless arm'. Prisoners were allowed to talk to each other only during a one-hour period; anyone caught saying a word outside that time was given a 'number of blows'. There was nothing to eat, drinking water was inadequate and polluted, there was no heating and shelter was totally inadequate. Every prisoner on release was forced to sign a paper stating they were never mistreated, had always eaten and drunk well, and were forbidden 'to speak about their treatment in the concentration camp, on pain of death'. Men returned from Dachau who lost thirty pounds in weight in one week. 'Fatalities are reported to the family so they can come and fetch the urn; the body itself is never returned.'[4]

Another prisoner described his mistreatment in Vienna and Buchenwald in a statement. He was taken to a school gymnasium in Vienna, where Jews had been brought since 2 a.m. They were met by police, SA and SS men, all of whom struck them with bullwhips and sticks. He escaped flogging, but was kicked so badly that he could hardly walk. A terrible picture presented itself. The blood of the 'poor, wounded people' who had been beaten sprayed out and their 'terrible screams of pain' were nerve-racking:

> After the beasts had staunched their sadistic lust we were ordered to knee-bend with arms raised, face to the wall so that they could shoot us. Moreover, what was about to happen was all the same to me. Now a new hail of beatings was deployed and blood sprayed about in such a way that my coat was completely spattered with the blood of other Jews. I was lucky again in this situation too, I received nothing, perhaps because someone amongst them wished me well.[5]

The violence accelerated official German action against the Jews. On 12 November 1938 Field Marshal General Hermann Göring told a meeting of senior German government officials at the Reich Air Ministry in Berlin, including Reich Minister of Propaganda Joseph Goebbels and Heydrich, that 'a Sühneleistung' [sin tax] of 1,000 million Reichsmarks was to be imposed on the German Jews as compensation for the death of vom Rath and to cover the costs of the pogrom damage. He also signalled another raft of anti-Jewish legislation to drive the final nail into the coffin of Jewish economic activity and extend the segregation of Jews from Aryans. In March

1939 Austrian Jewish men and women had to adopt the names 'Israel' and 'Sara' respectively, and use them in all official documents, a measure designed to identify and humiliate them.[6]

As the Nazi leaders discussed possible Jewish counter-moves to the financial measures to be taken against them, Göring assured them that there would be none, and made an ominous prediction: 'If in some foreseeable future an external conflict were to happen, it is obvious that we in Germany would also think first and foremost of carrying out a big settling of accounts with the Jews'.[7] Heydrich stressed that all measures should lead to emigration, and briefed the meeting using a report prepared by Eichmann:

> He pointed out that in the time it had taken 19,000 German Jews to emigrate, the *Zentralstelle* in Vienna had facilitated the departure of 50,000 Jews. It seemed that in a few months Eichmann had removed from Austria many more Jews than it had been possible to push out of Germany, despite the plethora of anti-Jewish laws and constant anti-Jewish propaganda.[8]

The point was well taken: on 30 January 1939, Göring decreed the establishment of the Central Office for Jewish Emigration for the Reich, with Heydrich as its head. Vienna was now a model centre of expulsion. Berlin's Jewish leaders were ordered to go there to see how the SS handled Jewish migration. They were shocked at what they saw in the Central Office for Jewish Emigration at the Rothschild Palace:

> The main hall filled with cowed and desperate Jews, the desks at which property, wealth and rights were exchanged for pieces of paper whose only value was to enable the bearer to get out of Austria. It was not an assembly line, but a disassembly line: professional men, property owners, families, all emerged stripped and shattered, their former lives smashed to pieces.[9]

Then they met Eichmann. He told them they were going to be responsible for the emigration of 1,000 Berlin Jews a day. The delegation leader, Heinrich Stähl, a brave World War I veteran, said the cost of emigration could be paid out of the 'flight tax' imposed on the migrating Jews, which infuriated Eichmann. That money was for the Reich. 'Germans would not pay for keeping you old bags alive', he said. Eichmann was further enraged when news of the 'terroristic methods' used against Austrian Jews leaked out in a Parisian Yiddish newspaper, almost certainly after details were given to the delegation in unauthorised contacts with local Jewish leaders. The article referred to 'the bloodhound Eichmann', who was described as an 'enemy of the Jews'. Eichmann recalled the delegation and demanded to know who had leaked details about his activity. When the groups stonewalled, Eichmann again singled out Stähl for abuse, calling him an '*alter Scheißsack* – an old shitbag'.[10]

On the night of 9 November 1938, in Vienna, Otto Goldberger, aged thirty-one, listened with great foreboding to the radio news about the death of Ernst vom Rath, with his parents, Hermann, aged sixty-two, and Malwine, aged fifty-six.[11] Next morning, Otto went to his small shirt factory at Rögergasse 12 and his female workers greeted him on the verge of tears, thinking he had already been arrested. They told him about the terrible events of the night before and added that several Jews had committed suicide.

Otto was popular with his workers and was a talented pianist and an outstanding swimmer. His brother Hans represented Austria as a swimmer at the Olympic Games in Amsterdam in 1928, where the legendary American Johnny Weissmuller won two gold medals before going on to play Tarzan in twelve films. Otto's father Hermann counted Theodor Herzl, one of the founders of modern Zionism, among his friends but regarded his ideas as 'half-crazy and unworkable'. Otto later wrote of his father: 'To him, trying to arouse a nationalistic feeling among the Jews may only awaken anti-Semitic counter actions and make matters worse. He was blind to the darkening clouds gathering over the horizon right to the bitter end.'

In October 1938 Hans left Vienna illegally on a ship sailing down the Danube to the Romanian Black Sea port of Constanza, planning to go to Palestine. Otto decided to go to Australia via London, staying there with his sister Fritzi. Luckily, he obtained a British visa within days. He tried to convince his parents to come, but they were determined to stay.

The day after Kristallnacht two men in civilian clothes arrived at the factory around 11 a.m. and arrested Otto. They walked in silence for twenty minutes to one of the city's main police stations. There he was pushed into a big room full of Jewish men. His heart nearly stopped at the sight of all 'those unfortunate and pathetic people'. Hundreds were lying on the floor, because there were only a few benches available, hardly speaking to each other, staring into space. They were locked up there all day without food. In a memoir written towards the end of his life, he wrote:

> It was getting already dark, when suddenly the doors were opened wide and in came about four or five SS men, sinister-looking characters in their black tunics, carbines around their shoulders and steel helmets. We were ordered to get up and move quickly and orderly to the big police yard outside, constantly pushed and shouted at. Once in the yard we had to line up in single file, in a few rows, and stand there in the cold November evening, motionless and waiting.[12]

After some time standing still, more guards arrived for a last inspection. It became clear to Otto that they were being sent to a concentration camp:

> As the guards passed us, I with a quick glimpse recognised an old school-friend, Franz Pokorny. Not knowing what I was doing, I stepped out of line and only said: 'Franz, do you remember me?' He had just passed me when he suddenly stopped and jerked his head, staring at me: '*Goldberger, aus der Reihe sofort an die Wand und bleibe dort.*' ['Goldberger, out of the line immediately to the wall and stay there'.] I went to the wall and remained silent. I was convinced this was the end of me, a few bullets in my back and it is all over. My fate was sealed. I was standing there, God knows how long. I heard lorries arriving and shouting and crying, but I never turned my head once. Then there was suddenly stillness, when I heard footsteps coming toward me and it was my friend, Franz Pokorny. He asked me to come with him. We went along to the big entrance gate and never spoke

one word. He ordered the guard to open the gate and as he pushed me out into the street, he just said in his Viennese dialect: 'Scram home as fast as you can and let no one see you for a few days'. I have never seen Franz, who saved my life, again. He probably perished like so many in the Russian snow-waste during the war in the East.[13]

In fact, Franz Pokorny would spend the war in Vienna and later face prosecution for his Nazi activities. Next day Otto learned that the Nazis had plundered the factory, taking everything apart from the machinery:

My sole and only worry was my parents, whom I would have to leave at the mercy of those beasts, the new masters of the new Germany. Even my father began now to realise the true situation and reassured me he would try to obtain a passport if he had to, as his only option. I look back in sadness at his unswerving optimism in the midst of dire calamity, always believing in the goodness of man.[14]

After considerable effort, Otto obtained all his travel documents. One day in mid-December 1938, his parents accompanied him to say farewell at the Westbahnhof station. Otto was nearly overcome with the worry of leaving them behind: 'I must have felt in my innermost being I shall never see my parents again … just before leaving I consoled them by saying we shall see you very soon, against my better judgement, and after a last look the train moved slowly out of the station.' Near the Dutch border, SS troops and German police took Otto and a Jewish girl from his compartment off the train, and searched their documents and luggage carefully. They were finally allowed to proceed to Holland.

When my Jewish female travelling companion enquired of the Dutch border police if this was now Holland, she just broke into tears, being let out of prison and breathing fresh air again. I nearly felt the same. The feeling of leaving the tyrannical regime of the Third Reich, SS butchers and Gestapo, was indescribable and took some time to take in. We were now in a free country, nobody asked questions such as 'where are you coming from?', 'where are you going?', or what your religion or racial origin was. You only appreciate freedom and democratic humanity when you have the misfortune to live in a ruthless dictatorship.[15]

When Otto reached London, he learned that his sister Fritzi was in a place called Londonderry, which was not a suburb of London as he thought, but in Northern Ireland. He also found that the Australian government had suspended immigration for all German and Austrian nationals. He could stay just four weeks in the United Kingdom, because his sister had only a temporary visa. After visiting the sights in London, he crossed the Irish Sea. His initial impression of Derry was a mixed one – 'a rather small Irish town, where everybody knew everybody and people greeted each other with a short twist of their neck, I thought first a nervous habit'.

Being reunited with Fritzi was a 'real blessing', and Otto began to relax. They phoned their parents in Vienna and begged them to get passports; they would do everything possible to get them out. Then Otto had to report his arrival to the police at Victoria Barracks on the Strand Road. He was apprehensive and arrived 'rather meekly', but was interviewed by a staff officer, offered a cup of tea and a cigarette, and asked about conditions in Vienna:

> The men were very tall and rather good-looking and above all, very polite and friendly. They asked me to get a photo and come back, when they would issue me with an alien certificate, which would give me permission to remain in Northern Ireland with no time limit. I thanked them very much and left with a great burden off my shoulders.[16]

He soon made many friends and believed the whole town knew him, even dignitaries such as the Lord Mayor Sir Basil McFarland, as well as Thomas Finnegan, the professor of classics at Magee College. He visited Finnegan regularly and was deeply impressed by him. Finnegan spoke near-perfect German and was, Otto thought, convinced of Hitler's thirst for reckless territorial expansion, a 'sure signal for conflict'. Otto also became friends with prominent members of the Jewish community and was struck by how orthodox they were, in contrast to his own 'more progressive and assimilated upbringing'.

He was impressed by the beauty of the nearby Lough Swilly peninsula, and even more by the imbalance between women and men at the Saturday night dances in a ballroom in the city centre. When he asked a friend, Jimmy Sherrard, what had happened to the men, he 'just laughed and told me there are no men available, they are all away looking for work elsewhere and I can have my choice and pick whomever I fancy, big ones, small ones, fat or thin ones. Paradise for the male.'

His brother Hans had undergone a nightmarish three-month voyage with 200 other Jewish passengers from Vienna to Palestine. When he finally reached the coast, it was swarming with Royal Navy ships trying to stop illegal immigrants from landing. Hans and some others swam 'the few miles to shore' where the Jewish paramilitary group, the Haganah, told them to destroy their papers to stop the British sending them back. Otto was now very worried about what would happen in Vienna. 'The uncertain fate of our poor parents, caught in the Nazi hell-hole bore heavily on our minds. Alas, we were unable to do anything about it.'[17] In Derry, Otto tried to get a part-time job, to be less of a burden on his sister, but unemployment levels were very high. He made contacts with staff in some shirt factories, who were interested in continental shirt-making, and earned a few pounds now and again. Fritzi and he kept writing to their parents, 'really concerned and constantly worried about the worsening situation, with it quickly becoming impossible to obtain travel papers to facilitate their escape'.

At a funeral in Belfast in July 1939, Otto met Thomas Sunderland, co-owner of a local clothing factory, who offered him a job as a tailor. The wages were 'rather small' but he gladly accepted, particularly since his knowledge of tailoring was then 'nil'. He stayed with a family named McCoy in Eglantine Avenue, in the university area of Belfast, for five shillings a week. They were very kind to him, and when he agreed to give Mrs McCoy's two daughters piano lessons, he was able to live rent-free. The McCoys were keen Irish dancers and later opened a successful dance school.

Another young couple, Miklos and Dora Szanto, also made it to
Derry in 1938 after a hair-raising escape from Vienna. Dora, born in
1907, had lived there all her life, while Miklos, a fashion designer, had
moved with his family to Vienna a year after he was born in Budapest
in 1901. Miklos and Dora married in 1933. A frightening incident
which took place after the Anschluss convinced them that they must
get out. Coming home from work one evening, Miklos saw a man
he knew, a Jew, on his knees at the feet of an SS officer, scraping out
the dirt between pavement flagstones with his fingernails. Miklos and
the Jewish man recognised each other and the latter shouted at the SS
officer, 'Him! Make him do this! He's a Jew too!' The SS man kicked
him in the side and ordered him to get back to work. The man kept
insisting, 'Make him do this, leave me alone, he's a Jew too!' The SS man
appeared confused for a while, then kicked him again, and said, 'Get on
with your work! I'll decide who's a Jew around here.' A terrified Miklos
walked away. His son George wrote: 'Years later he told me of the heart-
gripping horror and the sense of betrayal he felt, in equal parts.'[18]

Miklos immediately tried to arrange the emigration of Dora,
his mother Ottilie and mother-in-law Anna-Netty. His design skills
would help him find a job in many parts of the world. Their first
choice was the United States, where the majority of their relatives had
already settled. But the US quota system was based on a ratio of the
nationalities already in the country. If two per cent of US citizens were
of Austrian origin, two per cent of emigrants could be from Austria.
Dora would have no problem getting in. But Miklos had to qualify
on a Hungarian quota, and fewer than one per cent of Americans
were of Hungarian origin. It would be practically impossible for him
to obtain a visa. The couple next tried Canada, but Canada admitted
few Jewish refugees, only 5,000 between 1933 and 1948. Canada's
immigration minister, Frederick Charles Blair, was strongly opposed
to Jewish immigration. Most of Canada's political and business leaders,
including the Prime Minister, Mackenzie King, supported this policy.
'One of Blair's immigration officials, when asked how many Jews
should be admitted to Canada, replied, "None is too many."'[19]

The couple next considered Chile, where Dora's sister and her
husband had emigrated several years before, but they feared that
they would never see any of their family members again. Then

they heard that Britain was keen to admit people with Miklos's expertise in knitwear. Through a trade paper, Miklos applied and successfully obtained a job designing outsize women's swimwear with Gilfillan Ltd in Derry. He soon obtained a British visa, and Dora queued every day for two weeks for the coveted Austrian visas. Each time she reached the Nazi official in charge, she was told 'No, not possible':

> Finally, she resorted to placing a large bill [banknote] inside the covers of the British visa. She felt brave, but fearful as well – would she be put in jail for bribery? The Nazi slipped the bill into his pocket and smiled, telling her, 'But we didn't mean to have such lovely women as yourself leave, Fräulein.' In half an hour she had two exit visas.[20]

In October 1938 Miklos and Dora readied themselves to travel to Northern Ireland but they had to leave their mothers behind. Dora was told that getting their parents out would be easier from England. The mothers would follow when their visas were obtained, and hoped their possessions and furniture would be sent to Derry by Dora's firm. Dora had worked as a trilingual secretary with Schenker & Company, a large import-export firm, and was highly regarded by them. Her mother, Anna-Netty, had to pack at home under the eyes of an SS officer. She tried to include her silver candlesticks and when he moved to stop her, she said, 'Surely you wouldn't begrudge my daughter these? Surely you would want your own daughter to have her candlesticks.' He let her have them.

Miklos and Dora had their visas, but feared being stopped at the Austrian frontier and prevented from leaving. They came up with a daring plan. They flew from Vienna to Berlin with their skis. No Jews would risk flying into the heart of the Reich, so they would be safe, they thought. Pretending to be going on a skiing holiday, they took a train to Munich, then a local train into the Bavarian Alps, and stayed a night in a ski lodge. Next morning, with just their rucksacks, they climbed high into the German mountains and skied down into Switzerland. They then flew to London, took the train to Liverpool, the ferry to Belfast, and on to Derry.

But it proved much more difficult to get their mothers out of the country. Dora had to travel to London three times to sort out their visa problems, the last time at Passover 1939. Finally, both mothers managed to emigrate. They lived with Miklos and Dora in Derry, where, according to Dora, they bickered incessantly. In 1943, Ottilie obtained a visa to the United States, and she travelled across the Atlantic by ship, running the risk of being sunk by U-boats. Anna-Netty left Derry after the war ended, and lived the rest of her life with her daughter Kit in New York.

Miklos and Dora were lucky to escape before the horrors of Kristallnacht, but Miklos' brother Leopold, a jeweller, was not so fortunate. He was arrested and sent to Dachau. His wife Elly frantically tried to secure his release, visiting Gestapo headquarters eleven times and obtaining US visas before she succeeded. They left with Elly's parents in April 1939.[21] For the less fortunate, often jobless and penniless, it was now even harder to get out of Vienna.

9

'I IMPLORE YOU FOR THE QUICKEST HELP'

By December 1938 more than a third of Austrian Jews had been forced out of the country.[1] After the murderous Kristallnacht violence and mass arrests, the Nazis demanded an increase in Jewish emigration. This led to a second surge of letters at the Northern Ireland Ministry of Commerce. Despite the large number of applications rejected, they continued to arrive throughout the autumn.

Henriette (Hinda) Wollisch, aged sixty-four, of Liechtensteinstrasse 73, wrote in English on 8 December 1938, pleading for a permit for her 'miserable son' Alfred, aged thirty-eight, arrested on 12 November 1938 and deported to Dachau. He had never occupied himself with politics, nor was he guilty of any other crime. 'I implore you for the quickest help and intervention.'[2]

She said she was told by the authorities that he would be set free if he had permission to travel to another country, therefore a permit would be necessary. He had been living with her because he was single, and had been employed as a wages clerk for eighteen years with several large companies. He knew English and had worked in Vienna, Bratislava and Hamburg. She included references from companies which said he had been entrusted with 'very grave causes' and was a person in whom they had the greatest confidence. He had been let go in April 1938, 'due to the political subversion and to the change in the firm which he was connected with'. 'No reply' is written on her letter.[3]

A sign of the dire financial straits of some applicants can be seen in a letter from Artur Wald, from Nice, on 24 February 1939. He said he had sent five leather belts worth twenty Reichsmarks to the Ministry of Commerce in October 1938. He had emigrated from Vienna, and since he had no work or possibility of making a living, he found himself in greater need. He begged them to send as soon as possible the '1¾ pounds', or to return the belts so that he himself could make some money with them. A note on his letter said 'Regret'.[4]

Leo Friedmann, aged forty-two, a maker of buttons and buckles, wrote on 14 March 1939 from Lienfeldergasse 11–13, saying he had written on 7 January but had received no reply. He sought visas for himself, his wife Gertrude, aged thirty-six, and their son Kurt, just six weeks old. They had been all been moved from Pfeilgasse 48. The couple had been born in Czechoslovakia but were now naturalised German subjects. Friedmann also mentions a couple, Erwin Pollak, aged thirty-nine, and Regine, who had been living at Praterstrasse 52. All five were refused entry.[5]

Mathilde Fischer, aged forty-five, from Castellzgasse 20, Vienna, a ladies' clothing manufacturer for eighteen years, said she would apprentice a number of girls and employ them if admitted to Northern Ireland. She sought permits for herself, her husband Emil, aged sixty-one, Charles Günsberger, aged forty-five, an underwear manufacturer, and his wife Carola, aged forty-one, both then living in Vienna. All four were refused entry.[6]

Some applicants wrote seeking visas for themselves and their families to go to Derry, and promised valuable contacts to sell Ulster goods abroad. Arthur Haas, of Henrietta Platz 3, aged fifty-two, a leather goods master craftsman, married to Beila, with a daughter, wrote on 24 February 1939 seeking a job with Gilfillan and Neumann Ltd. Arthur Haas had worked for the leather goods export firm of Rabl and Grün, which employed nearly 300 workers in Vienna. The firm had Jewish commercial travellers in Asia and in Central and South America, and he had been in permanent connection with them since the 'changed situation' in Austria. 'I believe that I am able to acquire these Gentlemen for me.' The Nazis had recently liquidated the firm. He sent some information about Rabl and Grün: 'I take the liberty to ask the honourable Ministry whether another house or person of your country is interested in my proposal.' Arthur and Beila Haas and their daughter were rejected.[7]

Berthold Kohn owned a weaving company in Vienna and, as a Jew 'compelled to transfer my residence to another place', sought permits for himself and two assistants to set up a factory in Northern

Ireland. These were Hans Kraus, of Ingenhausz 4 and Emil Eckstein of Reisnerstrasse 15. They too were refused entry, and no note was written on their application.[8]

Hermann Arnold, a native of Hawrylowce in what is now Belarus, living at Denisgasse 4, aged forty-nine, wrote in German, saying he was an expert in making industrial filters, but as a Jew he had no possibility of earning a living and must seek work in another country. He had owned a business making household equipment and leather goods since 1918. He, too, was refused entry.[9]

Rudolf Berger, aged fifty-two, a master producer of jams and fruit juices, applied from Kriernhildplatz 1, saying he could bring over machines and could employ a large number of people, or at least could earn his own keep. A note stated, 'fruit juice. No opening', and he was rejected.[10]

Gertrude Bunzlau, aged thirty-six, a single woman living at Hollandstrasse 10, an exporter of industrial art articles, asked for entry and a work permit. She had been producing knitwear and other articles for eight years, and could train people in all kinds of work. Her application was rejected with the usual one-word note, 'Regret'.[11]

Elisabeth Fränkel, aged eighteen, who worked in applied art, knitting at home, was also rejected. She had written on 31 August 1938, and when she received no reply she wrote again on 15 October 1938, but again received no response from the Ministry of Commerce.[12]

Moritz Katz, of Silienbrunngasse 5, aged fifty-two, a corset maker, applied for permits for himself, his wife, Therese, aged thirty-seven, a cook, and their son Bruno, aged eleven. Their application was refused.[13]

Emil Löbl, aged forty-five, a bank official and widower from Strozzigasse 2, with a daughter, Ingeborg, aged eleven, enquired about job and visa prospects and said he was ready to do anything for a living for him and his daughter. They were rejected.[14]

Bernhard Mosonyi, aged fifty-three, of Stumpergasse 9, a belt maker, had come to Vienna from Budapest in 1912, served in the Austrian-Hungarian army and then had started a factory. He said he could bring out machines and employ ten to fifteen hands immediately. 'No reply' was written on his letter.[15]

Arthur Neumann (no relation), aged forty-eight, applied with his wife Hermine, aged forty-seven, on 14 September 1938; a note on his letter says 'not one of the best known'. They were rejected.[16]

Josef Neubrunn, aged fifty-five, of Erdgasse 29, said he was prepared to set up a factory to make novelties with the help of a partner, and also to set one up at his own risk and without any material help. He noted that the Ministry of Commerce had no opinion on the utility of his proposal in their reply to an earlier letter. He was turned down.[17]

Arnold Rosenberger, aged thirty-eight, single, a decorated World War I soldier working as a leather goods expert, of Arnezhofergasse 9, sought to come either as a workman or to set up a factory. He was refused entry and the sample of his work he sent was returned to him.[18]

People became increasingly desperate and made clear their willingness to do any work. Richard Rosenbaum, aged fifty-four, of Untere Viaduktgasse, described himself as 'tall and very strong', a Czech subject who had worked in his parents' distillery, then as a farm manager, and sought any job. He was not accepted.[19]

Simon Kleinberger, aged fifty, of Angelsgasse 39, was a maker of hats and hoods and his son was an electro-engineer. He asked if he could get himself, his wife Berta, aged fifty, and his son out, and transfer his machinery to Northern Ireland. A civil servant noted that he should be sent a letter explaining the rules. The family were refused entry.[20]

Ignaz Rothmann, aged thirty-three, of Wichtelgasse 20, wrote on 9 October 1938, and wanted to open a factory making knitted jersey garments. He worked with a female designer, aged thirty, who had opened her own workshop at the age of twenty-two. 'No opening' was written on his application.[21]

Max Seidner, aged thirty-seven, a hat maker, and his wife Margarete, aged thirty-three, a fashion worker, applied looking for jobs, but said they would otherwise work in a household. They were turned down.[22]

Dorothea Both, aged fifty, living at Untere Viaduktsgasse 53, a corset maker, wrote asking for permits for her husband Dr Benno Both, aged fifty-eight, a bookkeeper, her younger sister

Zofia Haber, aged forty-three, her husband Josef, aged fifty-six, and their son, Friedrich Haber, aged twelve, of Alserstrasse 71. The application was refused.[23]

Amalie Korn, aged forty-two, ran a knitwear business at Forstergasse 8, and exported the bulk of her products to 'the British empire'. She could bring some machines with her, but needed starting capital. She would use British raw materials and could easily train the necessary labour. 'Regret' appeared on her letter.[24]

Friederike Altstädter, aged thirty-nine, of Windussichlgasse 25, wrote saying she was trying hard to secure in England half the capital needed for her application and believed she could give a concrete answer within days. She asked for their patience. 'Regret' appeared on her letter too.[25]

Paul Stagel, aged twenty-five, and his wife Fritzi, aged twenty-two, a 'perfect applied arts worker', of Boltzmanngasse 18, wanted to set up a home-industry workshop making artificial flowers and belts. In a second letter Stagel said he had £20, an aunt in London would give him £20, and he would like to borrow £20, which he would repay as soon as possible. A note on their letter states, 'Same as N'ards [Newtownards], very small.' They were refused entry.[26]

Handicraft workers and skilled artisans, who had been described in the *Zionistische Rundschau* article as having a chance of a new start in Northern Ireland, fared little better than anybody else. Sara Schütz, of Neubaugasse 64, aged sixty, who had worked forty years as an applied arts worker, wrote seeking permits for herself and her husband Hugo, aged sixty-four. She sent a second letter saying she could employ forty to fifty women permanently. A note said 'No opening', and she was rejected.[27]

Two sisters, Ernestine (Erna), aged sixty-three, and Friederike (Frieda) Silber, aged fifty-six, of Neubaugasse 33, applied for visas together. Erna was an independent dressmaker who had managed a business for thirty years, and Frieda was a first-class milliner, who had also managed a shop. Frieda wrote that it was her 'wish to practise my profession in the same country with my sister because I am single and I have no other relations'. They included as a referee a Mr Zeiler, a hat-maker, who had been living in Galway since December 1937. They were refused entry.[28]

Szyfra Schneider, aged forty-two, a former Polish citizen living in Vienna for nearly thirty years, of Rueppgasse 7, was a manager of a 'great fancy goods workshop', and 'would prove useful to every establishment'. She was refused entry.[29]

Marie Rosenberg, aged forty-five, sought to emigrate with her daughter Lilly, aged nineteen, of Gumpendorfer Strasse 8A. She made art embroidery for clothes and could bring out her machines. She sold her work to exporters. A note on her letter said simply 'Not Required. No opening. Regret.'[30]

Sidonie Wolkenstein, aged forty-five, of Glasergasse 16, a fashion designer with markets at home and abroad, who had managed a company for years and could train unskilled workers in a short time, received the standard 'Regret' letter.[31]

Dr Max Neustadtl, aged fifty-one, of Argentinierstrasse 13, who ran a cosmetics factory in the city with his brother, Dr Rudolf Neustadtl, and sister-in-law Helene Neustadtl, wrote from Zurich on 30 August 1938 that they had a great number of 'practically tested prescriptions' to make cosmetics and could found a factory. They had help from friends with sufficient means to cover the costs. Supplying packaging would also 'offer a gain to the natives'. Their application was refused.[32]

One of the few applications that was not rejected immediately was from several brothers called Schafranek, from Werderthorgasse 17, who ran a plywood and furniture factory there. Friedrich and Jacques Schafranek applied separately on behalf of all the brothers and said they supplied furniture to England, where there was a chance of large sales. J. Clarke of the Ministry of Commerce noted that the application might be of interest to a firm called Duff in Lisburn. He added that experts in the manufacture of plywood were scarce in the UK. Nothing, however, came of the application.[33]

Rudolf Schafranek, aged forty, living at Liechtensteinstrasse 119, a foreman in the family furniture factory for thirteen years and the son of a well-known family of officers of the Imperial Austrian army, also applied separately for a permit. Owing to 'the political changes', he said, he had to leave Austria and try to find a new home. He had no money and 'only a call to a post [job], whatever it be, could be of any use for me'. He knew English and bookkeeping, was a car driver and in perfect health. He asked for his photo to be returned. He was rejected.

Another Schafranek, Isidor, aged fifty-six, had a factory making cordials and fruit juices but had been forced to give it up. He wanted to set one up in Northern Ireland and could engage a great number of workmen. He was rejected.[34]

Dr Heinrich Molnar, aged fifty-seven, of Ladenburggasse 78 in Vienna, had a brush-making factory and employed fifteen people. He was about to increase this by five more when his work was 'interrupted by the present events'. He said that in Northern Ireland he could soon employ thirty workmen, which would greatly increase after the first export results. He would need only two or three Austrian workmen. He wanted permits for himself, his wife Regine, his collaborator Hans Berger, and his mother. He enquired about the chance of obtaining a little credit, but a note by a civil servant ordered that he be sent a letter explaining that the Ministry could not grant more than half of the working capital. He was refused entry to Northern Ireland.[35]

Manele Bohm, aged forty-two, and Gottlieb Mendel, aged forty-five, of Greiseneckergasse 22, made knitwear and employed up to seventy workers in their factory. They were also sure they could employ a great many people if given permission to come and to found a factory. They were refused.[36]

Fritz Mieser, aged forty-seven, wrote from Berggasse 4 that he could set up a leather goods firm. He was also a specialist in gold-pressed Vienna goods, 'much favoured in all foreign countries, which could be a great export from Ireland, with many workers employed'. He had the necessary engines and instruments. He was the well-known leader of a school to retrain people, 'with very good results'. This suggests that he was probably a key worker in the IKG, which retrained thousands of sacked Jewish professionals. He was refused.[37]

Ernst Löbl, aged thirty-eight, was managing director of a shirt-making factory in Vienna, founded by his father in 1878, and run by Ernst since 1920. He offered to set up workshops or retail shops provided he could get the financial support. He could not transfer his machines because of the 'present laws'. This was noted by a civil servant, a Mr Foster, who wrote at the top, 'first class shirt making. Saturated.' He was not admitted.[38]

Ernst Percy Schablin wrote from Pulverturmgasse 7 and included the newspaper cutting from the *Zionistische Rundschau*. He was a metal jeweller and art worker and his wife Frieda, aged thirty-eight, was a 'perfectionist' in leather goods, an academic painter and drawer of ladies' fashion. He was convinced they could get business and employ people. They would have to start work without capital because it was impossible to transfer any to foreign countries. He asked for an answer as soon as possible because he would leave Austria within the next two weeks. The application was rejected.[39]

Dr Leo Adler, aged sixty-nine, of Mosergasse 11, wrote seeking a permit to set up a pharmaceutical and cosmetics manufacturing plant. He wanted to bring over his wife Johanna, aged fifty-five, and son Rudolf, aged thirty-one, who was his co-worker and also an electro-chemist. He had run a factory in Vienna for thirty years. He wrote again saying that he had sent the details requested on 15 September but had received no reply. One word in blue pencil is written on this letter, 'Regret'.[40]

Rudolf Fuchs, aged forty-six, wanted to set up a sweet factory in Ireland because his company, Fuchs and Berger, was no longer allowed to operate, since he was Jewish. His application was rejected.[41]

Arthur Fischer, aged forty-nine, of Taubstummengasse 6, was a self-employed tradesman producing leather goods and had at one time employed thirty people. He wanted to found a new company and to train Irish workers with the help of his relatives, his wife Jeanette, aged forty-five, daughter Anita Pecker, aged twenty, and son-in-law Max Pecker, aged twenty-seven. He had applied to Mexico but preferred to go to Ireland if he received a positive response. 'No reply, same as Newtownards', is written in pencil on his 15 September 1938 letter. He wrote again from Rue Verte, Brussels on 29 November, saying he had received no answer to his first letter. He had been forced to emigrate, and asked for the speediest favourable answer. He had sent two leather belts by separate post as evidence of the quality of his work. A note on this letter said only 'No reply'.[42]

Otto Neugebauer, aged fifty-three, from Stuckgasse 5, sought a permit to emigrate and open a factory making adhesives. He had employed up to sixty-seven permanent workers, and intended to employ only Irish workers. He needed few funds and could build the works himself. No note appears on his application, and he was rejected.[43]

Edgar Kisch, aged forty-seven, and his wife Edith, aged thirty-nine, of Lindengasse 51, applied on 27 August 1938. He was a paper manufacturer; his wife also worked in the business and his son Peter, aged eleven, was in the first year of grammar school. Kisch wanted to produce applied art articles but had no capital. A friend could put capital at his disposal in Ireland, and he would seek permits for this man and his family. 'Regret' was written on their letter.[44]

Many of the highly qualified applicants said they would start up new types of industries if they were admitted. Dr Oskar Grauer, aged forty-one, a chemical engineer living at Renngasse 14, wrote to the Ulster Development Council hoping to found a chemical factory in Northern Ireland. He asked which type of chemical or cosmetic products would be of any interest. He was refused entry. [45]

Heinrich Idelovici, aged fifty-three, and Charles Grüner of Raxstrasse 69, wrote asking about the chances of establishing a bicycle and patents factory. They had one in Austria and it was a growing industry which they thought would be very useful for Northern Ireland. They were compelled to emigrate. The Ministry of Commerce sent information and they replied asking whether they had to write to the Home Office in London. But 'No reply' is written in pencil on their last letter of 15 September 1938.[46]

Arthur Fried, aged thirty-five, of Wittelsbachstrasse, sought to transfer his business preserving tinned fish and vegetables to Northern Ireland. Friends abroad would put £150 at his disposal, leaving him with £100 working capital. 'If the Ministry of Commerce would help with an appropriate subvention, this would enable a modest and promising start.' This would give permanent employment for the local fishing trade, sales for farmers and gardeners, further employment in vinegar production, large requirements of tin or glass, wooden packaging, as well as labels and printed material. No note was written on the letter, and Arthur Fried was not admitted.[47]

Isak Seidmann, of Filienbrünngasse 9, aged fifty-nine, and his wife Golde, aged fifty-six, employed fifty permanent workers in Vienna and could bring with them six machines. He wrote seeking to set up a knitwear and hosiery factory in Northern Ireland. They were rejected.[48]

Jakob Sonnenfeld, aged sixty-eight, who had his own ladies' clothing factory in Vienna, sought a permit for himself and his wife

Jetti, aged sixty-two. He wanted to bring over his machines and to start a business in Northern Ireland, and he asked if the permit was free. The couple were rejected.[49]

Hermann Schattner, of Rembrandtstrasse 32, aged thirty-three, a co-worker in a firm making women's underwear, and his wife Sali, aged twenty-one, also an expert worker who could teach female workers, sought permits for themselves and their four-year-old daughter Edith. A note from a civil servant said only, 'Asks for job'. All three were refused.[50]

Samuel Weiss, aged sixty-four, who ran the family embroidery firm S. Weiss and Brüder, and his wife Marie, aged fifty-six, sought permits because they had to emigrate from Austria, being Jews, and they asked for a favourable response as soon as possible. Samuel and Marie Weiss were rejected.[51]

Wilhelm Band, aged sixty, had invented a dental apparatus which sterilised root canals, and wanted to open a plant making the machines in Northern Ireland. 'The apparatus is absolutely new and has never been manufactured as yet anywhere.' He didn't ask for money at that stage, but said he would look for an Irish backer. He would ask the government for money later on if he needed it to complete the project. He wanted to bring his wife Sally, aged fifty-six. A note on his letter said 'too specialised', and they were rejected.[52]

Solly Spitalink, aged twenty-six, of Schmelzgasse 12, a 'perfect' dressmaker, and Rachel Fisch, aged thirty-three, of Mariahilfer Strasse 99 wrote to the Irish Department of Industry and Commerce in Dublin, who sent their letter on to the Ministry of Labour in Belfast, and apologised for the delay in doing so. A second letter was sent by Spitalink, but he was not admitted.[53]

Irene Klein, aged forty, a skilled leather worker from Gonzagagasse 7 wrote in German sending an illustration of a weaving loom, but she too was rejected.[54]

Civil servants in Belfast set the bar on admissions extremely high. Individuals and families, no matter how talented or successful, had little chance of getting in, and even owners of large-scale enterprises who had capital, despite Nazi confiscations of their plant, were routinely refused. Factory owners or skilled individuals who had contacts in Northern Ireland, particularly with senior civil servants or influential émigrés such as Alfred Neumann, had a greater chance of success.

10
'LIKE WOUNDED ANIMALS, LICKING THEIR WOUNDS'

While applications from Vienna's Jews increased after Kristallnacht, by then the governments of western Europe had severely limited immigration. But in December 1938, a lifeline appeared. The British government agreed to admit children aged sixteen or under in groups rather than as individuals to the United Kingdom, including Northern Ireland, without parents or adult guardians, under the Kindertransport scheme. Strict conditions were applied. Jewish and non-Jewish organisations funded the operation and had to ensure that no child became a burden on public funds, guaranteeing £50 to finance their re-emigration, as the measure was regarded as temporary. Almost 10,000 children, the majority of them Jewish, from Germany, Austria and Czechoslovakia, availed of the scheme between November 1938 and September 1939.[1]

Among the first to come to Northern Ireland on a Kindertransport was fifteen-year-old Walter Kammerling. For Walter, Vienna was a paradise that had turned into a hell. He was born there on 27 October 1923, the youngest of three children, to Max and Marie Kammerling. Walter had two sisters, Ruth and Erica, two and four years older, and the family lived in an apartment in Ausstellungsstrasse 7, between the Danube canal and river in the Prater district, close to the large park where the Viennese loved, and still love, to relax. In the 1920s, Max had a small but very good chocolate factory. Ninety years later, Walter could still recall it:

I remember the lovely chocolate, such as pralines, being made in a big drum. But unfortunately Father wasn't smart in picking his partners, and the whole thing went bust because they robbed it. Then it was very difficult to make a living. He became just a travelling salesman. It was a hard life. He was talented, and came up with terrific ideas for inventions which could have taken off, but unfortunately didn't. We were always struggling.[2]

But like many Jews who grew up in Vienna in the 1920s and early 1930s, Walter remembered an idyllic childhood:

I loved the place. On Sundays we went on excursions into the Vienna woods. We would pack a lunch and though it was ages before we started off, it was fun. Or we would go to the swimming baths on the Danube. We were not only not very wealthy, we had precious little money. I got on well with my parents and they got on well with each other. It was a lovely family.[3]

Walter attended a *Realgymnasium*, a grammar school, where he studied Latin and English, but he also had a talent for maths and science:

There were a lot of Jews there and no problems about being Jewish. It was a fifteen- or twenty-minute walk to school, and thirty of the thirty-six pupils in the class were Jews. Other classes had more Christians than Jews, but all got on well. Growing up in Vienna when I was a boy, it was wonderful. It was a sunny time. We went to the Kinderfreunde [Children's Friends], a Socialist organisation, and to their summer camps. Father was not active in politics, but was a socialist.[4]

With the Anschluss on 11 March 1938, things changed overnight:

The non-Jewish friends we had, some stayed friends, but of course they had to be careful not to appear to be friends. But the majority turned away. It became very unpleasant. Going to school was running the gauntlet, because there were groups of Brownshirt stormtroopers and Hitler Youth roaming the streets and when they found any Jews, they beat them up or made them scrub the streets clean of pro-Schuschnigg slogans.

One day in March 1938 stormtroopers grabbed Walter and forced him to join Jewish men on their knees scrubbing the pavement. 'It was frightening. You know when you walk home and you hear people screaming behind you, you don't dare to turn round because you know if you do, you'll be among the ones that are screaming when they're beaten up.'

When he got home, Walter said little about what had happened. 'I don't think I cried but I was very unhappy. Father knew exactly what had happened, that I had been forced to clean the streets. But as a fourteen-year-old you get over it. We didn't talk about it. I had two sisters and we were all worried whether we would come home all right.'

Walter was astonished to see how many Austrians turned out to be Nazis, including 'a good number' of his teachers, now proudly sporting the party badges that had once been illegal. Jews were expelled from school within weeks of the Nazi takeover. His mother, Marie, had to give up 'a good job in an office', and his father was sacked from his post as a travelling brush salesman. His parents found work with the IKG. At home, Walter suddenly found himself pining for the education now denied him. He committed to Latin in a way he had never done at school. With few friends and time on his hands, he developed a hunger for knowledge that stayed with him all his life.

Max tried everything to get the family out of Vienna. He handed over money to a Colombian embassy employee for exit visas, which turned out to be worthless. 'Father got all ready to go and I remember how they packed all this stuff in the summer of 1938,' said Walter. The fraudulent official who ran the scam was arrested, tried and convicted. Within days of Kristallnacht, and probably because of their contacts at the *Kultusgemeinde*, Walter's parents managed to get him on the first Kindertransport out of Vienna. 'Next week you're going to England', Walter remembered being told:

It was a bit of a blow. Father was in hospital with an angina attack. I went to say goodbye to him. This was the first time I saw Dad cry. He knew that we would not see each other again. I was hoping we would. I didn't say much. He was in bed and then he hugged me. That was the last time I saw him. In the early evening, my mother and my sister Ruthie saw me off at the station. That was the last time I saw them too. I don't think we said anything. We just hugged each other. The station was busy, with a lot of parents saying goodbye. Parents were trying to keep a smiling face, which was very hard to do because they and their children didn't know when they were going to see each other again. And so it happened. I never saw them again.

I didn't like it on the train. I didn't like to be separated from my folks. I thought, 'I'm going to England now.' I was hoping to meet them again. On the train journey people tried to be light-hearted, but we couldn't be. I had no friends. I think I hardly talked to any of the others. Then in Holland a number of ladies gave us tea with milk and sugar, the first time I saw that. They smiled at us. We hadn't seen strangers smile at us for a long time. It made us feel quite good. In Vienna they called you 'bloody Jew'. When you walked on the pavement, you would have a group of Hitler Youth coming by and they just pushed you off the pavement onto the street. You were lucky if you didn't get beaten up. I obviously didn't have a Nazi badge and was dark-haired and brown-eyed, so they assumed I was Jewish and that was that.

But you're still full of home, of your parents and your sisters. I was the first one to leave in our family. I was extremely immature and was so spoiled by my sisters, the youngest child, and a boy. I only realised the change when I got to the camp at Dovercourt, outside London. The day after I arrived I had the feeling I wanted to tell Mum something, to go next door, and then realised there was no next door. Mum was not there.

Walter stayed for a few weeks at Dovercourt, a Butlin's holiday camp in Essex requisitioned by the British government. A number of women from Northern Ireland came to take him and two other youths to Belfast. He stayed first at the hostel provided by the Jewish community at 62 Cliftonpark Avenue. Walter had learned English at school in Vienna but had to get to grips with the spoken language. One day he asked a friend in Belfast, 'How is the time?' and he replied, 'Very well, thank you, how are you?' Walter realised his mistake, and worked hard to improve his English:

We were all in the same boat. We never talked about home, we never talked about our families. We were just like wounded animals, licking their wounds. You try to joke, you try to laugh, and you're not really laughing because you're always thinking about your family which you left behind, and the uncertainty, will you see them again, and how long, and when and what and so on. Of course, you have letters from home and you write letters when it is still peace time. They didn't describe what was happening to them, as the letters were censored; they wrote about personal things, but not about political matters.

After some months in Belfast, Walter was transferred to the Refugee Settlement Farm at Millisle, County Down, about fifteen miles away, which he liked:

I did everything. I worked in the bakery, I had a job in the kitchen, I worked as a labourer, with the chickens, and at the harvest, which was the nicest time. We worked from 7 a.m. to 10 p.m. There were several groups, children, teenagers and Chalutzim [Jewish teenagers training in agriculture for Palestine]. Some of them started Kibbutz Lavi in Israel.

Walter was too old to go to primary school but wanted to continue his studies. In Vienna he had planned to study engineering, and so he managed to get on an evening course in Maths for Building Construction at Donaghadee, walking the three miles there and back to Millisle.[5]

Gertrude Kessler's family was part of the Polish Jewish diaspora who migrated to Vienna to escape anti-Semitism. Her grandfather Salomon Kessler and grandmother had come to Vienna from Krakow, where he was a wealthy entrepreneur, with jewellery and coal businesses. The family had a large villa with several horse-drawn carriages to take them around. But Salomon, alienated by Polish hostility to Jews, decided to move to Vienna. His son, Leopold, was born in Vienna in 1902. Leopold was given the good education of a middle-class

Viennese. Intelligent and diligent, he worked as a government official. He married Ernestine Anna Schrekinger. Their first child, Gertrude, was born on 10 April 1924, and their second, Friedrich (Fritz), was born two years later.

Gertrude remembered a happy childhood, sheltered by her parents from the gathering storm. There were cycling trips and school holidays in the Alps. They celebrated a Jewish Christmas Eve with carp instead of turkey. Her father had given up the Jewish faith when he was twenty and Gertrude had been raised in a largely secular home.[6] An excellent student, she won high marks in school. Everything changed with the Anschluss, as she later told her son Charlie:

> I remember that very well. Because after Hitler came, we were still at school. And we came home all excited. We were going to join the Hitler Youth, we were going to get uniforms. Up until then we had never heard the word 'Jew' in our house. We didn't know. I mean, Dad was just like any other Dad. He wasn't like anything called a 'Jew'. And my parents said 'Sorry, but you can't join the Hitler Youth.' We said: 'Why? We have to,' and so on. Then we were told the reason why.[7]

The family was forced out of their apartment. Gertrude vividly remembered standing outside their Streffleurgasse home with all their possessions in a little cart, which Leopold pulled with him towards their smaller flat in the mainly Jewish twentieth district. Leopold lost his job and was forced to do manual labour in an abattoir, slaughtering pigs, an insult to a Jew. He had become a Catholic in an attempt to evade the anti-Semitic laws. On Kristallnacht, the Kesslers, like thousands of Jewish families, watched fearfully as crowds of SS and SA and their supporters thronged the streets of Vienna, attacking Jews, looting Jewish property, and burning down synagogues.

Gertrude, Fritz and their Jewish classmates were removed from school, which was taken over by the Gestapo for use as a temporary prison for Jews. 'We saw terrible things going on there,' Gertrude later told Charlie, but would not elaborate. They heard the jackboots of the German soldiers marching through their apartment building and prayed that they weren't coming for Leopold:

It was a family living in fear most of the time. Because every time a knock came to the door, we thought it was the Gestapo coming for Dad. He used to hide. That's the worst thing I have carried with me, this fear of the doorbell ringing. Even now, when I think about it, that's the biggest fear that I had then as a child. Was that them coming for my father?[8]

Thirteen months after the Anschluss, their parents told the children that they were sending them to Ireland, a place they had never heard of. Her grandfather told her, 'The only thing I know about Ireland is, there are no summers or winters. The weather is the same the whole year around.' She explains:

We were just put on the train, and that was it. It took three days and three nights, a nightmare journey for two children. The last thing I remember is my mum running down the platform with the train as it got quicker and quicker, she couldn't run as fast, and then I didn't see her any more. 'Stay always with Fritz, whatever happens. Don't be separated,' my mum told me just before we left.[9]

Gertrude believed it would be only a short time before they returned home. There were about 200 passengers on the train, including some much younger children. It was one of the last to leave Vienna before the war broke out, and it would be at least six years before any of the children came back.

Once on the train, Gertrude and Fritz were too nervous to eat. They cried a lot. The train stopped often, and children were sometimes taken off, Gertrude later told her son Charlie. It went from Ostend to Dover, then on to London, with Gertrude and Fritz wearing labels around their necks saying, 'Londonderry, Northern Ireland'. Gertrude remembered that people came and took children, and by the end only she and Fritz were left. 'I said, "This is great. Nobody wants us, we're going home!" We were sure we were going back home, but we didn't know we were only half-way to our destination.'[10]

Alfred Neumann (far right, back row) with six skilled Viennese Jewish workers he brought to Newtownards to train local people. James Stewart (far left, back row), secretary of the Ulster Development Council, recruited Neumann. *(Photograph: Northern Whig)*

Rabbi Jacob Shachter, leader of Northern Ireland's Jewish community, lobbied Stormont for the admission of Jewish refugees. *(Photograph:* Ingathering, *published by Jacob Shachter, Jerusalem)*

Jews are forced to remove pro-independence slogans from the streets of Vienna after the Nazi invasion in March 1938. SS men and police keep guard while Viennese residents enjoy their humiliation. *(Photograph: Alamy)*

The newspaper report about Stormont aid for skilled workers which prompted an avalanche of applications from Vienna's Jewish community to Northern Ireland in 1938. Almost all were rejected. *(Photograph: The Deputy Keeper of the Records, Public Record Office of Northern Ireland, COM/17/3/28)*

The Duke of Windsor leaves Anny Lewinter's fashion store in Vienna in 1932. She came to Belfast with her husband, Zoltan Frankl, in early 1939 and took over the Newtownards business of Alfred Neumann after Stormont sacked him over 'differences with staff'. *(Photograph: Vivienne Magee)*

Anny Lewinter and Zoltan Frankl made machine-knitted haute-couture garments for export in their Newtownards factory. Zoltan also quickly became the leading patron of the visual arts in Northern Ireland. *(Photograph: Vivienne Magee)*

Otto Goldberger, who was freed from a detention centre in Vienna by a school friend who had joined the Nazi stormtroopers. The other men detained with him after Kristallnacht were deported to a concentration camp, while Otto made it to Northern Ireland and set up his own clothing factory. *(Photograph: Mel Goldberger)*

Hermann Goldberger (centre), a friend of Theodore Herzl, the leading Zionist. Hermann's sons, Otto and Hans, escaped to Northern Ireland and Israel, but he perished in the Holocaust along with his wife Malwine, despite the best efforts of their children to get them out of Vienna. *(Photograph: Mel Goldberger)*

George Bloch, who escaped from Warsaw aged eleven with his family on the last train out of the city. The Blochs set up a lace-making business in Portadown, which employed 750 people after the war. *(Photograph: Noel Russell)*

Erik Utitz shows a tanned skin to the Prime Minister of Northern Ireland, Lord Brookeborough, during a visit to United Chrometanners factory in Shrigley, County Down, in the 1950s. Erik's father, Dr Alfred Utitz (fourth from right), founded the tannery with his brother Jacob (far right). Walter Weiniger, a Viennese exile (second left), part-owner of the factory, looks on. *(Photograph: Chris Hagan)*

Czech exiles Franz and Edith Kohner, who ran the Refugee Resettlement Farm at Millisle, County Down. The couple later set up a successful clothing business in Belfast. *(Photograph: Billy Kohner)*

Franz Kohner (rear, centre), with some of the young refugees who came to the Refugee Resettlement Farm at Millisle, County Down. *(Photograph: Billy Kohner)*

Tom and Agnes Finnegan, leading campaigners on behalf of refugees, many of them Jews, seeking admission to Northern Ireland, with three of their children, Ruth, Diarmid and David, pictured in 1943. *(Photograph: Dr Owen Finnegan).*

Ludwig Schenkel (left), who escaped Vienna and came to Derry in 1939 with his brother Paul. He set up a factory making bags and other goods. A talented photographer, Ludwig created 10,000 colour slides of Donegal, Europe and Israel, a valuable record of his life and times. *(Photograph: Bigger/McDonald collection)*

Loni Schenkel (right) was a qualified chemist. She was helped to procure a visa as a 'domestic servant' by Professor Thomas Finnegan. She met her husband, Ludwig, at his home. *(Photo: Bigger/McDonald collection)*

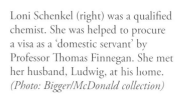

Walter and Herta Kammerling (left), Jewish refugees from Vienna, on their wedding day in Kent in 1944. Walter came to the Refugee Resettlement Farm at Millisle in 1938, met Herta at the Free Austria centre in London, and served in the British army in Europe. *(Photograph: Max Kammerling)*

Fritz ('Fred') Langhammer (left) with his father, Franz, and mother, Emilie, in a family photograph (right), taken in Czechoslovakia before they escaped and set up a factory in Whitehouse, near Belfast. *(Photograph: Eric Langhammer)*

The *Arandora Star*, which was carrying more than 1,100 interned Italian, German and Austrian 'enemy aliens' to Canada when it was sunk by a German U-boat off the coast of Ireland in July 1942. Among the dead was Alfred Neumann, the Austrian businessman who had rescued at least seventy Jews from the Nazis in Vienna. *(Photograph: Blue Star Line)*

Gertrude, holding Fritz by the hand, had to go round government offices to pick up the documents to stay in the United Kingdom. They were taken to Heysham, and then across the Irish Sea to Belfast. 'And then a lady came and met us and took us to Derry in the car, and just popped us there and never said anything. She never let me know anything. She just said. "This is where we're going."' The helper, from the BCGR, spoke German and left them at an isolated farm on the outskirts of Derry. 'I can't tell you who the people were, they took us to a room and gave us something for tea. It was a plate of rhubarb, which we'd never seen. We couldn't eat it … But then they took us up to the loft to go to bed.'[11]

The children had to sleep on the loft floor without beds or access to a toilet. They left early next morning without telling their hosts, and after some hours were picked up by a local man, a refugee helper, as they walked along a country road. He spoke some German. The Belfast Committee had earlier told him the children would welcome a visit and he was on his way when he met them. They stayed with him for a couple of days and remembered his kindness. Then they were taken to the Childhaven home outside Millisle, County Down, which was run by Methodists separately from the Jewish farm in the district. Though she and Fritz had run away from the Derry farm, Gertrude was grateful later that the family had taken them in:

> I was brought up without any faith of any kind. So, this was wonderful, to find that when I came here that people had a God that loved them and they took people like me in. Even for that family in Derry saying, 'we'll take two children', I mean they were going to feed us and look after us, I suppose. We didn't give them a chance. I'm sorry, but children will be children and we did not understand the situation. But to this day, only for them I wouldn't be here. We would have been dead in a concentration camp, my brother and I.[12]

Their parents quickly wrote to the children. In a letter dated 26 April 1939, sent via the Society of Friends centre in Singerstrassse, where the Irish writer Hubert Butler had worked in 1938, Leopold and

Ernestine tried to set their children at ease: 'Dear children! Warmest kisses to you. You need have no worries about us. We are healthy! We hope you are too! Are you still together in the home? We hope it's going well with you. So once again: have no worries! 1000 kisses.'[13]

Gertrude and Fritz committed themselves to learning English and attended Millisle Primary School, where they met some of the Farm children. Gertrude remembered the children there as Orthodox Jews, but while the Farm was leased by the Belfast Jewish community, many of the children there were, like themselves, from non-practising or even secular backgrounds: 'We were supposed to be Jewish but we had never heard anything. We had never been taught anything. It was most confusing. I mean, never to have been told anything – our parents didn't want us to know, and yet I think they were always fearing that Hitler might take over Austria, because he said he would get all the German-speaking countries – which he did.'[14]

Once she was eighteen, Gertrude had to leave the Millisle home. The Quakers managed to arrange nursing training for her, though as an 'alien' she was not supposed to work. She stayed at Derryvolgie Avenue, Belfast, with a Baptist couple who adopted her and Fritz, now calling himself Fred. The Burrowes owned two cafés, the Chalet Bonté and the Chalet d'Or in Belfast. Gertrude trained at Forster Green Hospital, Belfast, where she met Theodore Warmington, an Irish Quaker doctor of English descent. Theo was in his early thirties and Gertrude eighteen. They fell in love, and the Quaker married the daughter of a Jew, who had been registered as a Catholic, in a Baptist church under the auspices of the Methodists at Millisle.

Gertrude could not go more than two miles from her home, since she was categorised as an 'alien'. 'I was like a prisoner. Fortunately, I applied to do nursing, and I was too busy to go outside the two-mile limit.'

Fritz, now Fred, stayed at the Childhaven home until he reached the age of eighteen.

11

'BE STRONG AND COURAGEOUS'

As the numbers of Kindertransport children arriving in Northern Ireland increased, the need for accommodation for them also grew. In May 1939, the BJRC entrusted three prominent members, Maurice Solomon, Barney Hurwitz and Leo Scopp, to find a farm for young refugees then staying at the Cliftonpark Avenue hostel in north Belfast. Barney Hurwitz was friendly with Laurence Gorman, manager of Mooney's bar in Belfast's Cornmarket, who, as a sideline, bought damaged flax and took it to his farm at Balllyrolly, Millisle, on the Ards Peninsula. There it was reblanched and sold to merchants. Over a pint of Guinness, they agreed a twenty-year lease on the dilapidated farm and its seventy acres of arable land. Some of the young refugees who arrived from December 1938 were housed with Jewish families in Belfast, while others moved to the farm.[1]

The committee appointed Franz Kohner, a highly qualified Czech lawyer, as administrative manager of the farm. He left Prague in late July 1939 with this wife Edith and two young children, Dinah and Ruth. They arrived in Belfast on 7 August 1939, staying first with the Berwitz family on the Antrim Road. Edith's father, Franz Geduldiger, had a large linen brokerage firm in Trutnov, Czechoslovakia. Jakob's family had lived in a villa built to receive people from around the world who came to buy Czech linen. Franz Kohner's son Billy believes his maternal grandfather's linen industry connections in Northern Ireland helped smooth the way for Franz's appointment. The Trutnov area was famous for its linen production and, under the Habsburg Empire, was nicknamed 'the Austrian Belfast'. The Belfast engineering firm Mackies sold machinery to factories in the area.[2]

Franz Kohner was to play a key role in the Jewish refugee story in Northern Ireland. By the time he arrived in Belfast in the summer of 1939 he had already lived a highly eventful life. Born in 1898 to a prosperous Jewish family, Franz was conscripted into the Austro-Hungarian army while still a sixth-former. He served two years as a junior officer in an artillery regiment in Galicia and Russia, before being wounded when he trod on an unexploded shell on the Italian front in May 1918.

An exceptional student, he studied philosophy before becoming a Doctor of Law at Charles University, Prague in 1922. He was a successful partner in a legal practice in the town of Brüx, now known as Most, in a mining area of Bohemia in present-day Czechia. He took both civil and criminal cases, and defended miners and trade unionists, travelled widely across Europe, and became highly active in the Zionist movement. He attended the twelfth Zionist congress in Carlsbad, Czechoslovakia in 1921 and met some of the leading figures of the movement, including Chaim Weizmann, the first President of Israel, Abraham Ussishkin, President of the Jewish National Fund, and Martin Buber, an Austrian Jewish philosopher who deeply influenced his thinking. In Franz Kohner's candid unpublished memoir, he described how meeting these leaders affected him: 'Martin Buber: I listened to him and saw the fervour of his eyes. I saw others: wide, energetic heads, Jewish esprit and willpower – I submitted neither to personality cult nor to programme Zionism, but I had again images in my heart of strength, courage, masculine devotion – and self-confidence. I was enchanted without forgetting my weakness.'[3]

The memoir he wrote in the two years before his death in 1972 reveals a multi-talented man, highly energetic, but prone to occasional melancholy. He espoused a secular, tolerant outlook while retaining a consciousness of his Jewish heritage. Kohner was impressed by the early decision of a friend, Victor Grünwald, to settle in Palestine, but in a diary entry in the early 1920s, he was highly critical of his own indecision: 'I could spit on myself. This is no vocation for me. Will I still have the courage to change over and go to Israel? I shall be 25 years old THIS MONTH!' He visited Palestine in 1926, and again in 1934 with his young wife Edith, and they talked of emigration, but nothing came of it. He remained active, however, in Jewish organisations, including Makabi, a Jewish sporting club, and played a leading role in the foundation of a Jewish youth hostel, Maon Bahar ('House on the Hill' in Hebrew) near Carlsbad. In his memoir, he wrote: 'I am not exactly proud of my Jewishness, often it is uncomfortable to hear it, but I am a Jew and my forefathers were Jews and so there can be no argument about the fact.'[4]

In August 1933 Franz Kohner had attended the Zionist Congress in Prague and there met Edith Gedulgiger, a beautiful young Jewish woman from Trutnov. They married on 27 March 1934. Franz was thirty-five, Edith twenty-two. A daughter, Dinah, was born on 23 April 1936 and a second girl, Ruth, followed a year later. Franz gave up his presidency of the Makabi club, glad to be free of the obligation 'to represent, wave a flag, make speeches'.[5]

It was a happy marriage. But soon domestic bliss was overshadowed by the international tension caused by Hitler's designs on Czechoslovakia. German troops entered the Sudetenland in October 1938, just days after the signing of the Munich agreement was hailed by British Prime Minister Neville Chamberlain as guaranteeing 'peace in our time'. Franz loaded a huge van with the family's furniture, books, china and glass and other valuables and stored it in a rented room in a house in a remote valley in Bohemia.

He decided to get out of Brüx quickly after the Nazis 'did dreadful things to the Jews who had stayed behind'; for example, making a local doctor wash the main square (where the court was) on his knees. Franz took his parents, Heinrich and Valerie, to a small rented room in Prague, practically forcing his father into the car because he at first refused to go. He soon found a flat in Prague for them, his brother Rudolf, sister Bertl and her daughter Elsbeth, and Bertl's husband, Dolf, though relations between the couple were strained. Franz stayed in a rooming house in Prague.

Soon the family was struck by tragedy. On 7 November 1938 Bertl, aged thirty-seven, left the family flat and walked across the Charles Bridge to the old quarter of the city below the castle. She booked into a hotel. Next day her brother Rudolf was called there. Bertl had swallowed a bottleful of sleeping tablets. He found a note beside her body:

I cannot go on. I haven't the courage to start a new life. I'm not capable, only tired and ill. I haven't been a good mother to my child. It's no art to be kind and tender towards such a lovely human being. She always treated me better than I her. What can I do for her? She's to be taken to England to friends who have better hearts than me. Some day she'll be happy without me … I hope you won't find me too soon.

Putzerle [Elsbeth], your beautiful eyes, don't cry for me. My angel, don't cry, Forget me.

Cremate me or bury me secretly somewhere. I don't deserve any better.[6]

On 4 December 1938 Bertl's daughter Elsbeth, who was at school in England, wrote in her diary, 'Since 7 November … no more Mutti … since 7 October … no more homeland … no Mutti … never again … my Mummerl! … never to see her again!' Valerie, Bertl's mother, wrote in her prayer book: 'Our most dearly beloved child, our Bertl, parted from us in the accursed year of 1938. She died from loving too deeply and from a broken heart. She will live within me forever.'[7]

On 15 March 1939 the Germans marched into Prague, and the Gestapo raided the building where Franz was staying several times, and arrested the occupants. 'One could only listen to the drama and live on in fear for the next night,' Franz wrote in his memoir. He avoided arrest, and desperately tried to arrange visas to the United Kingdom for his family and parents, liquidate assets and establish contacts that might be useful. 'As the Germans marched into Prague, meantime, these tasks become more frantic and more difficult.'[8] Franz was put in touch with a black marketeer, whom he had met in the foyer of a large hotel. Pretending not to know each other, they took the lift and stopped it between floors. Franz handed over £500 in Czech currency, worth about £26,000 in today's money, and was promised £100 sterling to be collected at a house in the East End of London after his arrival. The man's job was to get the money out via Switzerland and change it into a valid currency.

In April, Heinrich, Franz's father, was accidentally struck by furniture removers on the street and broke his hip. He died on 7 May 1939. Rudolf returned from England for the funeral, putting at risk his chance of escape. He received an exit permit to England in July 1939, when Franz and Edith and the children reached London, then Northern Ireland. Franz's mother Valerie was alone now in Prague. On 30 July 1939, she wrote to Franz in Belfast and his brother Rudi in Bradford:

> My dear children
>
> I am anxious for news from you all and to hear you have arrived. Here everything is so terribly empty and desolate. It makes me shudder. True, friends are caring for me ... What is going to happen now? Edith will have such a struggle, and you my dear boy, what worries you will have. Be strong and courageous. I too am trying to be brave and am dealing with the various matters that now have to be settled. You should not have spared me so much in the past.
>
> Your flowers on Tata's [Dad's] and Bertl's graves are blooming beautifully and I have added some white flowers too ... It's all so senseless.
>
> My dear, good children, don't despair. I am praying for your happiness.
>
> Your Mama.[9]

It would not be until the war ended that the family would learn of Valerie's fate.

The farm became the main home for young Jewish refugees in Northern Ireland. The first children were moved there in July 1939, a night of howling winds and heavy rain. They slept in leaking tents and woke up drenched. The refugees, with the help of local tradesmen, quickly brought the farm buildings and the land into good order. Everyone had to work, and was paid a shilling a week pocket money, later rising to two shillings and sixpence. They included a group of Chalutzim, religious Zionists, who used the skills they learned at the farm in the kibbutzim of Israel after the war. The Ministry of Agriculture provided technical advice to the Northern Ireland Jewish Aid Committee.

The farm manager was Eugen Patriasz, a Hungarian Jew with a degree in agriculture from Vienna, but no practical experience. Several local people were employed to teach the refugee children farming skills. Among them were Bertie Muckle, who taught the older ones to drive a tractor and plough; Pat Beresford, who worked on the land; the Renners, including their daughter Marianne; Hugh Brown, who looked after the horses; and his brother John Brown. The Kohners became friendly with Bobby Hackworth, who was then a boy, but who in later years became an expert about the farm, and a historical guide.[10] Erwin Jacobi, a saxophone player from Vienna, was put in charge of the children's health and welfare because he came from a medical family. He was a warm personality who provided much-needed emotional support to the youngsters. The chefs were Josef and Alma Bamberger, who had run a kosher restaurant in Vienna, helped by another young refugee, Erna Horn.

The farm thrived. By October 1940 it was producing vegetables on sixteen acres and cereals from the rest. It had two Clydesdale horses, seven cows, and 2,000 chickens. Among the crops were potatoes, onions, turnips, cauliflowers, cabbages, Brussels sprouts, carrots, barley, wheat, oats and maize. A Ferguson tractor was acquired in 1941. The farm also had a dairy, a kosher kitchen, a sewing room and laundry, a machinery repair workshop, and tradesmen, including a carpenter and shoemaker. Food production increased as the war went on, and surplus produce was distributed to local military personnel stationed in the area. By 1941 more than one hundred refugees were working there.

Relations between the farm residents and local people were very good. They played football together, often on Saturday evenings between the end of the Jewish and the start of the Christian sabbath. The young farm children attended Millisle Primary School, where the headmaster, John Palmer, placed each refugee with a local child, to help them learn English. At age fourteen, many went on to local secondary schools, including Bangor Grammar, Bangor High, and Regent House in Newtownards. Some attended night school in Donaghadee. They joined local scouts, Red Cross First Aid classes, and, for boys aged fourteen to seventeen, the local Air Training Corps.

Jewish soldiers among the tens of thousands of Allied armed services personnel in Northern Ireland also visited. During the summer in the war years, young volunteers, many from Dublin's Jewish community, came to lend a hand with the harvest. Some refugees were invited to stay with the families of the Dublin friends they had made.[11] Members of the Belfast Jewish community also visited frequently. For recreation, the young people played table tennis, billiards and card games, and listened to the radio, especially to the BBC news, following events closely on a map of Europe pinned on the wall. They enjoyed playing Monopoly, particularly the Austrian and German versions they knew, and the boys especially liked making model aircraft. They listened to gramophone records, classical, swing and jazz. In summer they went swimming in the bracing waters of the Irish Sea at Millisle beach, often under the watchful eye of Franz Kohner, a keep-fit enthusiast. He ran fitness classes to build up the physiques of the young residents. There were concerts and dances which local people attended.

Occasionally the refugees made the three-mile trek into Donaghadee, where they were given cut-price admission at the Regal cinema, and to Nardini's café, where the owner sometimes treated them to free ice-cream. They travelled on foot and by bicycle, or, if they were lucky, horse-drawn cart. Petrol was strictly rationed. On special occasions, they visited Belfast to go to the cinema or shopping. As 'enemy aliens', though, their movements were restricted. They needed a permit from local police to leave the farm, even for one night. Many of the teenagers joined the British armed forces from 1943 onwards. Some returned on visits to the farm and were feted as heroes.

Franz Kohner was a dynamic leader and a polymath. A doctor of civil law, fluent in several languages, a talented violinist, widely read in European literature and philosophy, he was a liberal, progressive central European intellectual.[12] His wife Edith also spoke several languages and oversaw the farm finances. She acted as a surrogate mother to the refugee children, most of whom lost contact with their parents in occupied Europe when the war started. Franz bought the supplies, organised coupons, complied with blackout regulations, and liaised with the local and government authorities and the main Belfast Jewish community. He also found time to give lectures on Nazi Germany to troops stationed in Northern Ireland, while Edith taught some soldiers German. Together they made an outstanding success of the farm.

Relations between the cosmopolitan and liberal Kohners and the stricter Orthodox Belfast community were generally very good. Rabbi Jacob Shachter was a distinguished Talmudist, an expert on children's literature, a talented writer and broadcaster, the latest in a line of gifted rabbis to serve in Belfast (1926–54). Rabbi Yitzhak HaLevi Herzog worked there (1916–19) before becoming Chief Rabbi of Ireland in Dublin (1919–37), and later Chief Rabbi of Mandatory Palestine and of Israel. His son Chaim Herzog was the sixth president of Israel (1983–93).

During the Belfast Blitz of 1941, some members of the Belfast Jewish community, including refugees, fearing for their safety, moved to the farm at Millisle. Rabbi Shachter visited to conduct religious services on special occasions. But one episode soured the relationship between Franz Kohner and Rabbi Shachter. Franz gives his version of the event in his unpublished memoir:

A small incident happened at Passover time 1941 … which assumed a tremendous and, I must admit now, exaggerated but very far-reaching importance in my life. It was at the time after the German air-raid on Belfast. Rabbi Shachter, although his house had not been damaged or threatened, had deserted his flock, had come to the farm and quartered himself and his wife in the home of a nearby gardener, but ate and spent his day at the farm. We had built a big recreation hall at the farm, with a compartment serving as an office, and another adjoining one as some sort of synagogue. It was on one of these days that I typed applications for the Belfast 'refugees', mostly oldish people without British nationality, to be given permission to stay at Millisle, a 'prohibited area' in which foreign nationals could stay according to wartime regulations only by special police permit. I also had to apply for food allocations for them because it was the time of rationing, and food supplies had to be procured for them from local suppliers – all urgent jobs which to perform was my responsibility. While writing these lists and applications, I heard through the wooden wall that the Rabbi had come over from his residence and chanted his morning prayers in the adjoining room. Out of courtesy or consideration, I opened the shutter of my office compartment and apologised to Shachter if the typewriter was perhaps disturbing him. I explained I had to get food and residence permits for his flock who had come from Belfast with him, but he turned on me and said with wild eyes: 'I CURSE YOU, I CURSE YOU, I CURSE YOU.' He said so while wearing the Tallit [prayer shawl] and in front of the open Ark, containing the Torah scroll.

I realised only later on that this outburst was not merely a protest against my typing while he was praying at the open Ark (it was not a Shabbat [Sabbath]!) but an expression of the intolerant power complex of the orthodox against a Jew who was proud to be one without submitting to the tyranny of the rabbi. Whatever the explanation, the incident had a powerful, and as I am willing to admit now, a disproportionate effect on my relationship to Judaism. I was a rebel henceforth, and if I may anticipate years, I refused to become a member of the Jewish community of Belfast when I had started Belart Ltd and was asked to join. I never visited the synagogue in Belfast, my children did not get any Jewish tuition or upbringing. Although I confessed myself openly as a Jew wherever the question arose, I was equally clear about the fact that that I was not a member of the community. I maintained friendship with those members whom I knew, although some did not know or understand my reason for my negative attitude to the synagogue. My attitude has persisted now for 30 years although I regret it all and the consequences in my family.

Ruth Kohner also remembered another incident where her father's views clashed with the stricter orthodoxy of Rabbi Shachter:

At one Passover dinner, the Rabbi was invited. My father was in the middle and the Rabbi was next to him. I sat on one side of my father and Ella Smith, a local seamstress who came to the farm and helped out, was also there. The Rabbi said to me, 'And Ruthie, what is your favourite food?' and I said 'Sausages.' And he said, 'Oh, is that right? What sort of sausages?' I said 'Pork sausages,' and he was so shocked and about to be angry and Ella jumped at the other end of the table and said, 'Oh, Mr Rabbi, that's my fault, she had those with me when she had been visiting my children.' And my father stood up on the other side, and this is ironed in my mind, and he said, 'Ella, you have nothing to apologise for. You look after my children and they love it with you. My children can eat whatever they like and if they enjoy the food, that's fine with me.'

And that was the end of that. A very deep religious insight was for us ethics and tradition, but none of this other business. You don't have to go to *Shul* [synagogue], you don't have to go to Mass, or do any of those things. What you have to do is do right and be good inside. Daddy always said, 'You know, God is in the garden, you don't have to go to church to be true to God.' He was free-thinking. My parents got on well with everybody, but a few people didn't do the right things and he told them. He was straight up and he told them, including the Rabbi. He realised how valuable their work was.[13]

1 2
'I WILL SHOW YOU
THE WORST PLACE'

After the Nazi takeover of the rest of Czechoslovakia in March 1939, Czech Jews faced the same dangers as Austrian Jews, and, with others opposed to the regime, sought refuge where they could find it.

Two Czech Jewish brothers, Alfred and Jacob Utitz, and an Austrian Jew, Walter Weiniger, escaped the Nazis and started a new factory in Shrigley, east Down, which transformed the fortunes of one of the most deprived areas of Northern Ireland. They took over a derelict flax mill, once one of the largest in Europe, and the town's biggest employer. It had closed in 1930 and the area had experienced abject poverty for almost a decade. An education committee officer sent to check children for malnutrition at schools in Northern Ireland found on his visit to the area in 1931 'a considerable number of sub-normal nutrition cases among the 535 children in the Shrigley and Killyleagh schools'.[1] Alfred and Jacob Utitz had a family tannery in Prague, but when the Germans took over the Sudetenland, they lost a considerable part of their market. The brothers were aware of the high unemployment in the United Kingdom and travelled to London in January 1939 to enquire about starting up a leather-finishing plant to complement their Prague operation. Alfred's son Erik, who spoke English, travelled with them.[2]

The Utitzes were told there were two particularly deprived areas of the United Kingdom, the north-east of England and Northern Ireland. They travelled first to Durham, but the factory they were shown was 'awful' and unsuitable, Erik recalled.[3] They then made contact with James Stewart, the Ministry of Commerce representative at the Northern Ireland Office in London. Stewart told them, 'I will show you the worst place. If you take that, you can have what you like from the authorities.'[4]

They were shown the derelict linen mill in Shrigley, County Down. They told their Stormont guide that the five-storey building was too much for them, since they wanted only a small plant to finish animal skins. They agreed to take the ground floor.[5]

Alexander Gordon, Unionist MP for East Down and Parliamentary and Financial Secretary to the Ministry of Finance, supported the Utitzes, and they were given £14,500 in mortgage relief by the Ministry of Finance. Their company, United Chrometanners, was registered in August 1939. Its managing directors included Frank Klein and Alfred Utitz, who had been resident in London since 1918. His brother Jacob Utitz teamed up with Walter Weiniger, who had recently arrived in the United Kingdom. Weiniger and his wife Mary Meyer each owned shares in London, and he may have been able to use some of his capital in the new firm.[6]

While the Utitz brothers were setting up the factory in early 1939, Jewish families in Czechoslovakia now found themselves in the same bind as the Jewish community in Vienna exactly a year before. The Germans wanted to force out all Jews, but at a price. The Utitzes learned that their relatives were hostages to the Nazis, and the brothers had to find the money to get them out. They collected all the money owing to them in foreign currencies, which they gave to the Nazis. Only then were their family allowed to leave. The Northern Ireland authorities could have blocked the payments, but they didn't. For this measure, the Utitzes maintained a 'great love' for Northern Ireland, according to Erik.[7]

Initially, the new owners had planned to take on just a dozen local workers, but by November 1939 they employed 90, and at the business's peak more than 300.[8] A London expert, H. A. Daniel, adapted the old spinning mill and prepared rooms for use as a tannery, supervising the building of the giant drums used in the treatment of the animal skins.

When the Utitzes and Walter Weiniger set up their factory in 1939, local people regarded them as saviours. The work involved chemical processes to prepare the skins of sheep, pigs and goats for use in leather products, particularly shoes, and was smelly. But by local standards it paid well, and offered permanent wages instead of seasonal farming pay. One local man, Hugh Cochrane, remembered: 'Work in the tannery was much easier or at least not so heavy as on a farm. When I started in the tannery, I was getting £4.10 shillings, which was a big change from 35 shillings.' Another local man, George Watson, remembered the desperate times that preceded the factory opening. Then he earned sevenpence an hour when he started working as a teenager, which was regarded as good money. 'It was a God-send to the people. Eventually there were six bus-loads coming from Downpatrick alone.'[9]

The factory opened with an initial stock of 8,000 sheep hides from Northern Ireland and 1,500 from 'the British Empire'. One local newspaper report was optimistic about prospects: 'It is hoped that the annual output from 200,000 skins will be 1,500,000 square feet of leather for making shoe tops, fancy bags and clothing. The chief market will be England but 50 per cent of the produce will be dispatched to the Northern countries, France, Switzerland as well as South America.'[10] The firm's first order was in direct competition with the Utitz factory they had left behind in Prague, for garment leather for the Dutch army. Eventually, the family premises in Prague were destroyed by Allied bombing during the war.

It was a steep learning curve for local workers, who had been highly skilled in linen production but knew nothing about making leather. The Shrigley factory, like many businesses set up by Jewish émigrés, also pioneered progressive employment practices. The workforce was mixed, and inter-communal relations were very good. In the 1930s the population was divided 50/50 between Protestant and Catholic but it later became a majority Catholic village. The factory employed staff from across the district and buses brought workers from Downpatrick and Drumaness. Chris Hagan, local journalist and historian, said: 'There was never any bunting or flags on the machinery. The Utitzes treated each man as a worker, valued them according to just how they were at their job.' Intermarriage between Protestant and Catholic also happened and the district was largely free of the rabid sectarianism that scarred some parts of Northern Ireland.

Walter Weiniger soon started a handbag-making factory in Plantation Street, Killyleagh, but later left to set up his own business in Donegall Pass, Belfast, and was also extremely successful. When he transferred to the city, Alfred Utitz and his family moved into the Weiniger home at Shrigley Lodge.

Not only did the Utitzes employ many locals, they secured work permits for several fellow Jews who were then able to escape from Nazi-occupied Europe. An Austrian Jewish refugee, Erich Biss, set up a firm that took the tanned leather and made handbags and belts. He came from Derry with his wife, Friederike, and daughter, Hedy.

A Hungarian Jew, Nicholas Vermes, managed to travel across war-torn Europe to become a manager of United Chrometanners in Shrigley.[11] In Hungary in spring 1939 he met his cousin Lily, whose mother was already in Northern Ireland. She would soon join her. Nicholas asked her to inform any contacts in the leather business that he would love a job there.[12]

On Lily's first afternoon in Northern Ireland her mother introduced her to people who knew the Utitzes and Walter Weiniger at Shrigley. Four weeks later a postcard arrived for Nicholas offering him a job at the tannery. He accepted, and in the summer of 1939 began the anxious process of seeking a work permit and visa from the Northern Ireland authorities. In a one-hour television documentary produced by his daughter Vivienne for French television in 1996, Nicholas described his deliverance:

> When I was nearly at the lowest of my mental state there was a knock on the door and there was a postman, covered with snow and a letter in his hands with a foreign stamp … There was a chink, there was an opening. I said, 'I wonder, I wonder.' So, I opened the letter and read it and they said, 'Yes, your permit is granted, you have a working permit.' Of course, the whole thing changed then, all pessimism went out, optimism came in. When suddenly I realised, 'What am I saying? How can I leave my father?' He was in hospital. My mother said, 'Just you go ahead. Prepare yourself for the journey.'[13]

After six days on the train across Europe, with his passport often closely scrutinised, Vermes reached Liverpool and boarded the Belfast ferry. Next morning, 7 February 1940, a steward knocked on his cabin door, and said, 'Good morning, sir, a nice cup of strong tea for you.' I thanked him very much and he said: 'Oh well, we had a nice crossing. The German U-boats must have been busy somewhere else.' It was raining when Nicholas arrived in Belfast. 'It was a breath of relief, the fresh breath of freedom. I had arrived through the narrow gate.' He lodged first with a local woman, Annie Minnis, in Shrigley, but five years to the day after he arrived, on 7 February 1945, he married Josephine Morrow, in St Anne's Cathedral, Belfast. She was a local girl, one of a family of twelve, whom he met in the laboratory of the Shrigley tannery.

In May 1945 Nicholas received a short letter from his father, Eugene, through the Red Cross. It said, 'Mother died in Berndorf. Living now in Budapest, love Father.'

Nicholas arranged for his father to come to London and heard from him how his mother Anushka had died. After the German invasion of Hungary in March 1944, the couple had been taken as forced labourers to the town of Berndorf in Lower Austria. The German firm Krupp had a metal factory there and it is probable that the couple worked in it.[14] One day in January 1945 Anushka was in the kitchen cooking with other women. By then, they were surviving on rotten potatoes and carrots:

> My mother and a few other women stole a few potatoes. A German female SS guard stopped them and searched them outside the barracks and found three potatoes in each of the three women's pockets. They were arrested, unclothed, and searched everywhere. Then they were put out between two barracks without overcoats. They had to stand there for three hours in the frost. My mother was already very emaciated and thin. She had been sent out to work when she had fever. Then she collapsed, and she died alone that night.[15]

Nicholas's father Eugene took his own life in 1957, his traumatic experiences too much to bear. Nicholas could not face going back to Hungary to live: 'When you trust people and they kick you down, you never forget it. I will always be a Hungarian, even if the Hungarians kicked me out. You can't deny the place where you [were] born, the language you spoke, the teachers you had, the poetry you knew, the countryside you loved.' In the film, his wife Josephine says, 'I think there is a lot of hidden anger. He seems to be a very calm, quiet man, very gentle and I see glimpses sometimes of a volcano inside.'[16]

Czech specialists who taught the Shrigley workers the new skills needed for finishing leather products included J. Horenovsky, who became managing director after the war before going to Britain, and Joseph Mouchka, who spent his working life in the firm. United Chrometanners provided much-needed work in the area for almost 35 years, finally closing in 1972.[17]

Maurice Hayes, who became a Permanent Secretary in the Department of Health and Social Services, one of the most senior Catholic civil servants in Northern Ireland, was town clerk of Downpatrick Urban District Council in the 1950s and was friendly with several of the Jewish families who settled in the area. He vividly remembered Dr Jacob Utitz, the family 'patriarch', as a stately presence in the town.[18] He was friendly with his son Erik Utitz, and played football with him. The Utitzes had a patent for chrome leather, and Maurice believes this may have played a part in easing their admission and gaining government financial support to set up the Shrigley factory. He also knew Viennese exiles including the Bisses, Zoltan Frankl and Anny Lewinter. They were all regarded as good employers.

Maurice Hayes never forgot one episode which brought home to him the families' suffering in Nazi-occupied Europe. In the late 1960s, several Jewish families sought compensation from the Austrian government for Nazi plundering of their property and businesses. Family members came to him and filled in affidavits, authenticated and signed by him as town clerk and Commissioner for Oaths:

> They were heartrending, I could read a bit of German and here were these people reciting how peopled avoided them in the street, there was graffiti on walls, and eventually Kristallnacht came. I was struck by it because things were

just starting here [the Troubles]. You say to yourself, 'Christ, look at these people, I wonder do they [Northern Ireland people] know what they're starting, and where they're getting to.'[19]

The Jewish applicants were also adamant that there must be official stamps on their documents. Unless it was stamped, your signature had no validity, they insisted:

I remember this guy said, after I signed it, 'Where's the stamp?' I said, 'What stamp?' He said, 'Oh, if I go to these people, they don't know me, they don't know you, but if they have a stamp …' This document was about taking a dog back to Austria. 'If there's no stamp they don't take it seriously.' So I went and got the two biggest stamps in the office. It must have been the only dog ever certified under building bye-laws and the planning regulations of Downpatrick Urban District Council![20]

Two people in particular were extremely helpful to Jewish immigrants, Hayes recalled: one a middle-ranking civil servant in the Ministry of Labour who took a 'fairly urbane view of what was an essential worker' and facilitated their entry, the other a 'half decent police sergeant'.[21] He was also struck by the 'amount of anti-Semitism' he encountered, especially in Belfast, more than with country people. He played bridge in the 1950s and 1960s and the Bisses and other Jewish people also took part:

Whether it was because the Jews tended to be very good card players, or whether it was just another stone to throw at them, it wasn't virulent, but you could see a sort of thing where virulence could be tolerated. I couldn't understand how anybody could do that. It was just a half-sneer, or a word. It certainly wasn't manifest. They didn't show it in their treatment of these people, but when we were on our own, it was, 'Oh, you know …'[22]

Among the Jewish shopkeepers Maurice Hayes knew in Downpatrick was Isadore 'Izzy' Waterson, who had a shoe repair business in the town. Isadore was one of four sons of Samuel Waterman, originally Solomon Wasserstein, who had migrated from the Pale of Settlement in Latvia to Manchester in 1905. He left with his sweetheart, Rosa Birkahn, after being conscripted into the Russian army during the Russo-Japanese war in 1904. He set up a shoemaking business and had four sons, Lewis, Harry, Isadore and Simon, and changed his name to the less German-sounding Samuel Waterman when World War I broke out. He left heavily polluted Manchester in 1921 for health reasons and came to Downpatrick, where cousins of his wife, the Bass family, had stayed before they emigrated to New York.[23] He opened a shoemaking and repair business in the town, S. Waterman and Sons, and they won prizes on a number of occasions in the International Shoe & Leather Fair national shoe-repairing competitions in London:

> The family would go to synagogue in Belfast for the Jewish festivals and their kosher food had to come from the city by train. Both Solomon and Rosa are buried in the Jewish cemetery in Carnmoney, Co. Antrim. Simon remembered the respect that the people of Downpatrick showed on the occasion of their deaths, as each time hundreds of people followed the hearse until it reached the outskirts of the town.[24]

They had shoes in the window which had won prizes in London. Maurice Hayes, in his memoir, *Black Puddings and Slim*, described receiving a letter from one of Isadore's sons, then a professor of geography at Haifa University, with a photograph of Isadore. He described how Isadore had won a silver medal for his shoes, but not the gold one. He believed this was because he was a Jew: 'His father Izzy kept the shoes, and eventually retired to Jerusalem. He put them in a box above the wardrobe and every now and again he would take them down, look at them and say: "What fault could they find?" Isn't that a sad story?'[25]

Later Maurice Hayes met a grandson of Isadore's, who asked him, 'Is it true that when my grandfather died, people in Downpatrick walked in his funeral?' I said, 'Of course they did; he was a neighbour.' Once the war was over, there was such great relief that people obliterated memories of anything else. Local Jews did not go into details with him about what had happened their families in their homelands. He had warm memories of the families he knew and admiration for their contribution to society, 'nice people, very intelligent'. He lamented the steep decline in the Jewish population in Northern Ireland, which had 'gone like snow off a ditch'. Maurice Hayes believed both the Northern Ireland and the Irish Free State governments could have done more to help Jews seeking sanctuary from Nazi persecution:

> In 1937–38 there wasn't genuine knowledge about the concentration camps, or where the crisis was leading. Here are people who did have a fearful unemployment problem. At the same time, they were stopping people coming in from the South, although there was a vote thing going on there. It was just part of the protectionist thing of jobs and employment. 'We'll take them in if they can create jobs, but if they're coming to take jobs, we are not going to have them'. It wasn't anti-Semitism per se, but it did happen to bear more heavily on these people.[26]

A lot depended on individual civil servants, Hayes felt. 'Some of these guys were dealing with local people who claim they were crippled but they had a sore toe, so they develop a sort of carapace, really. Ireland, north or south, hasn't an awful lot to congratulate themselves about.'[27]

13
'HELP US TO SAVE
OUR PARENTS'

In 1938 two small groups of Viennese Jews managed to emigrate to Derry. The anti-Semitic violence and persecution which accompanied the Anschluss in March 1938 motivated the first group of sixteen workers. The Kristallnacht pogrom in November 1938 impelled the second group. They obtained jobs with local employers, Jewish and Gentile, largely in the clothing and handcrafts industries, and were helped by the small network of supporters in the city. These included Dr Thomas Finnegan, professor of classics and President of Magee University College, and Archie Halliday, who had come to Derry from Leeds in 1912 and owned a commercial college in the city, and who was also active in the city's Labour movement.[1]

The Jewish immigrants came to a city with the highest male unemployment level in the United Kingdom.[2] In December 1938 there were 5,407 unemployed.[3] Gerrymandering had guaranteed Unionist control of the local corporation since the foundation of the state in 1921, despite the majority of its citizens being Catholic.[4]

The new arrivals joined a small Jewish community in Derry which had fled earlier anti-Semitic pogroms in Tsarist Russia in the late nineteenth century. In 1891, 282 Jews lived in Northern Ireland, 205 in Belfast, and 5 in Derry, but by 1901 there were 899 Jews in Northern Ireland, 58 of them in Derry, as a result of this increased persecution.[5]

The majority of the Jews who first came to Derry had emigrated from the Pale of Settlement, the western region of Imperial Russia in which Jews were allowed to live, and outside of which they were largely banned. The Pale of Settlement comprised all of modern-day

Belarus, Lithuania and Moldova, much of Ukraine and Poland, and relatively small parts of Latvia and western Russia. Conditions had improved for Russian Jews under the modernising Tsar Alexander II, but his assassination by political radicals in 1881 provoked 'a fierce reactionary backlash that proved to be a catastrophe for the Jewish communities of eastern Europe'.[6] Persecution increased following the crowning of the anti-Semitic Tsar Alexander III, and, at least two million Jews emigrated between 1881 and 1914, mainly to the United States, but also to western Europe.

Like many of the Jews who came to Northern Ireland, the Derry émigrés were mainly from Lithuania. Many of them landed first in Glasgow before making their way to Derry. The first arrivals included the Robinson, Edstein, Wellshy, Spain, Fieldman, Fredlander, Gordon, Rubin, Lazarus and Danker families. They were mostly tailors, picture-framers and peddlers, but as business prospered they opened shops and started small firms. The Fredlander family came from Russia, and became horse breeders with a stud farm in Eglinton. The Gordons owned a picture-framing and art shop in the city centre.

The 1901 Census showed nine Jewish households in Derry, all involved in the commercial life of the city. Five of the families were in the drapery business. Barnett Robinson and Samuel Lazarus, both Polish, were furniture dealers and Samuel Philman, a Russian, was a commercial traveller. Ephraim Gordon, a Latvian, had a picture-framing workshop in Richmond Street. David Spain had a mattress factory in Bishop Street, and later he also had a factory in Carlisle Road, manufacturing artificial flowers.[7]

Many of the families lived in the Abercorn Road and Bishop Street areas on the south side of the city and the children went to First Derry School, a state school. There they were taught by Fred Logan, who became 'one of the community's staunchest friends and memorialists'. The school rolls for the period 1923–33 show thirty-seven Jewish children.[8]

The Derry émigrés were Ashkenazi Orthodox and Yiddish-speaking, and in 1894 they established a synagogue in Abercorn Road, which then moved first to Hawkins Street around 1900, and in 1940 to Kennedy Place in the largely Protestant Fountain Estate on the city side of the River Foyle. The synagogue closed in 1948, and was demolished after part of the building collapsed on 18 April 2013.

The first group who came in 1938 were joined in the months after Kristallnacht by a group who were mostly relatives from Vienna. These included Ludwig and Paul Schenkel, Robert and Elsa Sekules, Fred Szilogyi and Harry Lazarus, the Gold family, and Otto Goldberger. Szilogyi and Lazarus opened a factory that produced leather goods, shirts and uniforms for the British and Commonwealth armed forces.[9]

Fresh from his success in Newtownards, Alfred Neumann soon expanded his business interests to Derry. On 8 November 1938, the *Northern Whig* reported a 'New Industry for Londonderry' that would make knitwear from linen and wool and garments from art silk. The new firm of Gilfillan and Neumann had engaged Viennese experts, who would instruct local workers. It was hoped to employ a 'considerable additional number' by the end of 1939, the newspaper said.[10]

The directors were David Gilfillan, a well-known non-Jewish Derry hosiery and knitwear maker, Alfred Neumann, and Geoffrey Watt, a prominent Derry businessman. The firm had leased part of the Derry shipyard premises and 'their factory was equipped with the latest plant'. It had introduced three new branches of the textile industry to Derry: Viennese knitwear made from linen, wool and art silk; machine-knit gloves; ladies' blouses and frocks, and ladies' and gents' underwear made from Irish linen.

Alfred Neumann had contributed £200 in shares while the managing director, David Gilfillan, gave £1,800. On 2 November 1938 the Ministry of Commerce's advisory committee gave Neumann a loan of £2,500 for working capital, a grant of £125 for five years for rent of its premises, and repayment of the company income tax for the first five years.[11] He also received funding for a second Derry firm, Londonderry Continental Novelties. It was given a grant of £125 p.a. to cover the cost of rent, a £12,000 interest-free loan and a £1,300 interest-bearing loan. The company had a target of employing 150 people. The loans were not due for repayment until 1949.[12]

But the good news in Derry was quickly overshadowed by events in the Third Reich. The night after the new factory was announced, on 9–10 November 1938, Kristallnacht erupted. On 16 November the Ministry of Commerce's advisory committee noted that applications from Jewish firms were increasing. It granted a company called Fürst and Hoft the same financial backing as Alfred Neumann in Derry. On 7 December the committee granted Londonderry Continental Novelties £1,200 of the £2,500 loan to Alfred Neumann to renovate the premises of Londonderry Harbour Commissioners.[13]

Neumann was clearly highly regarded by the Ministry of Commerce, because they had rejected an alternative project for Derry. In September 1938 a German businessman, described in PRONI files only as Mr Goldschmidt, had applied to set up a fashion business there. The Ministry maintained there was room for only one such business in Derry, and Gillfillan and Neumann were already receiving government funding. Similarly, on 3 September 1938, Brüder Deutsch, a Viennese clothing and bedding manufacturer, wrote enquiring about setting up in Belfast, because as German Jews they were being forced out of business in Austria. An unsigned note in the margin of their application, written by an unknown official, said their business was 'no good for Northern Ireland – already plenty of firms in this enterprise'. They were rejected.[14]

Gilfillan and Neumann immediately tried to win visas for a small number of skilled Jewish workers from Vienna, most of them related to people already working for them. Some, including Otto Goldberger, were lucky enough to arrive in the United Kingdom quickly. But others faced strong opposition from Stormont civil servants, including eleven Viennese Jews who wanted to join sixteen relatives already working for Gillfillan and Neumann in Derry. The eleven were Leopold Szanto, Leopold Eisler, both jewellers, Marie Kohn, a cook, Marie Sobe, a domestic worker, Markus Mamber, a textile merchant, Max Filgur, a hairdresser, Otto Goldberger and his brother Hans, both shirt-makers, Willy Ehrenstein, a textile technician, Dr Arpad Neumann, a doctor of civil law and Friedrich Neumann, a travel agent for Thomas Cook.[15]

H. J. Campbell of the Ministry of Home Affairs asked the RUC to report on the character and status of the guarantors supporting the eleven applicants, including how many were Jewish, and asked, 'Are they all British subjects?' RUC District Inspector S. S. Hopkins replied on 23 December 1938 that three of the eleven guarantors were Jewish – J. E. Frieslander, B. Newman, and Ephraim Gordon. The eight others were local businessmen. No work was being provided, but friends in jobs would share their wages and the Jewish community and others would assist them. There appeared to be no objection to the aliens being allowed in.

Then Stormont civil servants lobbied against allowing the Jewish applicants' entry. Campbell felt that it was 'morally certain' that the applicants would want to work, 'which will conflict with the interests of British subjects'. Three weeks later he repeated his claim that refugees would sooner or later ask for employment permits. 'Their very occupations will conflict with local labour interests and it seems to me that feelings in Derry might be definitely hostile.'[16] Campbell was concocting local opposition where there was none. There is no evidence of public hostility to the immigration of these small numbers of Jewish refugees, but parliamentary secretaries at the Northern Ireland Ministries of Labour and Home Affairs soon united in opposition to admitting them.

While this wrangle continued, another four Viennese Jews sought to join their relatives in Derry. These were Wilhelm Szanto, a medical student and music teacher, Erwin Kohn, a goldsmith, Robert Eisler, a baker, and Hermann Sobe, a lithographer. Four Derry businessmen gave personal guarantees of the men's good behaviour and promised they would not be a responsibility on the rates. They said the applicants' relatives were training local workers at Gilfillan and Neumann in Derry on articles produced only in Germany and Austria before the crisis. Far from stealing work from local people, the émigrés would be helping create jobs for them.

The police had no reason to doubt their offer, and no objection to the aliens coming. But Campbell informed the Aliens Department that the four guarantors were unwilling to say to what extent they were ready to help, and so Home Affairs could not recommend that the applicants receive any special consideration. The applications were refused.

Despite initial objections, almost all of the eleven seeking to join their sixteen relatives in Derry managed to gain entry. Otto Goldberger came to Derry in December 1938 and stayed with his sister Friederike, getting work with Gilfillan and Neumann. His brother Hans escaped to Palestine after a grim journey along the Danube and across the Black Sea and the Mediterranean. Dr Thomas Finnegan helped to get

Ludwig Schenkel admitted, and it was through the Finnegan family that he met his future wife Loni (Leontine), who had been admitted as a domestic worker for the family.

As soon as they arrived in Derry, the refugees faced the increasingly arduous task of gaining visas for their beleaguered parents trapped in Vienna. On 30 January 1939 Paul and Ludwig Schenkel, who ran the handbag section of Londonderry Continental Novelties, applied for their parents Leopold and Berta, living in 'precarious conditions'.[17]

Erich and Friederike Biss applied for her parents, David and Rosa Neuman, to be admitted. David Neuman had been second reader and secretary of the Margareten Temple, which had been burned down during Kristallnacht, leaving him jobless. They supplied an undertaking of financial support from Professor Finnegan.

The Schenkel brothers and Erich Biss wrote again on 10 February to J. H. Craig, Deputy Principal Officer at the Ministry of Labour, saying the position of their parents in Vienna was growing worse and worse. They knew Geoffrey Watt, their employer at Londonderry Continental Novelties, had raised the matter with him and pleaded with Craig to 'help us to save our parents and to do our duty as children'. David Gilfillan also wrote on the Schenkels' behalf to the Ministry of Labour on 19 February 1939.

H. J. Campbell noted on 22 February 1939 that 'the list grows', while another writer, irritated by the efforts of the Schenkels and Bisses to bring their parents to Derry, took against them: '4 fussing. Disapproval.' But next day another hand, probably Campbell's, wrote: 'These elderly and more or less unemployable people perhaps merit special consideration.' On 4 April 1939 Paul and Ludwig Schenkel wrote again to the Ministry of Labour urging that body to speed up their parents' application. They described the great success their handbag section had achieved at the British Industrial Fair in London: Queen Mary was pleased with their beach bags and HRH the Duke of Kent bought two.

Another Derry Jewish worker, Ludwig Mandalss, whose Christian wife Mary, aged thirty-six, was stuck in Vienna and barred from working, had the solicitor for Londonderry Continental Novelties, F. G. Dickson, write to Craig on 14 March 1939 on her behalf. The Schenkels and Mandalss' applications were forwarded to the Home Office with Ministry of Labour backing. On 18 April Geoffrey Watt of Iriscot Ltd, Ludwig's employer, wrote to Craig on behalf of Mary. If she did not get an exit permit by 30 April, she would be unable to get a German tax certificate for another three months, a perilous delay.

At the same time Friedrich (Fred) and Rosa Szilogyi thanked Sir George Jones MP for getting Fred's parents out and requested his help for Rosa's parents, Rudolf and Flora Auspitz. H. J. Campbell told the Home Office they had no objection to them coming. But the process proved tortuous. Fred and Rosa Szilogyi wrote to Craig on 18 May 1939: 'Our parents are in Vienna in a terrible situation. They have no other children, for my wife is the only child and it is our duty to help them. They have no money enough to stay longer there and we cannot assist them from here. You will understand what a painful situation it is for children to know this, without any possibility to help.'

Geoffrey Watt wrote to Craig on the same day pleading their case. Craig informed Campbell, who told him he had recommended to the Home Office on 10 May that the applicants be admitted. Watt and F. G. Dickson of Derrycraft Ltd also wrote on behalf of Mrs Malvine Schwatzer, aged thirty-six, in Vienna, whose husband was an employee in Derry. H.J. Campbell backed this request. Finally, on 25 June 1939 the Home Office wrote to Derrycraft Ltd saying Mrs Malvine Schwatzer should apply for a visa to the British Passport Control Officer in Vienna, to whom a communication had been sent. It appears Mrs Schwatzer survived. Other Derry applicants who were refused entry were not so lucky.

The war provided much-needed work in the city because the factories supplied uniforms and other clothing to the British armed forces. The workforce had a large percentage of women, and many Derry men had either left to look for work in other parts of the United Kingdom or had joined the armed forces when war broke out.

The city was also a major naval base for the Royal Navy and the Allied armed forces. During the war it was rumoured that there were more servicemen than natives in the city. There were an estimated 20,000 British sailors, 10,000 Canadian and 6,000 American personnel, as well as British soldiers and RAF men defending the city. Many American Jewish servicemen were surprised to find a Jewish community in the city, and attended services at the local synagogue as well as enjoying hospitality.[18]

During the war, Lord Haw-Haw, the nickname for Hitler's Irish propagandist William Joyce, showed off his local knowledge by mentioning one of the city landmarks, a large golden teapot which hung outside McCullagh's grocery shop in Waterloo Place in the city centre. In one of his radio broadcasts, he called on the Royal Navy to come out from behind the teapot or Germany would blast them clear of it.[19]

However, the city escaped attack from the German air force, save for a raid by a single bomber on Easter Tuesday, 15 April 1941, the night of the first devastating blitz on Belfast. It dropped two bombs, but missed its apparent target of the shipyard and, instead, hit two civilian areas. The first killed thirteen people and injured thirty-three, nineteen seriously, in Messines Park, while the second damaged a Catholic church and other buildings in Pennyburn.

Other Viennese Jews not named in the PRONI letters who came to Derry after the Anschluss included Robert and Ellie Sekules, who opened a factory making artificial flowers; they were joined in October 1947 by Kurt and Edith Sekules, Robert's brother and sister-in-law, and their three children. The couple opened their own knitwear factory in Kilkeel, County Down in 1950, employing sixteen workers.[20]

When the war ended, several of the Jewish refugees left Derry and went to the United States. But those who stayed thrived, for the most part, and continued to play a significant role in the business and social life of the city. Ludwig Schenkel had first hoped to become a concert pianist, but his father Leopold persuaded him to enter the family leather business. When he came to Derry, he first worked in Hallidays' small factory in Lorne Street, which employed five people, rising to manager and then proprietor. In the early 1950s, the firm employed up to eighty people but by 1959 that number had dropped to forty. It produced 250 dozen articles weekly, including travel bags, school satchels and airline bags. The company carved out valuable markets in Africa, the West Indies and the Middle East.[21]

After some bureaucratic trouble, Ludwig married Loni Rauser, from an affluent family in Grunewald, Berlin, a graduate of the University of Vienna. She had been married in Austria to a Jewish army officer who had converted to Catholicism to help his chances of promotion, but he divorced her after the Anschluss.[22] The Finnegans had a holiday home in Cloonmass near Dunfanaghy, County Donegal, and later Ludwig and Loni built one beside it. Ludwig's father, Leopold, died in December 1943 at the age of seventy-five, and his mother Bertha died in January 1956 at the home of her son Paul in Goring-on-Sea in Sussex, where he had moved in 1943.[23] Paul married and stayed in England until his death in 1969.

Ludwig had a number of extracurricular activities outside his work. His love of classical music remained with him throughout his life and he regularly gave lectures on famous composers.[24] His collection of photographs taken since the 1940s is a valuable record of his life and times. The slides, archived by his friend David Bigger, number more than 10,000 colour images in high resolution taken in Donegal, continental Europe and Israel.[25] Ludwig died on 5 January 1988 and his wife passed away on 24 September 1998. They are buried in Altnagelvin cemetery, Derry. Their headstone carries an enigmatic, rather melancholy epitaph: 'And all the dreams I ever dreamt, they came to nothing, nothing meant.'

Other Jewish employers thrived in the city. David Spain, the last president of the Jewish community in Derry, donated £2,000 to Kibbutz Lavi in Galilee near Tiberias in northern Israel in 1961, which was set up by Jewish refugees from Nazism in 1949.[26] Many were Kinderstransport refugees who had come to the United Kingdom, some to the Farm at Millisle. Like the rest of the émigré Viennese Jewish community, the Derry refugees did not learn the fate of their extended families trapped in the city until after the war. But it seems they were able to help their parents escape, as the names of Malvine Schwatzer and Mary Mandalss do not appear in the DÖW in Vienna. The PRONI files do not reveal definitive details of all those who actually made it to Northern Ireland. One cannot assume that all those listed in applications got to Derry, even if they were granted visas. They still faced problems getting out of Vienna because of arrest, harassment or rejection by capricious officials on spurious grounds, and were sometimes unable to obtain the necessary paperwork on time.

One such case among the eleven who successfully applied to come to work at Gilfillan and Neumann involved Willy Ehrenstein, aged twenty-five. He wanted to get to Derry to join his fiancée, Lily Weinstein. His story epitomises the fate of the 65,000 Jews who did not succeed in escaping Nazi Vienna.[27] When he applied in 1938, he was living at Nordbergstrasse 6. He is described as a textile technician and draper and by 1942 he was living in Werdertorgasse 17 in the city's Leopoldstadt ghetto, crowded with Jews who had been forced from their homes. Willy Ehrenstein almost certainly lost his job due to Aryanisation, and lived for another four years in Vienna, but was deported by train to Theresienstadt, the former Czech town of Terezin, 70 kilometres north-west of Prague, on 9 September 1942. In the passenger list he is described as an *Angestellter*, a white-collar worker, and he might have received training for office work with the IKG, on one of their courses to improve the chances of getting a life-saving visa.

Theresienstadt was a former Habsburg garrison town with a castle, which was turned into a ghetto for Jews, many of them elderly, from several European countries. Overcrowded, filthy, and dangerous, it was home to up to 140,000 people. Epidemics of typhoid and other diseases periodically swept through the ghetto. But the biggest danger of all was deportation to one of the Nazi extermination camps. Willy Ehrenstein survived Theresienstadt for two years and was then deported to Auschwitz on 29 September 1944. He stayed there just eleven days before being deported to Dachau on 10 October. There he stayed three months until deported to work at Leitmeritz, a Czech sub-camp in the Flossenbürg concentration camp system, on 7 January 1945, according to the DÖW. A transport of 835 Jews left Kaufering, part of the Dachau system of work camps at that time, for Leitmeritz, and it is likely that he was on it.

Willy Ehrenstein's final journey took him back to a camp outside Leitmeritz, which was only five kilometres from Theresienstadt, where his incarceration had begun in 1942. This camp was opened in March 1944 by the Nazis to make tank engines. Conditions were so bad in the underground caverns that it was known by prisoners as 'the death factory'. During the month of January 1945, when Willy arrived, 934 prisoners died. In February 862 perished. Altogether 4,500 of the 18,000 prisoners who passed through the camp died from 'disease, malnutrition, and accidents caused by the disregard for safety by the SS staff who administered the camp. In the last weeks of the war, the camp became a hub for death marches. The camp operated until

8 May 1945, when it was dissolved by the German surrender.'[28] Willy Ehrenstein's forced odyssey through the concentration camp universe ended when he died a month after his arrival on 6 February 1945.[29]

Willy's fiancée Lily Weinstein's life took a different course. She was among the small group of workers who managed to travel from Vienna to Derry in 1938. She lived at 6 Baronet Street, and worked as an instructor in Gilfillan Hosiery factory in Derry shipyard in 1938. She was examined by an Internment Tribunal on 23 October 1939, when she was twenty-four, and granted exemption. In June 1940 she married Albert Moss in Willesden, London and gave birth to a daughter, Jacqueline Hannah Moss, on 14 December 1945. The family lived at High Street, Cheltenham, but emigrated to the United States three months after the child's birth. They arrived in New York by air on 27 March.[30]

We don't know if Lily lost contact with Willy, stranded in Vienna, where they had fallen in love. Given the difficulty in communicating once the war started, this is highly probable. But their different destinies proved one thing. Getting to Northern Ireland for a Viennese Jew was often a matter of life and death.

14
WHERE IS MR NEUMANN?

While Alfred Neumann was busy helping Jewish emigrants gain entry to Northern Ireland, in Vienna the Gestapo was trying to track him down. A letter from their Property Office on 14 January 1939 noted that 'the Jew Neumann has flown' to London. He now had an important role in helping the Ministry of Commerce choose which of the hundreds of Viennese Jewish applicants should be admitted to Northern Ireland. The Northern Ireland Government did not discuss the refugee issue at cabinet level; civil servants handled the applications for residency and work visas. But all did not run smoothly. Opposition MPs at Stormont disparaged the Newtownards scheme and the government's attempts to attract new industries:

> On 9 March 1939, Thomas Henderson, Independent Unionist MP for Belfast North, jeered at the notion that the scheme would provide work for 'hundreds and hundreds of unemployed women and girls'. Henderson asked what had happened to Mr. Neumann, who seemed to have left the business. Jack Beattie, Independent MP for Pottinger, pointed out that for all the grandiose claims of the Ulster Development Council, not one unemployed person had been absorbed as a result of the scheme.[1]

During the financial year 1938/39, the Ministry of Commerce had offered £270,000 in loans and annual grants of £3,000, as well as exemptions from or contributions towards the income tax payable by twenty-four firms.[2] 'For its part, the government was keenly aware of the poor performance of the New Industries Act,' noted historian John Privilege. 'In spite of its enhanced suite of benefits, by 1939 the new Act had led to the creation of only 530 new jobs. This was despite the establishment of twelve new companies.'[3]

But what had happened to Alfred Neumann? His role in the Ards factory was short-lived. A UDC memorandum to the Ministry of Commerce revealed that, 'owing principally to differences between Mr Neumann and his staff', the venture had ceased to be viable and government assistance was withdrawn.[4] It is not clear from the memo what the differences were between Neumann and his staff, but the Ministry of Commerce viewed them as serious enough to stop financial support for him. This had happened by January 1939.

After his sacking, Alfred Neumann wrote an impassioned, five-page letter in his defence to Rabbi Shachter on 15 January 1939.[5] He criticised Shachter's treatment of him, and the behaviour of some Viennese workers whose 'unjustified complaints' he believed had led to his dismissal. He also criticised Rabbi Shachter's wife for interference in his treatment of workers at Ards. The grounds for Neumann's sacking are not exactly clear, but one matter of dispute seems to have been meals for workers. He quotes Mrs Shachter as saying to his staff at Ards, 'but they must have two eggs for breakfast!' Neumann insists that no workers were getting two eggs, including many working harder than the complainants. Wages for workers in Derry did not allow for two eggs either, he said.

Defending himself as a truth-teller, Neumann informed Shachter that his handling of the case had been unjust. He said he had certain letters from the complainants which 'would give a far better light on the whole matter', but he had waited in vain to be asked to produce them. He said Louis Hyman, a member of the Belfast Jewish community, had the letters, which would show that the judgement about the case was wrong and against the laws of the Torah. Neumann said he had given his people everything they could ask for from the beginning. 'I had always declared again and again that the most important thing is to make it possible to bring always more people out [of] the hell …' He refers to a second incident, a dispute over a room involving two female refugees working at Newtownards. It showed that the complainants 'have not the smallest feeling for anybody else'.

Neumann said permits had been granted for seventeen key workers and their wives and children to come from Vienna to Derry, a total of thirty-two people. This would bring to seventy the number of people he had brought from Austria to Northern Ireland, not counting 'a good number of people' he had helped to other countries. Their wages would not permit everybody to buy two eggs for breakfast either. Nobody else could prove that through his own initiative without any assistance of any committee they had brought out such numbers of people. He dared to say that the whole Belfast community had not brought out seventy people. His daughter and wife were also working in the same spirit. People Neumann had saved had made complaints without any justification. He would continue to avoid bringing the matter into the public eye, but it might be impossible to avoid discussion of whether the [Belfast] Jewish committee had acted properly. When people heard of the refugees' behaviour – and of other cases – this would make a lot of people afraid to help refugees. He had given real help, not only in words but occasionally a dinner for a very important number of Jewish people. Neither Rothschild nor the German Jewish Aid Committee at Woburn House, London, nor other big institutions with millions of pounds had found the heart or the way to make people self-supporting, albeit starting in a modest way.

The 'proudest honour' of Neumann's life, when he was aged seventeen or eighteen, was to work with Dr Theodor Herzl, one of the founders of Zionism, and he had seen how often leading Jewish people had acted against Jews who wanted to do some good for Jewry. He was now over fifty-seven and had worked continuously for more than a year, often twenty-four hours a day without interruption, seldom getting five hours' sleep. He had not the slightest doubt that he would walk unhurt 'through the Red Sea' because he had the blessing of God to do very good things in the interest of Jewry.

Neumann also told Shachter that visas for the father of an E. Rapp, who had worked at Ards before emigrating to the United States, had been granted, and that his daughter had also procured one for Rapp's daughter. Six weeks later, Neumann urgently replied to a letter from Rapp asking him to answer nine questions with complete truthfulness. Had he, and others, had enough to eat at Newtownards? What had others reported about him in Belfast? Had he or others met Goorwitch and Lewis or Hurwitz, key figures in the Belfast Jewish community, and what had been said about him? Who of the Belfast people had spoken unfavourably about him? Had they heard Mr Craig, of the Ministry of Commerce, speaking unfavourably about him and what had he said? But all his efforts were in vain. He was not restored to his job.

By May 1939 the Ards business had reopened under the control of Nathan Goorwitch, a clothing manufacturer and prominent member of the Belfast Jewish community. The basis of the financial assistance provided was unchanged, but authority was given for the number of workers in training at any one time to be increased, thus shortening the period of the scheme.[6] The two Derry businesses continued to operate without a pause.

Goorwitch was soon joined in Newtownards by a recently admitted Viennese couple, Zoltan Frankl and Anny Lewinter-Frankl, who played a major role in the business and artistic life of Northern Ireland for the next fifty years. Born in 1894, Zoltan was the youngest of four children of Hermann and Regina Frankl. Hermann was a successful businessman, the owner of a grocery/haberdashery store in Csakova, now Ciacova, in Romania. Regina was a schoolteacher before she married, a 'highly cultured intelligent lady', according to her granddaughter Mrs Vivienne Magee.[7]

Zoltan Frankl served in a German Hussar regiment in World War I and was awarded the Iron Cross. He then went to work in the wool and knitwear industry in Vienna, where he met a brilliant young woman, Anny Lewinter, who owned one of the city's leading couture knitwear firms by the time she was twenty-one. They married in 1924, and the business quickly prospered, with two shops in the centre of Vienna, and by 1930 a substantial factory. It was a comfortable and stimulating environment. They entertained, attended concerts, visited art galleries, and enjoyed the rich cultural life that Vienna had to offer. Anny's sister Charlotte, a highly gifted designer, joined them and the company's reputation grew.

Anny was the dynamic entrepreneur and Zoltan the charismatic representative who brought in the orders. Anny's father, Karl Lewinter, a timber merchant, and her mother, Beila, a gifted seamstress, brought up Anny and her three sisters, Gisela, Charlotte and Felicitas, on a small farm near the Danube in Vienna's nineteenth district. It was a 'happy, wonderful childhood', and they were moderately well-off.[8]

The four talented daughters thrived, the eldest Gisela as a pharmacist, Anny and Charlotte in haute couture and the youngest sister, Felicitas, as a highly talented pianist.

Zoltan Frankl had no formal business school training, and though he and his father Hermann did not get on particularly well, he had inherited his economic acumen. His mother, Regina, said he had a 'brilliant' business brain and could instinctively make the right, difficult decisions. But Zoltan and Anny were forced to leave Vienna for England after the Anschluss in March 1938. Gisela escaped to Melbourne, Australia, and the family planned to follow her there, where they had many contacts in the wool industry. On 8 February 1939, the Home Office in London wrote to the Ministry of Labour at Stormont about the case of Zoltan, Anny and Charlotte. Zoltan and Anny were already in the United Kingdom, but Charlotte and Felicitas were still in Vienna. On 28 March, the Ministry of Labour passed on the letter to the Ministry of Home Affairs, who said Charlotte should apply to the British Passport Control Officer in Vienna.

'Daddy brought out his wife Anny. He then went back for Charlotte under the pretence that she was his wife. Then he went back to get out Felicitas, who at that time was a young pianist. That was very dangerous in those days,' said Vivienne Magee. Zoltan obtained a visa for Charlotte to come to Belfast, and Felicitas went to Scotland as a maid, the only path open to many of Vienna's highly qualified female Jewish refugees.

By 10 May 1939 negotiations had been completed between Zoltan, his wife Anny and her sister Charlotte, and Nathan Goorwitch for the establishment of a knitting concern. The Frankls had planned to open a factory in Liverpool, but the Stormont government persuaded them to consider Northern Ireland. They arrived in Belfast off the Liverpool boat, to be met by the personal Rolls-Royce of the Minister of Agriculture, Sir Basil Brooke, and, according to Vivienne Magee, by Sir Basil himself: 'They might have had plenty of other wonderful people from Vienna, but I think they were very keen to get him. I think that was because they must have found my father fascinating. If my father walked into a room, everyone would stop and look at him. He had such an aura about him. If he spoke to you, you were the only person in that room. That is a great talent.'

The Frankls stayed at the Grand Central Hotel in Belfast, but quickly found a house at 93 Malone Road, one of the most affluent areas of the city. They soon made a success of the factory. By April 1940 the Frankls employed 160–200 workers in Newtownards. As soon as they arrived, they made tireless efforts to get Anny's parents, Karl and Beila Lewinter, out of Vienna. A tortuous struggle to save them began.

Between June 1939 and April 1940 Zoltan and Anny wrote several letters to the Ministries of Home Affairs and Commerce at Stormont, who contacted the Home Office. Their letters received a sympathetic hearing in the Stormont ministries along with a firm statement of Home Office rules. Plans were made for their parents to leave via Vienna, Budapest or Milan, but these came to nothing. In the midst of all this stress, Zoltan's father, Hermann, was able to write to him on 24 August 1939, a week before the Germans invaded Poland, to congratulate him on the birth of a son, Peter, in Belfast:

> Vienna, 24/8/1939
> My dear Zoli!
>
> Just now received the surprising telegram. But as it unfortunately has not been granted to me to personally congratulate you on the happy event of the birth of your newborn son, so receive from me and your loving Mummy in written form the heartiest congratulations. May the dear Lord grant him good fortune, that you should all be healthy, your little son may be healthy with good fortune blessed, may you yourself with your lovely Anny have a healthy, happy life. Many greetings and kisses, your happy father,
> Good luck!

On 23 April 1940 Anny wrote again to the Ministry of Home Affairs for visas for her parents. By then they were living in Vienna at Doeblinger Hauptstrasse 72, having been evicted from their home at Formanekgasse 2. She said the Germans did not let her parents have their passports until after the outbreak of war, by which time the visas were null and void. She asked the Ministry of Home Affairs to raise the matter with the Home Office in the hope that that Department would be prepared to state that, if her parents reached neutral territory, favourable consideration would be given to the issue of visas to enable them to proceed to Northern Ireland. 'On compassionate grounds I trust that the Home Office will be disposed to accede to my request', Anny wrote, adding that she appreciated 'that at the present time, it is almost impossible for persons living in enemy territory to come to live here'.

The Stormont correspondence ended then, but Karl and Beila Lewinter kept writing to their children via the Red Cross. Their last letters came from Vienna in December 1941:

My dear children!

Since we have from you till today after several attempts received neither an entry permit to somewhere nor a favourable communication regarding one, and nothing further about it, we take it with certainty that with the best will in the world you have unfortunately found it impossible to fulfil our wishes. So we must accept that it was unfortunately not granted to us to experience the joy of being together with you. It seems that we will only with difficulty be together again. So it is our greatest wish my dear children and we fervently ask that all three of you be together with dear Zoli to live peacefully together and if dear C.[Charlotte] and F. [Felicitas] are married, God willing, as far as possible then also to keep together, just as we also ask that you keep in contact with dear Gisa. To you dear Zoli, we wish you a healthy happy marriage with dear Anny and that you bring up your golden child happily. Furthermore, we ask you that just as parents you care for your golden child, so we ask you to look after the two dear sisters, C and F, like a father, and if they should marry according to their wishes, that it is our wish that all of you be together as happily and peacefully as possible and we will with the love of the Lord be with you in spirit. We accept it as the work of Providence and so we must live with it and if the good Lord gives us life, then we will seek to communicate and to come together with you. And now dear children and golden little child we embrace you all with love in Spirit, with many, many greetings and kisses, God protect you always and everywhere, farewell, farewell,

> Your faithful parents Karl and Beila
> P.S. Please let dear Gisa see this letter.

In December 1941 Karl and Berta Lewinter also wrote to their daughter, Gisa, and son-in-law, Harri:

My dear Gisa and Harri!

As it has not been granted to us to live with you in your home and to congratulate you and to get to know you, my dear Harri, and your lovely little daughter, and to congratulate you and to experience that joy, do accept, my dear children, our sincere congratulations in writing. May the loving God bless you with a peaceful, healthy and happy marriage. Do bring up your golden, lovely, daughter with joy, and we would be delighted to receive your good news in writing from afar; we will always be with you in spirit, with paternal and maternal love. We must accept the divine will. We ask you, my dear children, to always stay together in peace with your beloved sisters, and always to keep in touch; that is our dearest wish. And now my dearest, we embrace you with love in the spirit and many, many kisses. God protect you always and everywhere, farewell, farewell.

> Your faithful parents
> Karl and Beila

Like all the refugees who came to Northern Ireland, Zoltan and Anny heard nothing of their parents' fate until after the war.

Karl and Beila were deported to Riga in Latvia on 11 January 1942, in one of four large transports from Vienna (3 December 1941, 11 and 26 January, and 6 February 1942), carrying a total of 4,200 Jewish men and women. After an eight-day journey, they reached Riga. The deportees were either brought into the ghetto there or had to do forced labour in the nearby Salaspils camp. Because of the terrible living conditions, the death rate among the ghetto residents, especially among the weak, the elderly and children, rose sharply.

From information in the files of the DÖW about the treatment of those on the last transport which arrived at Skirotava station in Riga on 6 February 1942, it is possible to piece together the likely fate of Karl and Beila Lewinter. Those deportees who seemed too weak for the kilometre-long march were offered lorries – in fact 'gas wagons' – for the journey. Of the 1,000 deported from Vienna, only 300 reached the ghetto on foot, the others being gassed. Only 800 of the 20,000 men women and children deported from Germany and Austria survived the selections, the ghetto and the various concentration camps at Riga, among them around 100 Jewish women and men from Vienna. So Karl and Beila were either murdered immediately on arrival or died of ill-treatment sometime later. Their children never learned exactly how or when they died, and no grave marks their passing.

In Vienna today, the names of Karl and Beila Lewinter are among twenty-nine people who died in the Holocaust listed on a memorial tablet on the exterior of the Karl Marx Hof building in Boschstrasse 9 in the Döbling district of Vienna. It says the twenty-nine were among sixty-nine people evicted from the building by the National Socialists in 1938–39 because they were non-Aryan. Karl and Beila lived at the address, one of several they had before they were deported and murdered.

15
'A MULTIPLICATION
OF CATASTROPHES'

By the summer of 1939 an estimated 67,000 Jews were trapped in Vienna under the Nazi dictatorship, with greatly reduced chances of escape. States across the world had made it much harder for them to be accepted. Refugee support committees and Jewish bodies had to finance those admitted, and visas were issued on the understanding that those receiving them would re-emigrate as soon as possible. But these support groups faced huge pressure on their funds because of delays in re-emigration, and refugees would soon rely on public funds, which the Home Office opposed.

A cabinet committee report advised offering public funds proportionate to private donations, as long as other states contributed, particularly the USA. The motive was financial, not simply philanthropic, as Louise London explains: 'The new position ... was consistent with the policy of keeping the United Kingdom as a country of transit. The proposed injection of British finance was aimed at increasing opportunities to emigrate from the United Kingdom, not at expanding the chances of escape from Nazi territory.'[1] The British cabinet agreed to the proposals in principle, and informed the Americans and the Inter-Governmental Committee of its funding move.[2] But it was too late. War broke out in September 1939, making such proposals impracticable, and the United Kingdom withdrew the offer the following month.

Re-emigration was the only way to reduce refugee numbers, but every month a few hundred left while several thousand arrived. The US government refused to relax entry controls for European transmigrants, who faced a near two-year delay before being considered. From April

1939, the Home Office tightened up entry rules for applicants in transit.[3] A large number of United Kingdom entry visas were issued but not enough to cater for the desperate people seeking escape from the Nazis. Between May 1938 and the end of January 1939, some 50,000 visas had been granted to refugees, many covering more than one person. Of those, 13,500 had been granted in Vienna and 34,000 in Berlin.

In Vienna, the process had improved enough by June 1939 to allow 100 visas to be granted and 200 people interviewed daily; the long queues and most complaints had been eliminated. But a new obstacle appeared. Both the Co-ordinating Committee and the Home Office expressed concern that they were giving out visas to 'unsuitable' applicants in Vienna; they wanted a more effective way to examine prospective candidates, and felt that the Passport Control Office was not properly vetting them. A senior Home Office official hoped the Co-ordinating Committee would choose British representatives to select refugees in Vienna. He felt it would be little short of disastrous if 'the Gestapo try to unload the wrong type of emigrant upon other countries'.[4]

In May 1939 the British government had dropped a bombshell when it published a White Paper limiting Jewish immigration to Palestine to 75,000 over the following five years, after which no more would be permitted without Arab consent. The Colonial Office also added a six-month halt to admissions to Palestine as a punishment for illegal immigration. The chief hope for Austrian refugees was now emigration to developed countries, apart from risky and often illegal efforts to get to Palestine or even to Shanghai, where refugees did not require visas. Emigrants had to scrape together the money to get out or rely on private support from refugee committees or relatives and friends abroad. Applicants faced terror and delay from the Nazi authorities while pressures grew on the refugee support bodies funding their exit. In Vienna, the city's Jews faced Adolf Eichmann's imposition of an impossible timetable.

In mid-August 1939 Norman Bentwich of the CGJ met Eichmann in Vienna, along with Josef Löwenherz of the IKG. In his report to the CGJ, Bentwich noted that by then the city's Jewish population had fallen from 165,000 in April 1938 to 67,000. In the Austrian provinces the number had dropped from 15,000 to 370.

An estimated 110,000 had been forced out and 3,500 had died. The death rate had leapt four-fold compared to 1937, one-eighth due to suicide.

Bentwich's report gave incontrovertible evidence of the dire plight of Vienna's Jews. The livelihood of almost all of them had been taken away. 'Every single Jewish shop or business has been Aryanized, destroyed or shut. You no longer see the sign "Arisch" [Aryan] on any business place, because it is superfluous.' Movable private property of value, such as gold and silver objects, had been taken away, and any form of private wealth confiscated or blocked. The Jews had been herded into a 'congested ghetto' around the Jewish quarter of Leopoldstadt:

> The poverty and destitution of the remnant of a great community are heartrending. Well over half of the 67,000 are fed daily through communal soup-kitchens, most of them collecting for their family their one square meal of the day from the kitchens. They have no meat; and a large number are glaringly undernourished. The hapless people cannot even enjoy God's air; it is an offence for them to enter a public park or garden, or to sit on a bench in the Ring. One small park near the Jewish quarter was reserved for them, but it is not safe to enter it. They cannot use any bathing place, nor go to any form of entertainment; not even attend a Synagogue. Every one of the Jewish places of worship has been destroyed or closed ... The cemetery has not been inviolate; the hall where the burial ceremony is read has been blown to pieces. Their libraries, which had famous collections, have been seized and confiscated. The principal religious school was burned down ...[5]

Bentwich said that, since mid-1938, 40,000 Jews had attended retraining classes in 'a thousand different branches of manual or domestic work', as preparation for emigration. 'There is a class, for example, for bar-mixers, and several for butlers, which are attended by lawyers, doctors and industrialists.' He described the 'elaborate procedure which requires reference to a score of

Government offices and filling in scores of forms' and praised the IKG for organising it 'methodically and expeditiously'. The Nazi administration had set up a Central Office for Jewish Emigration in the former Rothschild Palace, where the passports were given out and the certificates of 'no objection' obtained. The Jewish emigrant finally returned to the IKG to get the money for his ticket and the landing money for his destination.

But this was the organised emigration. Others, including the stateless or previously foreign subjects, such as Poles, were expelled 'at the shortest notice on penalty of being thrown back into a concentration camp. Driven from their homes – even from the hospitals – they are forced over the frontier anyhow, usually without visas.' Thousands had gone to Shanghai, some to the 'No-Man's Land' on the Polish frontier, others boarded ships which 'hopelessly' tried to land their passengers at a port of asylum. Hopes were raised when the Italian government admitted some 'thousand or two' on tourist visas, then repudiated the policy, expelled many of the immigrant Jews, and arrested members of the refugee committees. It was the policy of the Nazi authorities in Vienna to force out all Jews by the end of 1939 or the beginning of 1940. So far they had succeeded at a rate of 7,000–8,000 monthly. 'They prefer a disorderly to a planned emigration, as a means of making trouble for the Jews in other countries,' Bentwich wrote.[6]

Bentwich met Eichmann and pleaded for orderly emigration, to be carried out over a longer period. The Council for German Jewry was unwilling to carry out a policy that was only multiplying the problems of the countries to which the refugees were forced to emigrate, he said. The Inter-Governmental Committee had been assured that the German government would co-operate in an orderly emigration, and that policy must be applied to the Ostmark, as the Nazis had renamed Austria after the Anschluss.

Eichmann told Bentwich that orders had been given 'in the highest quarters' for the complete evacuation of the Jews in the shortest possible time, and the statement about ordered emigration did not apply there. 'He could not make any change in the programme.' Of the 67,000 Jews who remained in Vienna, between 20,000 and 25,000 were over sixty-five, and could not obtain emigration visas.

Pensioners and the very poor might stay: 'About 45,000 must be cleared out over the next six months,' Bentwich noted in his report to the CGJ.[7]

He said to Eichmann that the proceeds of Jewish endowments in the Ostmark should now be used to relieve the destitute, as was being done in the Altreich (Germany). The refugee organisations were no longer able to provide the support that the IKG needed to feed the majority of the remaining Jews, or for other forms of social work. Eichmann said he would consider the matter, but Dr Löwenherz told Bentwich later that he did not believe there would be any change. Bentwich noted that 3,700 emigrants could be taken out legally each month, 1,000 each to Britain and the USA, the rest to other countries, within a year. But this was only half the monthly figure Eichmann was demanding.

Bentwich made another grim prediction, reinforcing the one he had made on his fact-finding visit a year before. 'Unless some change is brought about, there is bound to be a multiplication of catastrophes such as those now taking place in Italy, the No-man's-Land and the refugee ships, which cannot land their passengers.'[8] Louise London sums up the crisis facing the bodies helping refugees in the United Kingdom: 'The Council for German Jewry faced an agonising dilemma. Should it try to comply with Nazi pressure for Jewish emigration while pleading for time? Or had the moment come to call a halt? Several weeks before war broke out, the Jewish refugee organisation decided to accept no more cases. It asked the British Government to halt new admissions.'[9] Just when it was most needed, a key avenue of escape was closed to Vienna's Jews.

16

'THERE WERE GERMAN
SOLDIERS EVERYWHERE'

In December 1938 George Bloch, aged ten, was looking forward to the summer. He lived in the beautiful Baltic city of Danzig.[1] Predominantly ethnic German, Danzig had been declared a free city under the Versailles Treaty in 1919, which made Poland an independent republic and gave it a large part of German West Prussia. This 'Polish corridor' isolated East Prussia from the rest of Germany. Danzig was a cosmopolitan port city, for centuries a key member of the Hanseatic League, which brought it wealth and status in northern Europe. Of all the losses of German territory under the Treaty of Versailles, the loss of Danzig and West Prussia to the Poles was among the most galling. When the Nazis came to power in January 1933, they set their sights on both.

George Bloch's paternal grandfather Mordecai was in the grain business in Kalisz in western Russia, but he moved the family to Danzig to escape anti-Semitic persecution. His son Kasriel, George's father, took over the business and developed others. Kasriel's father-in-law Hersch Szajnik owned an embroidery lace factory called Kalisz Textiles and Kasriel helped Hersch export lace to Britain. Kasriel built up links with a London company, Mayfair Manufacturing Ltd, and supplied them with clothes.

With his elder brother Richard, George enjoyed an idyllic childhood in Danzig in the 1930s. The family lived in a well-appointed house in its own grounds. There were trips to the seaside on the Baltic in summer, with its sandy beaches, warm temperatures and blue skies. At home they played tennis on their own court and in winter skated on it. The family businesses, including a clothing factory and an export agency, prospered.

Kasriel had fought bravely for Poland in the war against Russia (1919–20), but valued Danzig's independence and had no desire to see it handed over to either Germany or Poland. Nazi agitation over the Versailles Treaty increased and from 1936 onwards Danzig was in the eye of the storm. Ethnic tensions grew. One incident stayed in George's mind. He loved to go with his mother to cafés in the city centre, and one day they went to one of their favourites. On the door they saw a sign in German which read: 'Dogs and Jews forbidden'. His mother Karola took him home and they never went back.

Then in June 1938 something happened which changed their lives for ever. Kasriel Bloch's businesses included one in the entertainment sector. He had a franchise for coin-operated table football games in several bars and cafés. He employed a German called Löwenstein to service the machines and collect the coins. One day Löwenstein was emptying the coin boxes in a bar when another German, a right-winger whom he knew, bought him a beer and sat down with him.

'I've good news for you,' he told Löwenstein. 'We're going to pick up Bloch in the next week. We're going to take over this business. You'll do well out of it, you'll get your cut.' Löwenstein listened but said little. He went straight to Kasriel and told him what had happened. Immediately Kasriel ordered the family to pack a few essentials in suitcases and loaded up their Studebaker car. That night they left Danzig for ever, travelling on back roads through forests and isolated villages to the port of Gydnia in Poland.

With his home and businesses in Danzig, Kasriel was up against it. He could not live there, and Poland's three million Jews already faced native anti-Semitism, while Germany became increasingly belligerent. On a business trip to London with his brother-in-law Jack Szajnik (later naturalised to 'Shanik') in 1937, Kasriel had complained about the growing anti-Semitism in Danzig to a friend, Jack Posnansky, managing director of Mayfair Manufacturing Company, who suggested he open a factory in the United Kingdom. Kasriel sold their Danzig home and went to London to investigate a relocation. There he met Major J. M. Henderson, the Northern Ireland government agent in Britain, who suggested that he should consider setting up in

Portadown, in the heart of Northern Ireland. Kasriel visited and was impressed. He opened a factory at Edward Street in June 1939. But there was a problem.

The Nazis had promised at Munich that there would be no more territorial demands but in the summer of 1939, emboldened by western weakness over Austria and Czechoslovakia, they chose Poland as their next conquest. Getting into the United Kingdom was growing more difficult by the day. As the Nazis persecuted the Jews in Austria, Germany and Czechoslovakia, every country in western Europe along with the USA tightened restrictions on entry. Kasriel went to Henderson and told him the deal was off unless he could get entry and residence permits for his family.

'Give me a couple of weeks,' said Henderson. If he did not come up with something, he would understand why Kasriel would reject the deal. Back in Gdynia, the family were desperately trying to shift for themselves. George's elder brother Richard queued day after day at the British legation, waiting for the visas to come through. His mother, Karola, booked them tickets on a liner leaving Gdynia. But by the time the visas arrived, their ship had sailed. They were stranded in Gdynia as war fever grew. The Germans demanded access to Danzig, which would have meant crossing Polish territory. The Poles refused. Tension mounted.

In Gdynia, George attended a Polish state school, a big change from his Jewish primary school in Danzig. Polish schools operated a *numerus clausus*, a restriction severely limiting the number of Jews admitted. George and another Jewish boy were the only two in his class and were segregated at the back. They were regularly bullied. One winter's day, George was attacked by a group of bigger boys on his way home from school. They beat him up, stripped him naked from the waist down, and threw him into the snow. Bruised and shocked, he made his way home and vowed to Karola that he would never go back to school. 'You'll go back tomorrow. Otherwise they will have won,' she said.

Next day she went to see the headmaster, but he said he was not responsible for what happened outside the school. George also went back, and he was not attacked again. It was a lesson he never forgot. The family left Gdynia and moved to Warsaw to live with George's uncle Arek and aunt Hala Szajnik. Abandoning hope of an escape by ship, George's mother managed to secure rail tickets on the black market. It would mean travelling across Nazi Germany, with an invasion of Poland ever more likely. It would also mean travelling with Polish passports stamped with a 'J', revealing their Jewish identity.

On 31 August 1939 George, Richard and their mother boarded the train in Warsaw. It travelled across Poland without incident, then stopped at a Polish–German border crossing. The town was crawling with SS and SA men and she had to show their passports. She handed them nervously to the border police, who examined them closely but allowed the family back on the train. After a long wait, it set off into Germany.

What the eleven-year-old George saw next was unbelievable. They passed mile after mile of German army trains, crammed with soldiers, tanks, artillery, shells, and other war materiel. That night, these troops invaded Poland and two days later, on 3 September 1939, Britain and France declared war on Germany. The Blochs had escaped on the last train out of Warsaw. 'Talk about winning the lottery!' said George nearly eighty years after their escape. 'We were unbelievably lucky.'

The family reached Ostend in Belgium, then London, where they met their father. After a few days they headed to Portadown, and within weeks Kasriel's factory, Ulster Laces Ltd, was employing twenty-five workers. The factory produced embroidery lace for export to Canada as well as tens of thousands of army badges, shoulder flashes and uniform markings for the war effort. George enrolled in Portadown College. It was one of the happiest periods of his life. His extended family, though, were still in Poland.

A number of key refugee figures from Czechoslovakia also made it to Northern Ireland at the same period as the Bloch family. Zdenek Sochor was in England planning to open a clothing printing works, when the Ministry of Commerce offered him financial support to set up in Northern Ireland. He renovated a disused flax factory at Waterford Street, off the Falls Road in west Belfast, and opened the Belfast Silk and Rayon company, which at its peak employed 180 local people.[2]

The Sochor family employed nearly 2,000 people in clothing, wood-making and brick factories at Dvur Kralove Nad Labem, a Bohemian town about 145 km north-east of Prague. Josef Sochor had set up the family business in the nineteenth century, and it was highly successful. They were wealthy, with a modernist home, and were the area's main employer. Josef had five sons, Zdenek, Josef, Robert, Jaroslav and Pavel, and when Josef senior died in the 1930s Zdenek became the main man in the family business. He was in the United Kingdom when the Nazis took over Czechoslovakia in March 1939. His wife Eliska, who was not Jewish, and son Paul, aged five, were still in Dvur Kralove, but he managed to get them out. They travelled by train to the Hook of Holland, then to London and Belfast. The Nazis soon removed textile machinery from the Dvur Kralove works and turned it into an aircraft factory making Heinkel bombers.

In April 1939 Zdenek was joined by one of his cousins, Alfred Landsberger, who had escaped from Frydek in Czechoslovakia the previous month. His family also had a textile factory and Alfred, known as Fred, invested £5,000 in the Belfast Silk and Rayon Ltd. Fred had business contacts in the United Kingdom and went there. He was in London during the Blitz and also lived for a time in Hastings, but by mid-1941 he had settled in Belfast. Fred lost the firm in Frydek, and never returned there. Another Czech exile, Ákos Laszlo, was appointed managing director. In 1953, Fred set up Landsberger Ltd, a textile company selling mainly linen and cotton material such as tea towels and tablecloths. From 1957 its office was at 20 Alfred Street, Belfast. Fred died in 1964. The Sochors took over an aircraft factory in Newtownards and set up Crepe Weavers, which was run by Akos Laszlo.

Zdenek's brother Pavel joined the Czech resistance. On 27 May 1942 a group of Czech parachutists serving in the British army attacked SS deputy leader Reinhard Heydrich, acting Reich-Protector of Bohemia and Moravia, and one of the main architects of the Holocaust, in Prague. He died on 4 June. On 18 June his assassins were betrayed by one of their group and were either killed by the Germans or committed suicide in Prague. The Czech people paid a terrible price for the assassination of Heydrich. It is estimated that at least 1,200 people were murdered by the Nazis and up to 15,000 deported to concentration camps. The Sochor family believe Pavel may have played a part in the operation against Heydrich, though they are still seeking details of his Resistance activities. He was betrayed to the Gestapo by a local informer who knew of his activities, and executed in Auschwitz on 14

June 1942, ten days after Heydrich's death, aged twenty-nine. Pavel's brother Zdenek later received a coded letter from a friend, saying she knew the people who had betrayed him. She would not reveal their identities but described their roles in his capture, by giving each a letter instead of a name (A, B, C, etc). The writer promised at some stage to name names. A second brother, Josef, also died in the camps, but it is not believed he was active in the Resistance. A third brother, Robert, a doctor, was forced to work for the Germans but managed to escape from the camp where he was being held. Paul Sochor later took over the family business in Northern Ireland and it thrived.[3]

Czech Jews with a left-wing background also emigrated to Northern Ireland. Among them was Franz Langhammer, an active Social Democrat from Hradec Kolove in the Liberec area, and his son Fritz, aged seventeen. Franz hoped that his background as a printer would help him get work in the United Kingdom textile industry. Franz had fought in the Austro-Hungarian army in Albania during World War I. He was close to Wenzel Jaksch, the leader of the Social Democrats in the Sudetenland, who managed to escape to London. Franz's grandson Eric, who lives in Belfast, believes they escaped through the port of Gydnia around 21 December 1938, and made their way to London.[4]

After a few days they went to Dollar, outside Stirling in Scotland, and then Josef Sochor, the Czech Jew who had set up the Belfast Silk and Rayon Company, brought them to Northern Ireland. Sochor appears to have seen the names on a Red Cross list and helped them move. During the war the company was very busy making camouflage netting. Both Franz and Fritz, who changed his name to Fred, worked for the company.

Fred met a local girl called Margaret Gregg at the Floral Hall ballroom and married her. He joined the Czech army in the United Kingdom and worked as a dispatch rider. He served in Normandy after D-Day, and moved east into Germany with the victorious Allies. Fred recalled meeting Russian soldiers, their arms banded with watches taken from German prisoners. He said the only German words the Russian soldiers seemed to know were '*Uhre*' (watches) and '*Frau, komm.*' ('Woman, come.')

After 1945 the Sudeten Germans were expelled from Czechoslovakia, and in 1948 the Communists took over, so Franz never went back. Fred set up a firm called Radiant Fabrics which he ran with a close friend, Mackie (Mordecai) Gewing. Fred owned the factory and did the technical work, while Mackie carried out the administrative work. Franz also worked there. The business in Whitehouse, just outside Belfast, burned down, and as Fred had no insurance, he had to start from scratch. His factory did well and employed forty to fifty workers.

The Langhammers were committed socialists, but the extended family included Hitler supporters. Fred had a cousin called Erna Friebel, an ardent Nazi and 'cold narcissist', who worked for the Gestapo in Trutnov. She married a Wehrmacht doctor called Helmut Stiepel, who worked on the Eastern Front with German Army Group South. Helmut's brother was killed by the French Resistance in June 1944. He was a member of SS Das Reich, the division which carried out the massacre of 642 men, women and children in the French village of Oradour-sur-Glane on 10 June 1944. Franz also had a brother Walter, who had a son killed on the Russian front.

Fred was a warm, kind-hearted man, with a ready laugh, Eric remembers. Like most émigrés, neither Fred nor Franz talked about the war. Eric's paternal grandmother, Emilie, was more introverted, prone to depression. Her father was killed in the war. Eric takes a passionate interest in the history of his family and their birthplace, and has returned to Czechoslovakia to find out more. Eric met two sisters who had an antique shop in Bangor, County Down, who came from the same area of the Sudetenland as his father. 'Meeting them was like having an out of body experience,' Eric said.[5]

Eric's brother, Mark Langhammer, kept up the family's leftist tradition, serving twelve years as an independent Labour member of Newtownabbey Borough Council. Fred died of a heart attack on 18 August 1962 when Eric was four and his sister Helen was only a month old. Fred was just forty-one and had smoked seventy cigarettes a day.

Eric feels his life would have been different had his father lived. He has always felt an outsider, alienated by the sectarianism and lack of compromise in Northern Ireland. He was a punk, a backpacker, a traveller. He loves steam trains and has taken photographs of them all over the world, publishing two books, one called *Vanishing Steam*, and a second in German.

Another Czech family with a background in textiles who came to Northern Ireland, was that of Alf Dubs, who became a well-known Labour Party peer at Westminster and a prominent campaigner for refugees.[6] He was just six when the Nazis invaded his native Prague:

My Czech father Hubert was Jewish, and my Austrian mother Bedriska was not. And so, when there was a threat of Nazi invasion, my father said to his cousins, 'If the Nazis come, I'm getting out.' So, my father got out. My mother was refused permission to leave. She went to the Gestapo place and they said her exit permit was refused. They threw her down the stairs. She landed in a heap at the bottom and before she found out what was broken, if anything, she realised they had thrown her passport after her, which gave her hope.

When the Nazis occupied Prague, the first thing we had to do was tear a picture of the President, Edvard Benes, out of our schoolbooks and stick in a picture of Hitler. There were German soldiers everywhere. Father had disappeared quickly. Then my mother put me on a Kindertransport and I remember her taking me to the station and seeing her there with all the anxious parents, with a friend of hers, and German soldiers and swastikas in the background. Then the train went. That was June or July 1939.

We had an interminably long journey with hard wooden seats, but as a six-year-old you don't mind that. The German soldiers came in. They didn't harm us. They went into some carriages and tipped all the luggage out, but they didn't in my compartment. I didn't know anybody, I was just with children. We got to the Dutch border, when the older ones cheered because we were out of reach of the Nazis. I knew it was significant, but I didn't know why.

I was looking for windmills and wooden shoes because that's what I thought about Holland, but I didn't see any of those. We got to the Hook of Holland, then Harwich and then to Liverpool Street station, London, with our dog tags on. We all had to be ticked off and assigned to family and relatives. So I was lucky. About two-thirds of the children didn't have a parent waiting for them, but everybody had somebody waiting for them. Meeting my father was quite bewildering. He took me to Belsize Park, as all the refugees lived in Belsize Park or Swiss Cottage. He was living in a bed-sitter, so it was all quite complicated.

My mum packed a little knapsack with sandwiches for the journey, and when I got to London my father looked at them and said, 'You haven't touched them. You haven't eaten food for two days.' I must have been a bit traumatised. For a six-year-old boy not to eat is quite funny.

I know my father had permission to stay in Britain until October 1939, on a Jewish passport. His two cousins, an uncle and aunt, one had a cyanide pill and when the Gestapo came for them, that was the end, and the other was taken to Auschwitz. He didn't survive.

My mother eventually managed to fiddle an exit permit and arrived in London on 31 August 1939, on the last possible train before the Second World War. My father had been told by a friend of his from central Europe, who had some money and had been given permission to start a factory in either Northern Ireland or Scotland, 'If you ever get out, I'm going to offer you a job in Cookstown.'

My father told my mother, 'If you ever get out, we are going to Cookstown,' so my mother looked at the atlas and said, 'Good, we're going to Australia.' We got out and then travelled to Cookstown, in County Tyrone. I was lucky in a sense. Many children never saw their parents again.[7]

The company was innovative, and installed machinery 'at considerable expense' to make cotton goods not previously made in Northern Ireland.[8] But Alf Dubs' father Hubert, managing director of the Cookstown Weaving Company, County Tyrone, had only a short time to live. He died suddenly on 30 September 1940.

17

'COLLAR THE LOT!'

When war broke out on 3 September 1939, the British government ordered a register of adult 'enemy aliens', as refugees from Axis countries were then categorised, throughout the United Kingdom. In Northern Ireland this included 200 Germans, 32 Austrians, 24 Czechs and 155 Italians. The majority of the Germans and Austrians were Jewish refugees, and most of the Austrians had come from Vienna since August 1938.[1] These were called for examination in Northern Ireland.[2]

Across the United Kingdom, 120 tribunals were set up to categorise 'enemy aliens' according to their security risk. The tribunals heard the cases of 73,800 individuals, three-quarters of them refugees. A few hundred regarded as dangerous enough were categorised as Class A and interned immediately, including, mistakenly, some Jewish refugees; Class B, doubtful cases, were subject to some restrictions; and Class C, which included 64,244 cases, were thought to pose no security risk.[3]

Among the first to be interned was Alfred Neumann. He was questioned by an interview panel in London on 6 December 1939, and held initially at Dovercourt, a former Butlin's holiday camp near Harwich, Essex. In May 1940 he was transferred to the Isle of Man. His son Kurt, aged thirty-three, was also interned. Kurt was held for a time at Warth Mills camp, a filthy disused factory in Bury, Lancashire. Conditions were so bad that some of the internees described them as worse than Dachau, and a hundred of them staged a hunger strike in protest.[4]

Alfred Neumann's younger brother Julius wrote to Rabbi Shachter on 15 January 1940 appealing for his help in obtaining Alfred's release.[5] Alfred had worked 'with heart and soul to save as many people as possible from Nazi persecution', and to prove that refugees were not a burden but an asset to the country. As he knew, Alfred 'became highly nervous by the terrible strain of working by day for the business and by night to do all the correspondence to get people out of Austria'. He had succeeded in getting ninety-five people out of Austria, about forty to Northern Ireland. His scheme had cost him about £850 and a great deal of labour. He wanted it to be a success because this would make it easier for refugees to come to the United Kingdom. It had been largely due to his zeal and energy that Belfast had been the first place to open a refugee children's hostel: 'Now, the people who swore him eternal gratitude for bringing them out of Nazi Germany, have not only intrigued against him and have brought him out of the enterprise which he has created in thought and in action and with material sacrifice, they have also denounced him and that <u>denunciation is now the cause of his internment as an enemy alien</u> [underlining in original].'

Neumann's wife, Sophie, a delicate woman with a weak heart, was crying alone all the time. Alfred was loyal 'to this country' and could not justly be considered an enemy alien. He knew also that those refugees who had denounced him 'must receive eternal punishment'. He named one, Dr Kurt Schwarz, who, he heard, had 'found a terrible death in America'. He appealed to Shachter 'to tell the refugees that they should not forget to whom they owe their salvation from Nazi Germany and to be just by this man, who bears no grudge'. Any helping letter should be sent to him or his brother's solicitors.

But five weeks later, Julius still had not received any letter of support from Rabbi Shachter. On 21 February 1940 Julius sent him a letter he had drafted to rouse the consciences of the refugees Alfred had helped.[6] He also asked Shachter to write a separate letter supporting his claim that Alfred had persuaded the Belfast Jewish community to open the United Kingdom's first refugee children's hostel. Maybe he could influence other people too. He asked for the letters to be sent as quickly as possible before the Home Office Advisory Committee had heard the case.

Three weeks later, however, Julius wrote to Shachter saying he had still not heard from him.[7] Alfred's wife had received a letter from one of the six refugees who were then living in Bangor, Mrs Wilma Schlesinger, saying Shachter had told her and her daughter during a visit that 'nothing can be done against the decision of the tribunal'. Julius doubted very much that Mrs Schlesinger had reported the conversation correctly since he was sure that the rabbi was 'fully aware' that these cases can be put for an appeal. All twenty-three refugees Alfred Neumann had brought to Derry had signed a letter supporting him. It would make a very bad impression against the few people in Bangor if they would not show their goodwill towards the man who had helped them. He could not understand how people could have 'an hour's quiet sleep as long as they have not done their part by a man who has done such a service, and saved them from a journey to the Lublin area'. (Lublin was the centre of German-occupied eastern Poland, an area called the General-Government. An estimated two million Jews were murdered at the extermination camps of Sobibor, Belzec, Majdanek and Treblinka situated in it.)

On 10 March 1940 Julius wrote thanking Shachter for a letter of his, which he had received two days earlier, but asking him for a copy of the Bangor refugees' letter they had signed and sent to the Home Office, as it was essential to keep his brother's solicitor informed.[8] He also asked Shachter again to send him a letter confirming Alfred's key role in setting up the refugee children's hostel. 'The obvious charitable effort of this enterprise for which my brother got into trouble with Woburn House [German Jewish Aid Committee HQ, London] needs confirmation from your side of his zeal and energy in the matter and how he has taken this to heart.' In their signed, undated letter to the Home Office, the six Bangor refugees said Alfred Neumann had helped them to escape from persecution and they knew that 'he worked night and day to help to get persecuted people out of Austria'.[9] Mr Neumann was certainly strongly anti-Nazi, they wrote, and it must hurt him deeply to be considered an enemy alien and interned as one. They prayed that they would reconsider his case and free him from internment and all restrictions.

But the efforts of Julius Neumann and the refugees in Bangor and Derry to free Alfred were to no avail. His appeal was rejected and he stayed in internment. It is now easier to be more certain about why exactly funding was withdrawn by the Ministry of Commerce, and why Rabbi Shachter and the leadership of the Belfast Jewish community were unwilling to throw their weight behind Neumann's brother's campaign. Alfred Neumann's willingness to work outside the mainstream Jewish bodies was not well received. The German Jewish Aid Committee had cut all ties with him, refused to have anything more to do with him and dealt directly with the Jewish leadership in Belfast. When some of the Ards refugees complained, it seems they found people willing to give credence to their complaints. Both the BJRC, and in particular its leader, Rabbi Shachter, and the German Jewish Aid Committee in London, were careful about maintaining their leadership role in bringing refugees to Britain. Alfred Neumann's highly successful use of the New Industries scheme had brought out at least forty and up to seventy Jewish refugees from Vienna to Northern Ireland when it was extremely difficult to do so. The majority of the rescued had readily signed a petition appealing for his immediate release. Julius Neumann probably summed it up best. His brother, '– alas – sometimes rough outside has a remarkable good heart, and has not done anything but sacrificed his own and his family's peace, for the saving of human souls from persecution'. Like many others in his position, his good heart counted for nothing when the British government decided to intern Jewish refugees who had fled Nazi persecution. As historian Pamela Linden noted: 'Twenty-three refugee workers from Londonderry composed and signed a letter in support of Neumann, but no evidence in support of the businessman's refugee work or his good character was offered by the BHC or BJRC.'[10]

Though the multi-denominational BCGR was not involved in the Neumann case, it did its best to support other Viennese émigrés living in Northern Ireland. Margaret (Peggy) Fink, née Loewenthal, joint secretary of the BCGR, and Margaret (Peggy) McNeill, a Quaker, were allowed to sit on the Northern Ireland tribunals with a police officer to advise the chairman, Judge Marcus Begley KC. Peggy Fink wrote later that the refugee committee had 'an excellent relationship' with the Northern Ireland government, the Home Office and the police.[11] She said they were able to educate the locals in authority about Judaism; she was also a close friend of RUC District Inspector Bill Moffatt, who became head of the police Aliens Branch. All but one of the committee were sympathetic; however, she wrote that the chairman, Judge Begley, was 'ignorant and ill-informed, in spite of the fact that the Committee had at the start given him all the details about the rise of the Nazi regime in Europe and the history of the persecution of Jews and liberals in countries that had been overrun. This information was of little avail.'[12] After several weeks Judge Begley asked about the Kindertransport refugees in Northern Ireland, 'How is it that these children are here without their parents?' The two Peggys had to explain to him that the children were arriving at Victoria station in London, with the address of families or support groups attached to their clothing.

Otto Goldberger, because he had a German passport, was 'inadvertently labelled' an enemy alien. He appeared before a judge but registered in Category C, as a friendly alien, free of restrictions. He joined the National Fire Service. One night early in the war, he arrived back at his digs after a walk with friends to find himself locked out. He tried to get a room for the night in a hotel, but a suspicious receptionist contacted the police, who took Goldberger to York Road RUC station. He had no identity documents with him, and was thoroughly grilled, taken back to the hotel and told not to leave. Next day they took him back to his digs. His landlady was very upset and profusely apologised for his ordeal. So many drunks knocked on the door at night that it had reached the stage where she didn't even bother to look out of the window.

War raised suspicions about the most innocuous activities. Otto Goldberger swam occasionally at the Falls baths, and when regulars there learned that he had swum for Austria, they invited him to take part in a swimming gala. His story appeared in *The Irish News*, and a few days later, he got an 'ominous' phone call at work, telling him to report to the RUC Aliens Department as an Inspector Moffatt wished to speak to him.

Moffatt politely offered him a cigarette, and questioned him closely about his swimming history in Vienna and his connections with the Falls Road club. Then he asked: 'What if I put it to you that you are here under an assumed Jewish name and that you are not a Jew, what would you say to that?' Otto gave all the details he could, but Moffatt was still not convinced and asked him to see Rabbi Shachter for a letter of confirmation. Goldberger met Shachter, who asked him to read the Bible, but to his shame Otto said he could not read Hebrew. Shachter said, 'A Jew who does not know his own religion is not a Jew!' Otto was upset and said he was not to blame for his lack of Hebrew; his parents were. 'At this the Rabbi backed down and admitted that he knew immediately I was Jewish and was just provoking me for a reaction, but maybe he was also enjoying his exercise of power.' Shachter promised he would get in touch with Inspector Moffatt and settle the issue for him. In return, Otto had to promise to attend synagogue services, study the Old Testament, and learn the daily prayers so that he could eventually qualify as a 'good Jew'. In later years Goldberger and Shachter became 'well acquainted and quite friendly'.

On his release Goldberger got a job with James Faulkner, owner of Faulat Ltd, shirt-makers, and father of the future Prime Minister of Northern Ireland, Brian Faulkner, who employed hundreds of women in Belfast. Goldberger's salary jumped to £3 10s per week, and to £6 per week with overtime, 'good money in early 1940'.[13]

Some of the refugees found the tribunal interview frightening, after their experience with the SS and the German police. One woman who had escaped from Berlin with her seventeen-year-old son after her husband, a judge, had been killed, was shocked by Judge Begley's ignorance of the situation, when he asked if she had been forced to leave Germany.

Her son was arrested and taken as a Category A prisoner to a police station, but the committee had him released later that day because he was under eighteen. Peggy Fink took him straight to a weekend outing in a Mourne Mountains youth hostel. He later joined the Pioneer Corps and was killed at the Battle of Arnhem in 1944.

Walter Storch, from Vienna, was interned in both Dachau and Buchenwald, and after his release managed to make it to Ireland. He was among seven Dublin-based refugees who travelled to the Millisle farm to help in June 1940. Storch and another of the seven, Thomas Nachmann, were quickly interned and he was held until 18 November 1940.[14] Walter's father, Chaim, aged sixty-one, was deported from Vienna to Buchenwald on 2 October 1939 and died there on 17 November.[15] His younger sister Alice, aged twenty-one, had also come to Dublin but by the autumn of 1939 was working in Belfast as a domestic servant, which gained her exemption from detention. The tribunal noted that she had received permission to go to America with her parents, and wished to go. Walter stayed in Northern Ireland after the war and built up a successful chiropody practice in Lisburn, County Antrim.[16]

Others had better experiences of authority. One young German man teaching at the Berlitz school, Belfast, was the only one at the start of the war to be judged a Category A prisoner, liable for immediate internment. Peggy Fink described what happened:

> An apologetic young policeman went to see him explaining the situation and asked, 'Would Thursday week suit you?' He was picked up by a very sympathetic District Inspector who 'pub crawled' all the way to the prison. On his arrival at the gaol he found the cell prepared for him with flowers and fruit. That evening I received a phone call from Margaret Green, wife of the first secretary of the Home Office [Permanent Secretary of the Ministry of Home Affairs, Ronald Green], asking if Günther was Jewish. I said I thought not but why this question? She said she had made sausage rolls to send him in gaol and she feared that he might keep kosher.[17]

When the threat of invasion increased in June 1940, twenty-eight male refugees, most of them Jewish Austrians and Germans, were arrested and held in Crumlin Road Gaol, Belfast, and twelve women were detained in Armagh women's prison under 'enemy aliens' legislation. The men were shipped to the Huyton internment camp near Liverpool and then to the Isle of Man. Among them was Dr Kurt Sachs, the Viennese psychiatrist, who had hoped to qualify in medicine at Queen's University Belfast.[18] Peggy Fink wrote: 'It truly was a very difficult time, as no one knew whether or not Hitler's armies might invade our islands and the refugees once again fall into his hands. As it was, quite a number of the men under our care were shipped to internment camps on the Isle of Man. A few were even sent to Canada or Australia. We saw each of them off with a sleeping bag and a food parcel.'[19] The Austrian refugees brought over to work in Newtownards and Derry were safe from internment, but others were not so fortunate.

The twelve female refugees were classified as Category B and were held in a separate unit in Armagh women's prison. Peggy McNeill, a Quaker, volunteered to join them as a welfare officer and lived in Armagh Gaol for two months.[20] Ronald Green, who was also a Quaker, visited them with deckchairs and bags of oranges. The 'unfortunate and distressed women' were all 'terrified that Hitler would invade and they would be caught'.[21]

Otto Goldberger was among those detained in June 1940 in Crumlin Road Prison. He shared a cell with a very angry Frenchman, the master of a cargo ship arrested after it docked in Belfast. 'He could not speak one word of English, spending the day screaming and shouting and cursing in French.' After a few days Otto was going crazy, and he asked guards for a change of cell. He was happy to share with Jurgen Strauss, a German Jew from Stuttgart. Life was 'not too bad' over the next few weeks. 'We were very well treated as civil internees, allowed to spend most of the day in the prison yard, playing football or other games with Czechs, Dutch and even a few Germans.' With his sister Fritzi's efforts and some persuasion 'of a few Stormont ministers', Otto was soon released back to his old job and life. He tried to join the RAF in Belfast, and was accepted, subject to certain conditions. They wanted him to serve in civilian clothing using his native speaker's command of German and 'deep knowledge of Germany and Austria':

> Basically, they wanted me as a spy doing intelligence work, and making contact with the resistance on the other side. It all seemed very dangerous and risky as well as not even being in a uniform in case of capture. They gave me a week to think it over and emphasised that it was all totally voluntary. However, I had never claimed to be the hero type and being awarded the Victoria Cross posthumously had never been one of my ambitions in life. So, in the end I decided to turn down the invitation and just went back to the Auxiliary Fire Service.

Otto served during the Belfast Blitz in May 1941, which provided him with 'enough danger and excitement'. He and Fritzi rented a large house in Marlborough Park. Fritzi married Isaac Ellison in December 1942. Otto married a Dublin girl, Celia Blumberg, within weeks of meeting her at a dance at the Jewish Institute in Belfast in October 1943, the start of 'a wonderful marriage and life'. Fritzi and he continued to write to their parents in Vienna in mid-1942, but began to fear the worst.[22] Another Jewish refugee, Abraham Zukor, was held in Crumlin Road Prison until July 1940 when the Home Office released him on the grounds of ill health after Rabbi Shachter had pleaded his case.[23]

Some distinguished refugees avoided internment, including Paul Ewald, a leading German crystallographer who had taken up a lectureship at Queen's University, Belfast. He had given up the post of Rector at Stuttgart University in 1933, but kept working there as an academic. After continuing trouble with members of the faculty, he left and was appointed as a research fellow at Cambridge University in 1937, and later moved to Belfast. He became a close friend of the Loewenthals. Peggy recalled one day when a special meeting was held at her house attended by the physicists Erwin Schrödinger, and, Peggy believed, the Danish Nobel prize winner Niels Bohr. 'I am not certain as to what they discussed, but I believe it was about keeping nuclear findings from the Germans.'[24]

Another of the Belfast refugees interned in June 1940 was the Ukrainian-born artist Paul Nietsche, a friend of Zoltan Frankl, who included his work in his exhibitions.[25]

In February 1939, when he applied for British citizenship in Northern Ireland, three of his brothers were in Berlin and a fourth was living in Athens. But Nietsche did not gain British citizenship at that time. He lived in Belfast until he was interned as an enemy alien on the Isle of Man, where he painted crayon sketches of fellow internees. He was held until 1942, and, on release, Nietsche spent the rest of the war in Belfast and afterwards reapplied for British citizenship. The RUC believed he would prove to be a loyal subject. He was granted his certificate of naturalisation on 3 June 1946 and lived in Northern Ireland, becoming a prominent member of the post-war Ulster renaissance in painting until his death in 1950.[26]

Jewish refugees were not held in large numbers in the autumn of 1939, save for Category A 'enemy aliens', such as Alfred Neumann. The situation greatly worsened for refugees in May 1940 when the threat of a German invasion of Britain induced panic.[27] Prime Minister Winston Churchill wanted mass internment and demanded deportation for internees. He apparently issued the infamous order 'Collar the lot!' After the German conquest of Holland, on 16 May 1940, British police arrested 3,000 men born in the German Reich who were living in Britain. A total of 27,200 men were arrested in May and June 1940, the vast majority of them friendly to Britain, and a great number of them Jewish refugees, including German, Austrian, Czech and Italian socialists and anti-Fascists. A very small number of right-wing 'aliens' hostile to Britain were among those detained, a tiny minority of the total. The British government also rounded up around 1,400 Mosleyite Fascists and other pro-Nazis in Britain at this time. While the Northern Irish refugees were few, in comparison to those from England, internment created considerable bitterness among them and those who tried to help them. Moya Woodside, a compassionate wife of a local doctor and an acute observer, joined a committee helping refugees and kept a diary which recorded their experiences. On 27 August 1940 she described entertaining the first of the Northern Ireland contingent to be released from Huyton internment camp, Liverpool:

> The physical hardships and deprivations were bad enough, he [the released man] says, but 'they were nothing in comparison to the mental agony we suffered in being cut off for weeks from communication with our wives and relatives outside'. He also said how inevitable it was that they should become embittered, when the country which gave them refuge from Nazi persecutions and which now proclaims that it is fighting for liberty and justice etc, locks them up behind barbed wire and treats them worse than prisoners of war. On asking if any Nazi agents or sympathisers were interned, he said, it didn't take them long to spot these people. He put the number of suspects in Huyton at about 40, out of over 3,000. If the Government really want to separate the sheep from the goats, this seems to be the answer.[28]

On 14 October 1940 Moya Woodside noted that the refugees' troubles really began when they were released from internment: 'Mostly their jobs have gone; some employers are unwilling to take them back; and the atmosphere of suspicion is such (in spite of their credentials) that no-one wants to have "aliens" in their house. It is the Government's fault that this situation has arisen … An enlightened policy towards refugees would have swung people into line behind it.'[29]

On 30 November 1940, Moya Woodside wrote: 'We know from the police that there isn't a single refugee out of the 400 or so in Ulster who hasn't at one time or another been accused (without proof, naturally) of being a Nazi spy.' On 22 January 1941 she noted that new restrictions for 'enemy aliens' had caused great difficulties. They had been ordered out of coastal areas, which were declared a protected zone. It affected fifteen refugees, either people in jobs or those staying with locals: 'Two of them, after eighteen months of hard work and hand-to-mouth existence, had succeeded in building up small businesses; and about twenty others [from the Jewish community] were employed running a successful farm. We simply don't know what to do for these unfortunates. If only the military mind could see what these decisions of theirs mean in human suffering.'[30]

Woodside also praised the improved working conditions that refugee employers had brought to their factories. On the same day she wrote about her visit to an artificial silk factory started by refugees in the summer of 1939: 'A derelict linen mill has been turned by them into bright cheerful workrooms, and the original 25 employees now increased to over 300. I was tremendously impressed by the ideas which these people have for the welfare of their workers. Frankly, no Ulster employer would ever have dreamt of them!'[31]

The employers had introduced free hot midday meals because the juvenile workers were undernourished and listless, and the 'difference in appearance – and output – is astonishing … Chief difficulty is food prejudices and ignorance. White bread, pastries, chips and fried fish are eaten with gusto; but often the nourishing stews and milk puddings etc. are found thrown in the bin. My refugee friends are in despair to know how to educate these children.'[32]

Jewish refugees were not the only people imprisoned in Crumlin Road Gaol. An internment order was introduced on the first night of the war, and forty-five republican suspects were arrested. British government visitors to Northern Ireland had initially regarded its war preparations as lax, apart from one field of expertise, internal security – in particular, detaining republicans. Internment had last been used in November 1938 when all the leading officers of the IRA's Belfast Brigade had been lifted. The Stormont government asked Westminster to open an internment camp at Ballykinlar, County Down, both for enemy aliens and in the defence of the realm. In May 1940 a further 76 republican suspects were interned, with plans to arrest another 700. By 1942 the number detained had risen to 802, 450 of them held in Crumlin Road Gaol, and the rest on the prison ships *Argenta* in Belfast Lough and the *Al Rawdah* in Strangford Lough, off Killyleagh. By then the Jewish internees had long been released. The republicans were held until the end of the war.

A small number of Irish republicans were also held as political detainees with 'enemy aliens' on the Isle of Man. Two of them, Joseph Walker and John Joseph Barry, escaped along with a member of the British Union of Fascists, Arthur L. Mason, from Peveril Camp, near Peel, in September 1941. The three tunnelled out of a house in the camp, commandeered a boat and headed off into the Irish Sea. They spent three days at sea before being picked up by the Royal Navy. The two republicans were brought back to the camp, but were refused food, which led to a serious riot. The affair attracted heavy criticism in the press; Isle of Man newspapers condemned the Home Office reaction and canvassed the transfer of control of the camp from the military to the police. The three men received jail terms of between six months and a year under the headline 'Irish Desperadoes Sentenced'.[33]

Almost all the internees from the Reich classified as 'enemy aliens' were victims of Nazi persecution, particularly the Jewish prisoners. Some had survived concentration camps, and many had relatives in mortal danger in their former home countries. All these were hostile to the Nazis, and willing to do everything possible to defeat them. They now found themselves behind barbed wire in the country that a few months before had welcomed them.

18
'WITH YOU IN SPIRIT'

Almost all the Viennese Jewish emigrants who had made it to Northern Ireland before the war left behind parents and siblings facing increasing dangers. The conquest of Poland had made land available and the SS immediately set about imposing a new plan: the forced deportation of the Jewish populations of central Europe, including those of Vienna, to the east. Ethnic Germans (Volksdeutsche) would be brought 'home to the Reich' to replace them. Eichmann was to be the enthusiastic organiser of the expulsion.

In October 1939 two transports carrying 1,550 Jews left Vienna for Nisko, a swampy area in the Lublin district of Poland. Those chosen for labour were ordered to build a camp, and the others chased away under SS gunfire towards Russian-held territory. The project failed, and only 300 Viennese Jews survived. Among those deported on 20 October 1939 were the brothers Wilhelm and Leopold Wohlfeiler, and Ignaz Rothmann, who had all been rejected by the Northern Ireland Ministry of Commerce. All three perished at Nisko.[1]

In November 1939 Hans Frank, Governor-General of the occupied territories in Poland, made clear what treatment the Jews of Vienna and elsewhere could expect:

2.5 to 3 million Poles and Jews – they are not used to living cleanly and in an orderly fashion … The winter will be rough. When there is no bread for the Poles, I don't want to hear any complaints … Short shrift with the Jews. A pleasure to take physical measures against the Jews at last. The more who die, the better … The Jews are to feel that we have arrived. We want to have between half to three-fourths of all Jews east of the Vistula. We will oppress them wherever we can. Everything is at stake here. The Jews from the Reich, Vienna, everywhere – Jews in the Reich – we have no more use for them.[2]

After the Nisko tragedy, Eichmann and his colleagues in the Vienna SS kept up their pressure to force more of the city's Jews to migrate. By July 1939, 104,000 Jews had left Vienna, but only an additional 13,000 had emigrated by that December, when there were still 58,000 Jews in the city. On 13 November Eichmann told Josef Löwenherz, director of the IKG, that the 'emigration' of Viennese Jews must be completed by 1 February 1940. The leaders and staff of the IKG would be allowed to leave after this task was finished. Löwenherz replied that between 20,000 and 30,000 Jews could not emigrate under any circumstances because they were too old. Eichmann ignored this information.

Negotiations continued between December 1939 and January 1940, involving the main funders of Jewish migration, the AJDC. They pledged more money to the IKG, but insisted that deportations must stop. On 26 January 1940, Löwenherz told Eichmann that the 'Joint' had promised to transfer $100,000 to the IKG to facilitate emigration. But as the war continued, it became increasingly difficult to obtain visas from countries willing to take refugees.

The Nazi regime also increased anti-Jewish legislation. By September 1939, 250 discriminatory and oppressive laws had been passed. They included an 8 p.m. Jewish curfew and a ban on Jews owning radios. They were allowed on the streets and to shop in their own stores only at certain times; they were banned from parks and places of entertainment, and they faced abuse and often physical assault from anti-Semites, including the SA and SS, on the streets and on public transport. In May 1940 Löwenherz wrote to the Vienna police headquarters asking for two parks to be opened to Jews. The request was refused.

The Nazi authorities also set about increasing the segregation of the Jewish community, by moving them into three areas, the first, second and nineteenth districts, centred on the city's old Jewish district, Leopoldstadt. Jews were forced out of their apartments and into overpopulated accommodation. On 25 November 1940, Löwenherz made an appointment to see Dr Leopold Tavs, a deputy in the Vienna city administration, to inform him that the overcrowding was increasing the risk of epidemics. Tavs refused to meet him because, for 'ideological reasons', he did not receive Jews. Löwenherz had to make his complaint in an outer office. The Jewish population had fallen by more than two-thirds since 1938, but they were now crammed into a ghetto without walls:

> Married and unmarried, young and old, men and women were living in the same room. They were being forced into premises without bathrooms, heating or cooking facilities. Some had been assigned to apartments that were already occupied; many had to leave accommodation that they had only just moved into. The dispossessed and evicted Jews lived in extremely cramped conditions. The housing situation changed the mental state and outward appearance of the victims, who began to resemble the stereotype of the abject ghetto Jew. The victims of eviction were moved from one place to another.[3]

In 1938 Aryans had taken over 44,000 of 70,000 Jewish apartments in the city; 5,500 apartments changed hands from March to September 1939, and some 6,000 eviction cases were pending in October. Jewish residents were threatened with deportation to concentration camps unless they left their flats.[4]

Some Jews evicted in favour of non-Jews were not allocated new accommodation, and became homeless. Others were attacked in their own apartments and were forced to sign a document promising to leave within a day. They could not usually take their furniture with them, and it ended up in the hands of the Furniture Disposal Office of the Gestapo Administrative Office for Jewish Property Removals, or Vuguesta. This department had originally been set up to confiscate the property of emigrating Jews, and was soon used to rob the evicted. Valuables were sold cheaply to museums and to Nazi clients. In 1938 Jews had been allowed to take some of their belongings out of the country on payment of a tax equivalent to the real value. When war broke out, they had to leave everything behind. The Vuguesta dealers used forced Jewish labour to clear the apartments and their warehouses, and paid them a pittance. 'Between 1938 and 1942, around 70,000 apartments were vacated through the expulsion and forced emigration of Viennese Jews. This was 10,000 apartments more than had been built under the Red Vienna housing policy until 1934.'[5]

By early 1939 the Jewish community was deeply impoverished. The IKG was feeding 21,000 people daily, and Löwenherz expected this number to rise to 30,000. Between the Anschluss and Kristallnacht, confiscated Jewish wealth was estimated at 2.3 billion Reichsmarks. When war broke out in September 1939, the Germans introduced conscription and before its end 600,000 Austrians had served in the German armed forces. This led to a shortage of labour. Women were introduced into the workforce in large numbers, taking on traditional male roles. Jews were forced into road works and rubbish collection, paid paltry wages and allowed to do only menial labour. On 13 October 1940, the Gestapo told Löwenherz that a ration card register was to be established for the city's 58,000 Jews, and the IKG was responsible for collecting the names for it. Doron Rabinovici noted: 'Anyone, young or old, who wanted to eat had to be registered. The Jewish administration was successfully deceived. The register that had been ostensibly created to centralize the organisation of food rations was used to keep a record for the exploitation of the Jews, their deportation and murder, for the machinery of exploitation.'[6]

While the plight of Vienna's Jews had worsened as soon as the Nazis arrived, things had improved for the city's Aryans. Between May 1938 and May 1940, unemployment dropped from 220,000 to 15,000, just 7 per cent of the May 1938 total, of whom 2,000 were 'fully functioning' and ready to work. Some 4,000 of the unemployed were Jews, and 'the non-Jewish 11,000 were the dregs of any large city.'[7]

Once the war started, conscription and the expansion of war industries brought the Aryan jobless figure down rapidly, even leading to a labour shortage. But in spring 1940, Walter Rafelsberger, an economic advisor to the Nazi regime, felt that the treatment of Vienna's Jews was too lenient:

Jews were still getting away with much more than they deserved or that the laws allowed. Jews had been seen buying in stores at all hours of the day, not just in the times set aside for them. Store personnel sometimes gave Jews preferential treatment, explaining that after all, Jews were people too … In general, he continued, regulations covering sales to Jews were honoured more in the breach, and Jews had been buying unrationed items in great quantities.[8]

By the autumn of 1940 price rises, shortages of fruit, vegetables and other staples had led to a 'generally depressed mood in the city', an SD report said. This led many *Volksgenossen* ('people's comrades', those of German blood) to 'look with such concern at the coming second winter, especially with wood and coal so tight'.[9] For the city's remaining Jews, though, the future was much bleaker. The opportunities for emigration plummeted, living conditions worsened and dangers grew daily.

In Belfast and Derry, the lucky few who had arrived made continuous desperate efforts to bring out their relatives from Vienna. But it was difficult to maintain contact with them, and impossible to send them money or other support. Those who came to the attention of the Gestapo were particularly at risk. Walter Weiniger had left Vienna and linked up with the Utitz brothers to run the tannery at Shrigley, County Down. He was joined by his wife Mary and two children in 1939. But his parents, Salomon and Gisela, and brother Ernst and partner Grete were trapped in Vienna. Ernst and Grete were forced to give up their spacious apartment in Haizingerstrasse in the affluent Währing district. Salomon and Gisela were also evicted from their home. Ernst was an architect and interior designer, but after the Anschluss had lost all his valuable furniture and fittings, which he had used to equip apartments for clients. He found a ground-floor flat with one room and kitchen, and took in his homeless parents.[10]

The Nazis had forced all Jewish business owners to sell their firms at rock bottom prices or had confiscated them, and sacked Jewish workers. To survive, these now had to live on whatever money they could keep from the Nazis, and on their wits. They could not send currency abroad and to get into the United Kingdom they needed a visa and £50 to pay for their fare out again. They were allowed to bring out only 10 Reichsmarks in currency, less than one pound sterling.

As always in times of shortages, a black market opened in foreign currency. In the hope of getting his relatives out, Ernst Weiniger began to try to move money abroad, which he thought would help him get the much-sought-after visas. He approached several people and, through an acquaintance, met a man called Fried, who promised to help him. Fried agreed to carry out a foreign exchange transfer for Ernst, without asking for money in advance. Ernst heard nothing more and because he had no address for Fried, approached his original contact again, and gave him a letter. In it, he urged Fried to hurry the matter along and assured him that, if he was successful, Ernst would return the favour and do anything he could for him. Time passed and Ernst heard nothing more, so he approached his contact again. He told Ernst that Fried had been arrested by the Gestapo. Ernst assumed that his letter or possibly his address had been found with Fried.

He was right. The Gestapo had his new address. One morning in October 1939, two men in civilian clothes appeared at his flat. A friend of Ernst's mother was the only one at home, and they enquired about Ernst, then left. His parents returned. In a statement he made twenty-five years later, Ernst described what happened next:

> My mother knew where I was and, with a dreadful foreboding, ran straight out of the house in order to warn me. My first thought was not to return to the flat and so I hung about the streets until evening, not knowing what to do. However, fearing for my parents, I decided to return after all. The two German gentlemen had come back to the flat around midday and were guarding my parents, as well as my wife, who, in the meantime, had joined my parents. When I returned in the evening, there was great agitation because the Germans did not want to wait for me any longer and were going to take away my parents and my wife in my place. So, I returned just in time and was arrested, a fate that otherwise would have been that of my relatives. I was remanded to Moabit Prison in Berlin and taken into solitary confinement.[11]

Ernst was held in a wing for serious cases for two months before being taken to his first interrogation by an examining magistrate. Only then did he learn why he had been arrested. His bill of indictment was pages long and the charges ranged from breach of exchange control regulations to subversion of the Wehrmacht, and treason:

> Various interrogations followed, degrading and torturous. I only want to emphasize two of them. One of the interrogations ended with a confrontation with Mr. Fried, whom I now saw again in prison. He was told to directly confront me with the crimes that I was accused of. They made us face each other; horrified, we stared at each other and suddenly, our common fate was clear to us both.
>
> Fried was so badly beaten, so tormented and down and out that my heart was bleeding for him; and the way I felt, he most probably felt, as well; he broke down during this confrontation. After four months came the second interrogation. I was shown a long list of names and was told to confirm in writing that these people had committed the same crimes I was accused of. I refused to sign – as I did not even know the names of these people – I did not even sign when I was promised various benefits in return.
>
> As a result of this, the examining magistrate changed his tactics and handed me over to two SS men for further treatment. I was returned to my cell covered in blood, battered, with my abdomen kicked in. With the exception of a short interruption, being taken to a different prison and then returned, I stayed in solitary confinement throughout my imprisonment. Then the trial started. I was accused together with three other men. Their names were Wetzl or Wetzler, then Baker and the aforementioned Fried. As I found out later, Wetzl was in charge of the 5th Espionage Team for America. Originally, he was a German spy, but he changed sides and had recently been spying for America instead of Germany. The trial lasted two weeks. Two of my co-defendants were given prison sentences; I

believe that Wetzl or Wetzler was sentenced to death. After
having been imprisoned for one year, I was acquitted due
to a lack of evidence.[12]

Ernst returned to Vienna. He had been so badly tortured that he spent
several months convalescing at home, because there was no hospital
bed free. Finally, he was admitted to hospital, where he stayed for a
year and had two operations. It was now March 1942, and somehow
Ernst found out that the Gestapo had taken up his case again:

> I secretly left the hospital and went underground. I remained
> underground until liberation in 1945. To the best of my
> knowledge, I do not know to this day the reason for my
> arrest. As mentioned above, it is true that I wanted to take
> foreign currency abroad with the help of Mr. Fried. It is also
> a fact that I had heard news about failures of the Deutsche
> Wehrmacht [German army] and similar things from different
> people and that I passed this on to acquaintances. Fried also
> knew about this. So, it is certainly possible and likely that
> Fried talked about it under torture.[13]

Dr Ursula Schwarz of the Documentation Archive of Austrian
Resistance in Vienna confirmed to the author that Ernst Weiniger
was imprisoned in Berlin-Moabit on suspicion of treason, but that
he was never charged. It is possible that his court appearance was a
preliminary hearing but was noted by Ernst as a trial.[14]

Back in Vienna, Ernst obtained identity documents from a Josef
Jelinek, and lived under the alias of Jelinek at several addresses in the
city during the war.[15] He may have taken as his alias a Josef Jelinek
who had been arrested in Vienna. If so, his alias was not so lucky.
A Josef Jelinek was among 229 political prisoners massacred at the
prison of Stein an der Donau in Austria on 6 April 1945.

The prisoners were shot dead by the local Kremser Volkssturm,
the Wehrmacht garrison and the SS. A further sixty-nine prisoners
captured after escaping were shot dead by the Waffen SS at the
cemetery of Hadersdorf am Kamp next day. After the war, fourteen
of the ringleaders and the Kremser Volkssturm commander were

charged for their part in the massacre; five were sentenced to death, five others jailed for life, one for three years, and four were acquitted in Vienna in 1946.

While Ernst was in prison, his mother died at home in Vienna in 1940. His father was living with Grete in Argentinierstrasse. But the Gestapo had not finished with the Weiniger family. In 1941, Grete was transported to Poland, where the mass extermination of the Jews was already under way. Salomon was deported to Theresienstadt in Czechoslovakia in 1943. Prospects for their survival seemed bleak.

Like Walter Weiniger, Walter Kammerling had escaped to Belfast, in his case on a Kindertransport, but his parents and sister Ruth were unable to get a visa. Nearly eighty years later he recalled his family's plight:

> When I left father was just forty-four and mother was just forty-four. They were pleased I got out of Vienna because they knew I had gone to safety, but they never made it. Erica got a permit as a domestic servant and came out in July 1939. But Ruthie was a year too old for the Kindertransport at seventeen and a year too young for a domestic permit. My parents tried to get out to anywhere but they couldn't get out, it was quite hopeless. If you had money you could probably get out, but if you didn't have money, it was very hard. On 16 September 1939 I received my last letter from my parents. They just gave me advice on how to behave. I was an extremely young fifteen, my age would have been more thirteen. You had to grow up fast. Unfortunately, I don't have their letters now. I still regret that because I usually keep things and I didn't keep the letters, and it breaks my heart. Sometimes I think I should have done more to get my parents out, go round houses to get money to get them out, or something.[16]

After three years on the Millisle farm, Walter Kammerling moved to Carshalton in Surrey, where his sister Erica had managed to get him a job as a lathe operator in a garage, then to an engineering works in North Finchley, London.

He heard about an Austrian War Workers hostel called Free Austria, which had a youth group Young Austria, and he moved there, a decision he called a 'life-saver'. It was a pleasant place, with German and Austrian refugees. There, in 1942, he met Herta Plaschkes, also a young Jewish refugee from Vienna. 'It was wonderful meeting Herta. She was a lovely girl, she is a lovely girl. I fell in love. We got on very well.' Herta's mother had died of childbed fever just after giving birth to her on 9 February 1926, and her father, Heinrich, had married his wife's sister, Gertrude, one of four sisters. Herta recalled: 'My father Heinrich Plaschkes, known as Heini, was a sausage skin cleaner. It was not the perfect job, not one for gentlemen's clothes. The animal guts were sorted and picked and rolled.'[17] Heinrich had a little factory in a garage, and had one man to help him, but the Nazis took that away from him. Herta was forced to leave school.[18]

Eighty years after leaving Vienna, Herta, like Walter, vividly remembered the dangers on its streets. She would hold her brother Otto's hand so that when a group of young Nazis, wearing uniforms and swastika armbands, singing and shouting, approached, they would cross nonchalantly to the other side of the road. If they didn't, they would be pushed off the pavement: 'They called us either bloody Jew or bloody pig. We were not in any physical danger because it was daytime and there were grown-ups about. But you were frightened. Then we heard on the grapevine that people might get out on the Kindertransport, but it was kept pretty quiet as we didn't know if the Germans would stop the trains leaving. The "transport" word wasn't even mentioned.'

Herta left Vienna by train on 10 January 1939, a month before her thirteenth birthday, with her younger brother Otto:

It was a dark evening at the Westbahnhof railway station. The men sort of disappeared, because if they were spotted on the street, they were taken away immediately. Mama said to me, 'Take care of Otto,' because I was the older one, supposed to look after him. Mama was heavily pregnant, and when the train left, she went straight to the hospital and gave birth to my brother Erich two days later. We didn't know where we were at first, but apparently it was Holland. It was the first time I saw people smiling at us. That was the only difference we noticed, all of us. Nobody smiled at us in Vienna. Everyone you met was either hateful, or we crossed the road to avoid them. We were thrown out of our flat as well. We had nowhere to go. The Nazis in Vienna left us nothing.[19]

Herta's parents and younger brother Erich, who was only about eight months old, got out in August 1939, just before war broke out. Herta and Otto lived in Liverpool at first, but then moved to London. She found work as a seamstress. 'Then I met Walter and we were friendly, but I wasn't sure how serious it would be. Then of course I wanted to get married in Vienna. We were all going to return, we would be free, there would be a new Austria and new people, all with changed minds. It never happened.'[20]

After Walter and Herta met, Walter joined the British army as an infantryman in 1943. On a week's embarkation leave before he left for France in 1944, he went with Herta to say goodbye to her parents in Salisbury, and convinced her to get married immediately. Walter recalled: 'We knew we were going to get married, so why not get married now? I was in love and I still am. She is the centre of my life. Everything goes round that, and from there we branch out to other things, but she is the most important thing in my life; she has been and she is now. I'm only sorry I couldn't introduce her to my parents and my sister, Ruth.'[21]

19
'A MIGHTY HISS, A CRY – AND ALL WAS OVER'

While the war demand for leather, clothing and military kit enabled the Jewish refugee employers in Northern Ireland to take on more local workers, for those unlucky to be held as 'enemy aliens', prospects were much less appealing.

In May and June 1940, after the fall of France, a German invasion of Britain seemed imminent, and the Whitehall panic and mass detentions might arguably be excused as a precaution, indiscriminate and callous as it was. It is much harder, though, to justify the next British government move. On 11 June 1940, a policy of deporting aliens to the Dominions, primarily Canada and Australia, was presented to the cabinet as a fait accompli. The idea seems to have been Churchill's. The British government equivocated with those of Canada and Australia and its own supporters in Parliament, and 'broke its promise to internees who volunteered to sail on the understanding that their wives and children would shortly join them'.[1]

Altogether, just over 11,000 internees, classified as 'dangerous characters', were deported. Four ships sailed to Canada between 21 June and 7 July, carrying 'A'-class internees and prisoners of war, but over a quarter were 'B' or 'C' category Germans or Austrians, along with many Italians. Among those selected for deportation to Canada was Alfred Neumann.

When he was put on board the 15,000-ton former luxury liner *Arandora Star* in Liverpool on 30 June 1940, he had been interned for seven months. His son Kurt was also interned on the Isle of Man, but did not embark on the *Arandora Star*.

Alfred Neumann was one of 1,673 men on the ship. Canada was deemed a safer place to house 'enemy aliens' than the United Kingdom. The total comprised 734 Italians, 479 Germans and Austrians, 86 German prisoners of war, 200 military guards, and 174 officers and crew. Most of the Italians were expatriates who had long been settled in Britain and who worked in the restaurant trade, or as shop owners, barbers or market salesmen. The Germans and Austrians were a very mixed group: the majority were refugees from Nazi persecution, some of them Jewish businessmen, as well as socialists and communists, along with a very small number of fervent Nazis. Some were German merchant seamen taken off their ships by the Royal Navy.

The *Arandora Star* was built in 1927 by Cammell Laird at Birkenhead and was considered by her Blue Star owners to be the most luxurious and exclusive cruise liner afloat. While the Cunard line *Queen Mary* accepted second- and third-class passengers, the *Arandora Star* accepted only first-class. Among its notable passengers were the Prime Minister of Northern Ireland and his wife, Lord and Lady Craigavon.

When war broke out, the *Arandora Star* was three days out of Southampton en route to New York with 441on board. On her return, she joined the merchant shipping fleet that had been taken over by the Admiralty. She was too heavy to act as a merchant cruiser, but in December 1939 she was chosen to take part in anti-submarine trials in the English Channel. German U-boats had already sunk 100 British ships, and the vessel was fitted with nets for stopping torpedoes short of their target. She performed well, blocking all the dummy torpedoes fired at her. The nets, however, did not come into widespread use.

The *Arandora Star* helped rescue British soldiers from the failed operation at Narvik in Norway, surviving several air attacks. Her convoy, carrying 10,000 soldiers, narrowly avoided running into the main German naval squadron, including the deadly battle-cruiser *Scharnhorst*. Almost immediately, the *Arandora Star* was sent to evacuate 300 men at Quiberon in Brittany, landed them in Falmouth, and returned to rescue 3,000 Polish troops and British refugees from Bayonne and Saint Jean de Luz. She arrived safely in Liverpool on 27 June 1940.

She did not wait long for her next voyage. Armed with a 4.7-inch cannon and a 12-pound anti-aircraft gun, she sailed from Liverpool on 1 July 1940 with the internees. She steamed at full speed up the Irish Sea, past the Isle of Man, and through the North Channel. The prisoners got on well with their military guards, 'nice chaps, just returned from Dunkirk,' as one passenger, Gerhard Miedzwinski, a Jewish engineer from Silesia who had come to Britain in 1936, noted.[2]

Passengers could move freely, the food was good, and some even bought drinks from the stewards. 'In the evening we drank a lot, pink gin and beer, played a gramophone, and generally had the best time since our internment. How considerate of the Government to move us to Canada, we thought,' wrote Miedzwinski later.[3] They were escorted for a while by a British submarine, and a flying boat flew over and exchanged the time of day using light signals. Around midnight, the *Arandora Star* rounded Malin Head, the northernmost part of Ireland, and turned west into the Atlantic.

Heading east for Germany after a highly successful three-week voyage in the Atlantic was U-47, commanded by Günther Prien. Since 19 June, he had sunk eight ships using just thirteen torpedoes. He had one torpedo left. Prien was known in Germany as the Bull of Scapa Flow for sinking the British battleship *Royal Oak* at anchor there on 14 October 1939, with the loss of 833 lives. (Prien was also popular among some Kerry fishing boat skippers, who read about him in the press and displayed his photograph on their wheelhouse walls[4].) Hitler presented him with the *Ritterkreuz*, the highest order of the Iron Cross, and an American journalist who saw him that day described him as 'clean-cut, cocky, a fanatical Nazi, and obviously capable'. He had almost sunk several British warships in the Narvik evacuation, but faulty mechanisms prevented the torpedoes from exploding. The fault had been fixed and now U-boat wolf packs were sinking Allied shipping almost at will in the North Atlantic.

At 6:29 a.m. on 2 July Prien saw a passenger ship to the east, coming towards him and travelling 'reasonably fast'. He dived and observed her through his periscope for twenty-five minutes. He noticed her guns, and her zigzagging convinced him that she was an enemy ship. The wind was light, the sea calm with a light westerly swell, the sky was cloudy and visibility good. 'At 6:58 and 28 seconds,

Prien fired his last torpedo. The range was an ambitious 2,500 metres. Ninety-seven seconds passed, and then Prien saw a column of water arise from his victim amidships. It was a perfect hit.'[5] The torpedo had struck the *Arandora Star*'s engine room on the starboard side, flooding it to sea-level; those crew not killed by the explosion were drowned. The ship's turbines were wrecked and stand-by generators disabled, plunging the deep interior into darkness and disabling communications. This hampered the issuing of emergency orders and added to the confusion on board. The nearest land was 125 miles away to the south-east at Bloody Foreland, County Donegal.

Ten lifeboats were successfully launched, by both the ship's crew and a group of German merchant seamen, led by Captain Otto Burfeind and his officers and men from the *Adolf Woermann*, who had been captured by Royal Navy warships earlier in the war and interned. Burfeind and his officers had already inspected the lifeboats and survivors believed that they had marked out those in the best condition. Those who made it into the lifeboats had by far the best chance of survival. Other passengers jumped overboard and clung to life-rafts and flotsam. Some of these were hit by deck furniture and life-rafts thrown from the ship; others suffocated in the heavy black oil on the surface. Many perished in the water, too weak to withstand the prolonged cold. The older prisoners, many of them Italians, who found it hard to reach the deck or could not face jumping into the sea, died on board. Among these victims was Giuseppe Forte, the leader of the Belfast branch of the Italian Fascist Party.[6] He was among sixty Italians suspected of fascist sympathies in Northern Ireland who had been detained as enemy aliens.[7] The ship went down by the stern after half an hour. Miedzwinski later recalled the end of the *Arandora Star*: 'A huge beam tore loose and swept along the ship's side, squashing the men hanging on the ropes in its path. Down, down she went, faster and faster; her bows rose; we saw people running up the steep decks like flies. Suddenly, a mighty hiss, a cry – and all was over.'[8]

The *Arandora Star* had sent off an SOS which was picked up by Malin Head radio station. Two hours after the sinking, an RAF Sunderland flying boat found the survivors and dropped a box containing food, cigarettes and a message saying help was on its way.

At 1:30 p.m., a Canadian destroyer, the *St Laurent,* arrived to find ten well-filled lifeboats in a group and many survivors clinging to rafts and wreckage spread across two or three miles. The captain, H. G. de Wolf, picked up the last survivors by 4 p.m. and headed east, reaching Greenock on the Clyde in Scotland at 6:30 a.m. on 3 July. Altogether approximately 800 men had died (446 of the 734 Italian civilians, at least 175 of the 479 Germans and Austrians, while crew members, army guards, and German prisoners of war made up the remainder).[9] The ship's commander, Captain Edgar Moulton, his second officer Stanley Ransom and fourth officer Ralph Liddle all died. They were later awarded the Lloyd's Medal for bravery at sea, the citation stating that 'having done all they could to save life and having no boat or raft to save themselves, they took to the water as the vessel sank.' Captain Burfeind, the German prisoner who had led his crew in lowering lifeboats, stayed on the bridge helping Captain Moulton to the last minute, and the two men perished together in the water.

There was no panic on board the ship after it was torpedoed. Despite immediate stories in British papers claiming that the Germans on board had fought Italians to escape first, there were no such incidents. On 9 July the Minister of Shipping, Ronald Cross, claimed there were more than enough lifeboats and life-rafts for all passengers and crew. But this was not true. The *Arandora Star* carried fourteen lifeboats, enough for 1,000 passengers, but there were 1,673 men on board that day. Twenty rafts were thrown overboard, though the three biggest rafts were filled up and the rest were in such poor condition that they were practically useless. While there was no panic on board, there was confusion. No boat drill or lifebelt training had been carried out, and no instructions for an emergency given. The shortage of lifeboats, failure to instruct passengers, and the initial explosion accounted for the loss of 50 per cent of those on board.

Günther Prien did not know who or what the *Arandora Star* was carrying. In his eyes, the liner's behaviour as an 'enemy' gave him sufficient cause to sink her. At midday on 3 July, he learned the ship's name from German monitoring of British radio. But when he reached Kiel on 6 July, he still did not know details of the passengers. When the news emerged, German propaganda soon criticised the British for sending German prisoners to sea, conveniently forgetting that a

U-boat had sunk the ship. Prien was killed when U-47 was sunk on 7 March 1941, after sinking five merchant ships. It was initially thought the British destroyer *HMS Wolverine* had sunk the U-boat, but it may have been hit by one of its own circling torpedoes.[10] Prien had sunk 31 ships and damaged eight others in his wartime career.

Some 868 survivors were rescued, 586 of them detainees. Bodies were washed up on the coasts of the west and north of Ireland and western Scotland for several weeks afterwards, and buried there. Cycling through Donegal in July 1940, Rodney Green, a Belfast student, came across a 'row of very old taxis driving up the hill in the rain, each with a thin yellow box on its roof, tied down with string'.[11] Alfred Neumann's body, like those of the vast majority of victims, was never found. His widow Sophie received his effects. His son Kurt, who had recently married, was lucky not to have been on the ship.

Incredible as it seems, within days of being sunk by U-47, at least 400 of the 868 survivors from the *Arandora Star* were among 2,550 internees sent by ship to Australia. They went on the *Dunera*, an 11,000-ton troopship launched in 1937. The vast majority were classified as 'B' or 'C' internees, the latter supposedly the least dangerous category.[12]

The internees and their wives were promised that if the men were sent to Australia, the women would be allowed to join them. The promise was never kept. On the dockside in Liverpool the men were ordered to hand over money, valuables, clothing and personal effects. The searching soldiers pocketed much of this, and threw the empty wallets on the quayside. Most of the valuables were never seen again.

Once on board, the *Arandora Star* men were rigidly segregated from the rest, being placed first in a barbed-wire enclosure on the deck of the *Dunera*, and then led to the lowest level of her stern, with no bedding of any kind. The overcrowded and filthy holds were soon crammed with hundreds of disoriented men, a lucky few in hammocks while the rest slept on the floor for the entire voyage. 'On the first night, no one was allowed out of the cabin, and buckets were provided as lavatories. They soon overflowed and the deck was awash with a mixture of vomit, urine, and excrement … Conditions became even more foul when attacks of diarrhoea spread through the ship.'[13]

The ship sailed from Liverpool on 11 July 1940 and took a circuitous route to avoid the threat of U-boats. At 8 a.m. the next morning Oberleutnant zur See Harms, commander of U-56, spotted the *Dunera* twenty miles west of the island of Barra in the Outer Hebrides. He fired two electric torpedoes from 1,500 metres, well within their range. Luckily, the ship had just performed a routine evasive manoeuvre, unaware of the torpedoes fired at it. Neither struck and the ship sailed on undamaged. On board, though, the passengers heard the torpedoes. The survivors of the *Arandora Star* knew exactly what had happened. Panic spread and some passengers tried to get out of the hold. Some of the survivors had even planned for this scenario. One man charged at the door of the hold and broke one of the panels, but was bayoneted in the arm by a soldier on guard:

> The ship sailed on, the prisoners unaware of their destination until they passed Freetown in west Africa. Most of their ransacked baggage had been placed in the hold, creating a great shortage of toiletries such as toothbrushes and combs. Shaving was forbidden for the first five weeks. One piece of soap and one towel was shared by every ten men for a week at a time. Internees of all ages had an exercise period of fifteen to twenty minutes during which they were subject to oaths and sometimes rifle-butts from the guards. No evacuation drill was carried out. At night soldiers appeared in the cabins and robbed the internees of their remaining valuables, including wedding rings, under threat of violence. One internee, Jakob Weiss, learned that his visa for a country in South America had been destroyed during a looting raid by guards. He committed suicide by jumping overboard.[14]

The commander of the military guard on board, Lieutenant-Colonel Scott, put on record his view that the Nazi Germans on board were 'of a fine type, honest and straightforward, and extremely well-disciplined', whereas his Jewish charges were 'subversive liars, demanding and arrogant'. Conditions on board were hardly better, if at all, than those endured by convicts on the same route a hundred years before.[15]

The ship arrived in Melbourne after a two-month voyage, and 2,100 of the internees were transported by train to an internment camp at Hay, one of the hottest places in Australia. When the truth of the voyage emerged, the British government sent Major Julian Layton to Australia to look into the scandal. Layton, who was Jewish, was a stockbroker who had extensive links with refugee welfare groups before the war. He had been to the Continent several times to ensure that refugees received the correct visas needed to come to Britain. 'In Austria he had dealt directly with Adolf Eichmann, whom he described as chillingly courteous and efficient. He was in Vienna in November 1938, and Eichmann telephoned him on the eve of Kristallnacht and warned him to get out.'[16] Layton offered the internees compensation and invited them back to Britain. The British government ultimately had to pay out £30,000 to the detainees.

The sinking of the *Arandora Star* led a to a public inquiry which was highly critical of the deportation policy. The treatment of refugees on the *Dunera* also provoked a backlash. Large numbers of internees in Britain were freed, particularly category B and C prisoners, including Kurt Neumann, who was released in August 1940.

Alfred Neumann had helped Viennese Jews escape persecution and find work in factories in Newtownards and Derry. Hundreds of local people were trained and worked in these firms during the war and for decades afterwards. Within less than two years of being lionised in the Ulster press for setting up the Newtownards factory, he too became a victim of the Nazis. Like all who perished on the *Arandora Star*, he was also a victim of the British government's ill-judged and hasty decision to send a vessel easily mistaken for a warship across the Atlantic when U-boats were regularly sinking merchant ships. In the case of the Austrian and German passengers, many of them Jewish refugees, it was bitterly ironic: they had managed to escape the anti-Semitic hellhole that their countries had become, and almost to a man they were fiercely anti-Nazi. But they found themselves being held in internment camps before being sent across the Atlantic infested with killer U-boat packs. The survivors were then sent out to face the same dangers, and narrowly avoided being sunk again. It was a brutal policy against persecuted people who, far from being 'enemies', were the state's most grateful residents.

20

'THE ONE PLACE WHERE
WE HAD SAFETY'

Six weeks after the Allies invaded Normandy on 6 June 1944, a major group of evacuees began arriving in Northern Ireland. The 7,000 men, women and children who came in July and August 1944 were from Gibraltar, and among them were 250 Jewish evacuees, by far the largest single Jewish contingent admitted to Northern Ireland before, during, or after World War II. The Gibraltarians had been evacuated from London to escape the German V-1 flying bomb blitz. Initially glad to elude the deadly rocket attacks and warmly welcomed by the local population, within months the entire community was seeking a return to their homeland.

Four years earlier the British war cabinet, fearful of a German attack, evacuated all non-military personnel and fortified the Rock. In June 1940, 13,000 of Gibraltar's 20,000 inhabitants were brought to French Morocco. After the Royal Navy attacked the French fleet at Oran on 3 July 1940, the Vichy regime evicted the Gibraltar evacuees. They were sent to Madeira, Jamaica and Britain, mainly to London, where some initially found themselves put up in luxurious hotels. But when the V-1 rockets began to land without warning in 1944, the British government ordered a partial evacuation 'to prevent wholesale slaughter'.[1] Soon 7,000 of them found themselves in camps in Counties Down, Antrim and Derry.

In June 1940 the Jewish population of Gibraltar was around 700, and an estimated 570 were evacuated, 332 to London, some 200 to Madeira, 36 to Jamaica, and a handful to Tangiers. In July 1944, of the 332 Jews in London, 82 were repatriated and 250 were transferred to Northern Ireland.

'The Jewish evacuees carried with them a "Scroll of the Laws", which they have clung to in all their vicissitudes. They are from the Sephardics or Spanish Jews,' the *Belfast Telegraph* reported.[2] 'All the evacuees are ultra-British in outlook and think only of the day when they can rejoin their able-bodied menfolk, who remained on the Rock to play their part in its defence.' The unnamed reporter was clearly impressed by the female passengers. 'Dark-haired girls peered through open portholes and there was one face in its encirclement of raven black hair that recalled the conception of an Italian master painter.'

The first 3,600 evacuees, mainly women and children, received a warm welcome on arrival at the Belfast quayside and travelled by bus and train to sixteen camps. These had been built to house local people made homeless by the four devastating Luftwaffe air raids on Belfast in April and May 1941, which claimed 1,100 lives and destroyed over 56,000 houses (53% of its entire housing stock), made 100,000 people temporarily homeless, and caused £20 million damage to property at wartime values. When the Belfast evacuees were later found accommodation elsewhere, the camps stood vacant.[3]

The four County Down camps were sited at Clough, Cargagh Cut, Crossgar and Saintfield. A fifth camp was built in 1944 at Carryduff. Most of the Jewish evacuees were brought to Saintfield, which became known as the 'Jewish camp', and was also the home of Reverend Banzibra, who ministered to all the Gibraltarian Jews in Northern Ireland. There was close contact between the Jews at Saintfield and the Belfast Jewish community. Rachel Beniso, née Cohen, whose father Abraham Cohen became a close friend of Rabbi Jacob Shachter, remembers visits from young men and women from Belfast and going on outings with them.

Altogether, around 325 evacuees, the majority Jewish, were housed in 40 Nissen huts at Saintfield. Conditions were spartan, as local historian Gordon McCoy notes:

> The roofs were made of corrugated tin, the floors were uncovered concrete, and heating was provided by pot-bellied stoves fuelled by coke. Water was supplied by a well ... and the [river] Glasswater via a water tower ... Pollution of

the Glasswater by flax production rendered the river water stinking and undrinkable at times, and water had to be brought to the camp from elsewhere at considerable trouble.

Unfortunately, the Nissen huts were hot in summer and cold in winter; they rusted easily and were in constant need of repair. They were also very gloomy, having been painted black inside ... Electrification was introduced gradually and was only provided for the kitchens, canteens, recreation hall, sick bays and staff quarters ... Electricity was not provided for the accommodation huts, where it was needed most. Only Camp 17 at Carryduff was fully electrified, being on the Belfast grid.

In London, the evacuees had used private, flushable toilets. In the camps toilet facilities were primitive, more public and unheated. One evacuee, Charlie Tribello, wrote: 'We had no toilet in the huts and had to go for some distance to a wooden shack with a hole in the ground.'[4]

A serious problem for the evacuees was lack of money. In London, the evacuees were allowed to work, but in Northern Ireland they had to be resident for five years before gaining that right. They were not allowed the 'dole', but were 'given a weekly allowance of 8s 6d a week for a married couple, 5s for a single person over 15, and 2s 6d in respect of each child ... The evacuees felt these sums to be paltry and considered themselves to have been rendered both poor and idle at one fell swoop.'[5]

Evacuees managed to earn a little money in the camp as cooks, cleaners and labourers on rota, as the work ban was laxly implemented. Some of the men laboured in Belfast and on local farms, especially at harvest time. Camp children obtained eggs from the farms and picked wild fruit along a local railway line, 'a dangerous pastime', as Gordon McCoy noted.[6] The authorities employed local people as administrators, groundsmen, delivery drivers, nurses and cooks. Staff members who stayed on site lived in better accommodation, made either of red bricks or concrete. The evacuees' dining hall was a larger Nissen hut, which was also used as a recreation hall for dances, film shows and concerts, and as a synagogue. Charles Tribello remembered the food distributed not being to the residents' liking, so they cooked and ate their own food in their huts.

At first, the evacuees were positive about their new life, as a *Belfast Telegraph* reporter wrote after a ministerial visit to the Saintfield camp in July 1944. The evacuees were delighted with the warmth of the welcome they had received and were rapidly adapting themselves to the new conditions. The Minister of Health and Local Government, William Grant, told members of the camp committee that the Ministries of Health and Labour were considering the problem of finding work for the men. Plans were being made to provide elementary education for the children and technical education might also be arranged. The camp warden, S. O. Osborne, was similarly upbeat:

> The majority of the children spoke English and Spanish fluently and often filled the role of interpreter for the adults, some of whom could speak Spanish only. By way of entertainment, dances and concerts had been organised, and the visitors had their own orchestra. A farmer had placed a field at their disposal for playing football and there were other forms of healthy recreation available … The peculiarities of diet had given rise to some difficulty, but these were being overcome. A suggestion book placed in the dining hall at the camp had produced some useful hints from the evacuees as to what they liked and how they liked it cooked. One thing which had particularly pleased the evacuees was the plentiful supply of milk arranged through the Ministry of Agriculture.[7]

The reporter described the evacuees as 'obviously fit and happy and are making many friends amongst the Ulster community, but they are of course looking to the day when they can return to their homes'. By term-time, each camp had a primary school, in which the children were taught by Gibraltarian and local volunteers:

> Some went on to attend technical colleges or secondary school in Belfast where they felt that the education provided was superior than that available on 'the Rock'. One beneficiary was Joshua Gabay, who attended Methodist College and after a successful career as a teacher served in the Gibraltar Parliament for four years. His sister attended Victoria College.

Joe Gingell, a historian of the evacuation, writes of the Gabays: 'They were very pleased with the kind help they received and with the understanding attitude of the teachers toward the Gibraltar evacuees, many of whom had to struggle to catch up with the number of subjects, in English, owing to their numerous schooling interruptions in London during the war.'[8]

At first the change from London, where they had endured four of the five years of war, delighted the Jewish families. 'The Gibraltarians were townspeople enjoying the novelty of living in the countryside for the first time, and Charlie Tribello noted, "One of the things that impressed me very much as a child was the cattle fair held in Saintfield village. We Gibraltarian people were not used to seeing so many cattle before the evacuation."'[9]

But the summer of 1944 was a brief honeymoon period because of good weather, the peaceful surroundings, and the evacuees' relief at escaping the V-1 flying bomb attacks on London. The Gibraltarians, used to the sunny Mediterranean, found the damp, cold, Irish climate harsh. They became unhappy on learning that they would not be repatriated before winter. A correspondent from *The Times* visited the Saintfield camp in December 1944, and captured the change in mood:

> They complain bitterly of the cold, of their small allowances, the primitive sanitary arrangements, and lack of essential amenities … Most of the evacuees are not too badly clothed, but all are finding that their present living conditions are very severe on clothing, especially shoes. The W.V. S. [Women's Voluntary Service], who have a representative at each camp, assist the most needy with gifts of clothes and footwear, but the supplies are said to be far from adequate … No carpet or boards cover the damp concrete floors. A stove and oil lamp supply heat and light. The camp toilet, which consists of about 20 cold water taps pouring into long wooden troughs, is unheated and totally unsuitable for the women.
>
> At present there is no electric supply in the camp, but electric light will shortly be installed in the dining-rooms, kitchens, and recreation rooms of all centres. It will not be installed in the living quarters, where it is needed most.[10]

In November 1944 Miss Florence Horsbrugh, Parliamentary Secretary of the British Ministry of Health, visited two camps in County Down, and was left in no doubt about the strength of feeling there, as the *Down Recorder* reported. A surprise awaited her in the first camp. Slogans including 'Back to Gib' and 'We want to go home' were painted on the walls and roofs of the Nissen huts:

> ... placards, bearing similar messages were brandished by men and women, who, while appreciative of the hospitality extended to them, flinch at the thought of spending the winter here. Miss Horsbrugh was sympathetic; she understood this nostalgia for the shores of the Mediterranean; but they must wait a little until they could be repatriated like friends who had preceded them. At another camp, looking back on their short spell of war work in England, men complained of their present enforced idleness. Continuing her tour of the camps, Miss Horsburgh went on to Antrim and Derry, the scenes of similar demonstrations.[11]

While it is not clear whether Miss Horsbrugh visited the Saintfield camp, photographs taken there show the slogans, 'Back to the Rock', and, 'We want our country, is time now we were back'.

Some Unionist politicians would also have liked to have seen the evacuees back in Gibraltar. In an editorial, *The Irish News* criticised Sir Ronald Ross, Unionist MP for Derry, who raised the issue with the British Home Secretary. The coming to the North of a large number of people evacuated from Gibraltar was one of the many examples of the grave inconveniences caused by war. These people deserve and received widespread sympathy, the paper said. 'He wants to know why these people have been allowed to come to Northern Ireland in preference to Northern Ireland residents in Great Britain. We hope no one suspects that the arrival of the natives of Gibraltar constitute a fresh threat of "peaceful penetration".'[12] As the historian Eamon Phoenix noted, *The Irish News* feared that the religion of the Gibraltarians, the vast majority of them Catholic, was behind Unionist protests.

The Gibraltarian evacuees' complaints were also taken up by local trade unionists. Representatives of the Amalgamated Transport and General Workers' Union met the Minister of Health, William Grant, at Stormont over complaints from their members about camp conditions and the lack of jobs. Grant said the general conditions of the camps were as good as could be provided. Some of the Gibraltarian evacuees did manage to find work at United Chrometanners in Shrigley. A farewell party was held for them, at which the 'Señors' and 'Señoritas' added grace to the programme of songs, dances and games. 'Dr Alfred Utitz, welcoming them to the factory, spoke of the trials, owing to the war, which had been endured by his brother and himself and many of their own people. So the present guests were not alone in their adversities. He looked forward to a happy ending of all the troubles which the war had brought in its train, but which had also brought them many firm friends.'[13]

But pleas for repatriation fell on deaf ears. At the end of the war the evacuees from Gibraltar were still stranded in Northern Ireland:

> The Stormont authorities pleaded with the Colonial Office to move the evacuees back to England where they could find employment and better accommodation. However, there was an acute shortage of accommodation in England; one official communication I read suggested that the only accommodation available in Britain was in prisons. The Northern Irish blamed the British authorities for not helping them by accommodating the evacuees; in turn the authorities in England blamed those in Gibraltar for the delays of the repatriation programme.[14]

There were occasional surprises which lifted morale, if only temporarily. In March 1946, young evacuees from Saintfield were among 200 Gibraltarian children chosen to go to Comber to see Princess Elizabeth, on a royal visit which included the launch of the aircraft carrier HMS *Eagle*. 'The Royal car was stopped and a bouquet of flowers was presented to the Princess by Miss Ivonne Abudarham on behalf of the Gibraltarians. Her Royal Highness in reply said, "Thank you. This is very kind of the Gibraltarians."' [15]

Nearly two years after the war ended, there were still over 2,000 Gibraltarians in Northern Ireland. In March 1947 A. Creech-Jones, the Colonial Secretary, said the last of them might not be able to return for two years. 'I understand', he said, 'that they are not happy about the climate in Northern Ireland.'[16] It is believed the Saintfield camp closed by July 1947, and the last Northern Ireland camp, at Carryduff, closed on 21 July 1948. *The Down Recorder* reported on 5 June 1948 that they would soon see the last of the evacuees who had been 'hurriedly dumped into Ulster in 1944':

> So a striking chapter of social history has practically come to an end. During this strange interlude the exiles had 227 babies born to them here, and the deaths, of all ages, numbered 104. Communal life, however well organised, was by no means a holiday, though not without its lighter moments; discomforts and difficulties were accentuated by the constant sense of banishment. And the majority of the country folk were inclined to look askance at 'them foreigners'.[17]

Most of the evacuees, however, found the locals friendly and welcoming. Rachel Beniso remembered making friends with local girls who worked in the camp while her mother made friends in Saintfield village. She told Gordon McCoy, 'Nobody looked down on us or anything like that.' Charlie Tribello remembered relations with the Saintfield people and Women's Voluntary Service were 'very good indeed' and recalls invitations by a Mrs Coulter to visit her farm for dinner on many occasions.[18]

There are examples of local sympathy for the plight of the Saintfield evacuees, who found the Northern Irish welcome to be warmer than that of London. Rachel Beniso and other evacuees were often invited by local landowners, the Armytage Moore family, to visit their home at Rowallane House. Despite the often primitive conditions and desperate homesickness suffered by the Gibraltarian evacuees, they escaped the Holocaust, unlike so many of the relatives of the Viennese Jewish émigrés who made it to Northern Ireland. One Gibraltarian, Henry J. Ramagge, who had stayed at the camp at Cargagh Cut, outside Downpatrick, when he was a boy, returned on a visit in July 1971. He summed up what many of the evacuees felt. 'You know, despite the slogans on the wall that remind me of the women's impatience to get back to Gibraltar, this was the one place where we had safety during the war. And I'll never forget it.'[19]

21
BACK TO VIENNA

When the war ended in May 1945, the Jewish immigrants in Northern Ireland did everything possible to make contact with loved ones they had been forced to leave. Correspondence had continued sporadically for some until late 1942, but ended as early as 1939 with others. Few knew exactly what had happened to their relatives, but many feared the worst. They were desperate for news.

Among the first to return to Vienna were Walter and Herta Kammerling.[1] Walter was demobbed from the British army in November 1945 and went into a government training centre as a draughtsman, but he didn't finish the course:

> We were told we could be repatriated to Austria, and as we wanted to return there, Herta and I said, 'Oh, wonderful.' We returned in June 1946, only eight years after I left. I went to where my family had lived at Ausstellungsstrasse 7, in the second district. That was a very painful thing. At that time the gates to the houses were still open. Nothing had changed, only the buildings were a little dilapidated. I started to go up the stairs to the first floor. About half way up the stairs, I realised, *The people I love are not there. What am I doing?* So I turned around and never went back. I didn't know at that time that my parents and my sister were already dead, but I knew they weren't there anymore, they had been taken to the camps.
>
> Sometime later, a good friend of mine, Felix Schwarz, whom I had been with since kindergarten through grammar school and in London, gave me a book, *Deathbook*

Theresienstadt [*Tötenbuch Theresienstadt*] and there I found the names of my father, mother and sister and what exactly had happened to them.

They were moved out of their flat to Grosse Mohrengasse 38 in the second district, where they shared one room with five other families. They were deported from Vienna to Theresienstadt on 24 September 1942. My father was transported to Auschwitz on 29 September 1944 and my mother and sister on 23 October 1944, so that was the end of them. I know they didn't stay alive long in Auschwitz. They went from Theresienstadt straight to the gas chambers.[2]

Walter, marked by the loss of his parents and sister, was more affected by the return than Herta. He recalled:

We lived in Vienna for eleven years, from 1946 to 1957. I never went back to any place I knew before the war, not to my schools, not to where we lived, save that one time. It was completely separate, because I think it was too painful. You try to live the past down somehow, but it's really impossible. It's always with you. The interesting thing is when we came back to Vienna we recognised the sounds, the smells and the sights. It was sort of home and it wasn't home. When we came back to Britain, we also recognised everything, such as eating fish and chips out of a paper bag. It was home in a way that Vienna never had become, because my folks were taken from there.

I had a precious poor opinion of the Viennese because, as it turned out, whoever you spoke to weren't Nazis, none of them were, and I remembered that all of them were. They may not have been very strong believers, but they went with it, they all went with it. Very few didn't. I only knew one person who was anti-Nazi. He had to go with it, but he was not Nazi. We tried to kid ourselves that Austria was the first country over-run. No, they were Nazis.

It wasn't really difficult to start again. I did the matriculation and enrolled in the Technical University, but I couldn't go full-time as I had to work. I worked with AEG designing electric motors, which I always wanted to do. I was quite happy, but I knew basically underneath they were still the same Nazis. They did not talk about me, but they did about other people. There was a Jewish chap called Reichard, who worked on the floor below. One day I heard one Austrian say to another, about Reichard, 'Ah, that's another one who slipped through the grating,' meaning the grating of the crematorium. I went home that night and I felt, *I don't really want to bring our sons up here in this atmosphere.* Peter was eight, Max was just about two. It was under the surface, it was open, the anti-Semitism was there. They knew I was Jewish. I think they said it on purpose so that I should hear it. Herta and I discussed it and it made me decide, 'I think I had better go back to England.'

My friend Felix Schwarz stayed there, but when we discussed things, he said: 'You watch out, if you keep on talking you will one day be at my front door, saying, "Put me up."' He was a very decent guy and there were other decent people who tried to make a living.

The Viennese hadn't come to terms with what they had done, despite all that had happened. There is a saying in Austria, 'The Germans were the better Nazis, but the Austrians were the better anti-Semites.' And it's very true. I'm afraid it's still there more or less. I think the Germans have more character than the Austrians, though I am Austrian myself. I do believe that. Of course at the present time they don't know about the Nazis, what happened and so on. But I can't forget it.[3]

Herta, too, vividly remembered her time in Vienna:

We were housed with army personnel, who were Jewish. Walter found work but he really wanted to study. I always wanted to be a kindergarten teacher. That was a nice time. I joined a three-month course, and that is where I drank my first real coffee, downstairs for the 'ten o'clock break'. When I left I missed that coffee.

> Vienna after the war didn't affect me the way it affected Walter, because I went back open-minded and purposeful. They would rebuild and there would be a new democracy, so I wasn't afraid to go back. It was different, it was bombed a little but not much. The Viennese were suffering terribly, they said, forgetting that London was bombed to bits of course.[4]

Herta recalled two events which brought out Vienna's frightening past. They entered a repair shop to have a faulty fountain pen of Walter's checked. The owner was formally polite, dressed in the black outfit of a retailer. But something about his manner, which suggested he sensed that they were Jews, made goose-pimples run down their backs. Outside, without even speaking, they each sensed that he might have been an SS man, possibly even one who had served in concentration camps.

On another occasion, one of Herta's uncles, Oskar, and his wife, Emmi, who had escaped from Vienna before the war, paid them a visit not long after they had returned. Oskar had worked as an electrician, and Emmi, who had refused to divorce him as she was entitled to as a non-Jew, had been a chambermaid in the 'best hotel in town' in Semmering, a famous alpine resort in Lower Austria, about sixty miles from Vienna. For old times' sake they visited Semmering and walked past their former workplace. It had been a favourite haunt of leading Nazis from 1938 onwards. The porter noticed them and said, 'Hello.' Oskar replied: 'Do you know me?' He replied, 'Yes, you're the electrician.' Oskar was taken aback, but pleased that he had been recognised. Nothing else was said and Oskar and Emmi walked on, but realised that the porter must have been a Nazi sympathiser, because only a trusted supporter would have been allowed to work at a hotel frequented by the Nazi elite. Such incidents were a reminder of how things turned out after they left Vienna, said Herta:

> We weren't aware how unpleasant things would become during the war and how they would end. It's a time we don't think back on often. We don't discuss it, not any more, but when something crops up in the papers, whether it's in

Rwanda or another country in the world, it's not nice. When you read in the paper, a Jewish man was killed here, a Jewish man was killed there, that's when it comes back to you.[5]

Walter took part in events such as school visits to keep the memory of the Holocaust alive:

I visited Ireland to speak through the Holocaust Educational Trust. I think it is important to speak at events to prevent anything like that happening again, so that young people will be aware of what is happening, making up their own minds, and don't just follow, don't say, 'yes, yes, yes!' Make up your own mind and do what you think is correct. Watch out what they say to you. As Goethe said: '*Ursprunglich eigenen Sinn laßt dir nicht rauben / Woran die Menge glaubt ist leicht zu glauben.*' [Of your own mind don't let yourself be robbed / It's easy to believe the beliefs of the mob.] And that's very important. Because there are certain forces, undemocratic forces, who go for that. You must not let your guard drop one minute, because if we lose the democratic element, we're lost. Because once it happens, it's too late. Each young person has a life and they are responsible for it, and they can make what they want of it, not go suddenly and say 'yes, yes, yes!'

It should be more taught in schools, what happened. Though the interesting thing is it would be harder in Britain to follow mob leaders than it would be on the Continent. On the Continent, people are more likely to follow. In Britain, people are more likely to make up their own minds and say, 'I don't want that,' and that's the beauty of it, people are more independent. People think more for themselves. In Austria, they are more 'follow the leader'.

Plays and books should be written because it is important to have a full report of what happened, how it crept up, how one has to be very careful to let it not take over, because, if it does take over you're back to fascism, you're back to the one-party State and that's no good.

The difficulty of my life was rather lightened by being married to Herta. I still love her as much as I did when I first met her and I'm very sorry I couldn't introduce her to my parents. Their loss is with me every day. Poor Ruthie, too young to get a working permit and too old to go on the Kindertransport, and therefore she had to die, to be murdered a week or two before her twenty-third birthday.

I'm bitter against the Nazis, not the Germans, they are very different. Can I forgive them [for] what they did? Forgiving is not my thing. Who am I to forgive? If I forgive, the culprit thinks he's forgiven. No, I can't do that. Forgiveness is divine. It would be presumptuous of me to say, 'I forgive you.' How do I know what else he has done? No. The German people are alright. It's the culprits. We mustn't make that mistake. It's only the ones who actually did it.

On the continent, anti-Semitism has a long history. It's almost built in. They built on the remnant of anti-Semitism which was there, and they reinforced it. Unfortunately, so many people senselessly followed hate. We have it today as well and it doesn't have to be against Jews. If one starts generalising about people, then it becomes prejudice: 'You can hate him because he's done that, or not.' As it's a prejudice, you judge before you know.

Now when I visit Austria, they are very nice, the people, and I think they have absorbed democracy. There probably may be some hard-core Nazis there, but I think democracy is there to stay. I think if you taste democracy long enough, you get caught. You can forget about the past, unless you're a very convinced Nazi who keeps working towards the great past that never was. We must always remember what happened to the innocent, which unfortunately people are liable to forget, which is human nature.[6]

After the war, Herta and Walter discovered the extent of their families' losses in the Holocaust.[7] Walter lost his parents, Max and Marie, and sister Ruth; Herta learned that two of her mother's sisters, Valerie and

Alice, and one of her father's sisters, Ernestine, and an uncle, Lejos Haas, had been murdered. She also lost two cousins, Peter Blödy and Suzi Suranyi.

Herta's maternal Aunt Valerie had married Stefan (Pista) Suranyi and they had a daughter, Gertrude Suzanna (Suzi). All three managed to get to France, and were trying to reach Toulouse in the unoccupied zone by train when they were arrested. They were held in the transit camp at Drancy in Paris, and Valerie and her daughter Suzi were deported to Auschwitz on 7 December 1943, while Stefan was deported there on 30 May 1944, just a week before D-Day.

A paternal aunt, Ernestine Plaschkes, married a German Jew, David Weissmann, from Freiberg. He had a stammer, but was a fine singer and worked as a cantor in one of Vienna's synagogues. Herta remembered them: 'Auntie Erna [Ernestine] was getting older and was asked to marry, and she did, and they had a life together running a little shop selling ladies' underwear and haberdashery.' They were taken from their last home at Zwerggasse in the Jewish second district on 31 August 1942, and deported to Maly Trostinec, near Riga, where they were murdered on 4 September 1942. Her other paternal Auntie Fanka obtained a domestic permit to London, but her husband, Leopold Haas, was deported from Vienna to Maly Trostinec on 14 September 1942 and murdered four days later.

Walter and Herta and their two sons, Peter and Max, returned to England in 1957 and lived in Bournemouth. Herta worked as a kindergarten teacher, and Walter as chief engineer in a local company. He was awarded the British Empire Medal in 2020. He died in January 2021. They named Peter after Herta's cousin, the only son of her aunt Alice and uncle Arpad Blödy. Alice and her son Peter Blödy perished in Theresienstadt, when Peter was eight years old. Herta recalled visiting them in Prague before the war when Peter was a toddler. Arpad survived the war, and went looking for his wife and son afterwards. He found out they were dead, but he married a nurse who had known his late wife and son. They moved to Israel. Walter named his son Max after his father, a loving father full of good ideas, whom he saw cry for the first and last time in a hospital ward in Vienna on 10 December 1938, when they hugged each other goodbye for ever.[8]

Gertrude Kessler and her brother Fritz had reached Northern Ireland from Vienna as teenagers in 1938, but their parents, Leopold and Ernestine, could not escape. The children wrote letters, which often took months to reach Austria and to be answered. The correspondence petered out in 1942. A short reply from Vienna dated 31 July 1942 sees Leopold and Ernestine trying to set Gertrude's mind at ease, despite their grim experiences of more than four years of Nazi persecution: 'Dear children, we are healthy, don't worry we are doing well; stay good and healthy, write where you now are, a thousand kisses.'[9]

It was not until the war ended that the children learned a little of what had happened to their parents. And it was seventy-five years later before Gertrude's son Charlie learned how his grandmother Ernestine had miraculously survived. It was only after Gertrude's death in 2015 that Charlie found out what happened to his grandfather. Leopold and Ernestine Kessler were among 999 Jewish men, women and children deported from the Anspangbahnhof in Vienna on transport train 4 on 5 March 1941 to Modliborzyce in the Lublin district of Poland.

The DÖW website states that a ghetto was built at Modliborzyce to house both local Jews and deportees from all over Poland and the rest of Nazi-occupied Europe. Some deportees were also placed with Jews in surrounding villages. The majority were housed in the homes of local Jews or in mass quarters such as a synagogue. The living conditions in the ghetto were very difficult. A number of men capable of work were taken to a forced labour camp, while those left behind tried to survive by selling off their last valuables. Malnutrition and illness caused a high death rate, and regular attacks by SS and German police claimed more and more lives, according to eyewitness reports.

The ghetto was liquidated, along with others in the Lublin district, in the autumn of 1942. On 18 October 1942, the surviving inhabitants were brought to a railway station in Zaklikow near Modliborzyce and deported to an extermination camp under Aktion Reinhard, the Nazi programme for the murder of Jews in the General Government in south-east Poland. The old and sick were murdered in the ghetto. It was not known for certain exactly when or where Leopold died, and the family initially believed it was at Belzec, one of three extermination camps built in 1942, along with Treblinka and Sobibor. Of the 999 Jewish deportees to Modliborzyce from Vienna, only 13 survived. Altogether an estimated 1.7 million Jews were murdered in the Aktion Reinhard programme between the summer of 1942 and September 1943.

The DÖW website states simply that Leopold perished, but shows that Ernestine miraculously survived the war and returned to Vienna. It carries a handwritten letter sent on 17 September 1945 to Ernestine, from a fellow deportee, Paul Messinger, who survived and was also living in Vienna. In it, Messinger reveals that he was also on Train 4 to Modliborzyce, the one on which Leopold and Ernestine were deported. He stated that Leopold had been employed as a clerk by the Jewish Council in Modliborzyce, was moved at the end of September 1942 to Zaklikow, and was then deported on the first transport from there. As he later found out, these transports were sent to Treblinka. 'It is therefore to be taken that your husband unfortunately is no longer alive.'

But how did Ernestine manage to avoid transportation to Treblinka, a certain death sentence? Ernestine later told her daughter Gertrude that Leopold was in a queue for deportation and she gave him her coat because it was cold. Gertrude believed this was in Vienna, and March weather there is cold. But it could have been in Poland.

It seemed impossible to clarify where Ernestine was between March 1941 and September 1945, when she was back in Vienna. That was until January 2020. Following correspondence between the author and Dr Ursula Schwarz, an archivist at the DÖW in Vienna, part of the mystery was solved. Dr Schwarz confirmed that both Ernestine and Leopold were deported from Vienna to Modliborzyce on 5 March 1941. 'A letter in her file tells us that she was able to flee with another woman. They went by feet [sic] back to Vienna.' She added that the whole family had been dismissed from their flat owned by the city of Vienna in the twentieth district at Leystrasse 23.[10]

So, one mystery had been solved. Ernestine did travel to Poland but made her way back on foot to Vienna with another woman. How did she manage to do this? Poland was under the jackboot and by the spring of 1941 the Nazis had already murdered hundreds of thousands of Jews in the country. Their extermination of Jews had started immediately they invaded the country in September 1939. Had Ernestine escaped from Modlyborzyce in 1941 or later? Who was the unnamed woman who escaped with her? How had she survived such a dangerous journey back to Vienna and on foot? One question may have been answered but the answer had thrown up even more questions. Dr Schwarz quickly provided more answers.

She forwarded via email a sworn statement made in July 1945 by the woman who had escaped with Ernestine from Poland. Her name was Helene König. She said she got to know Ernestine with her husband in February 1941 at the Sperl school in Vienna, one of the collection centres for deportation. They were transported to Modliborzyce via Lublin-Krassnick in Poland in the early days of March 1941 on the second transport from Sperlgasse. 'After we decided to flee homewards from the ghetto owing to extreme beatings and hunger, Frau Kessler and I succeeded following weeks of privations to return to Vienna on foot at the end of the year 1941. Helene König, Vienna 1, Seegasse 9, Returnees' home, Room 119.' Their remarkable escape – two Jewish women crossing Poland under the genocidal Nazi occupation – showed astonishing courage and resourcefulness. Had they been caught, there is little doubt that the Nazis would have murdered them.

Ernestine's grandson Charlie Warmington had also long believed that members of her family, the Schrekingers, 'uncles' or possibly male relatives of some kind, had been involved in a plot to assassinate Hitler, probably in Vienna. According to the story, they were betrayed to the Nazis and executed by being thrown into a pit of wild dogs. A memorial of stones had been erected somewhere in Vienna, but he did not know where. Dr Schwarz in her email to the author revealed that a man called Nachmann Schrekinger, who lived at Kluckygasse 7 in the twentieth district of Vienna died in the city on 30 March 1941 and was buried in the central cemetery of Vienna. There are other Schrekingers mentioned in the DÖW database but she could not find out if these were related to Nachmann Schrekinger. She could give no other details. So the mystery about a plot to kill Hitler and the role of Ernestine Kessler's family remains.

Ernestine Kessler picked up the threads of her life alone in Vienna after the murder of her husband in Poland, and survived the war against all odds. Both her children were in the United Kingdom. Her daughter Gertrude and her new husband, Theo Warmington, moved first to Dungannon, County Tyrone, where he was a houseman in the local hospital. The Northern Ireland Tuberculosis Authority then appointed him to the Erne hospital, Enniskillen, County Fermanagh to lead one of four tuberculosis sanitoria, and he was among a small group of doctors who had a key role in eradicating the disease. Theo became seriously ill himself at this time, and had a lung removed in a London hospital. A son, Alan, was born in 1947 and he became a doctor like his father. A second son, Charles (Charlie), born in 1950, trained as an architect, but he has had a distinguished career as a radio producer and editor with BBC Northern Ireland, and later as a columnist with the *Belfast News Letter*. Gertrude had difficulty tracing her mother Ernestine in the chaos after the war, but managed to contact her, Charlie recalled: 'Ernestine just didn't want to talk about it. I can't tell you any details. She was a broken woman after.' In an interview with Charlie, Gertrude described the gulf that had developed between her and her mother:

> The connection wasn't anything like what we had when we left. No, Mother was more of a stranger, and I suppose I was a stranger too. And then you see, we had trouble when Mum came over a few times to us here, and she objected to us speaking in English. It was difficult for us. She was old, and she had lost a husband. She had 'lost' two children. She had nothing. She lost everything. Vienna was bombed, by the very people who were taking care of me in this country.[11]

Charlie remembers Gertrude packing a big cardboard box with rations every Thursday to send to her mother in Vienna, which still had food shortages and bombed-out buildings. 'Granny Kessler was sending us things like a wonderful toboggan sleigh, a leather school bag, and German books,' he recalled.[12]

But the sufferings of Ernestine and her daughter Gertrude were not over yet. They began again when Ernestine came to visit Gertrude and her family in Enniskillen for the first time in the 1950s. Charlie's paternal grandmother, Edith Warmington, was staying with the family then. She was the first woman pastor to work on a Christian mission in the East End of London. Charlie was just three or four years old when Ernestine came for the first time:

Once Granny Kessler appeared on a visit, that was the cause of it because she wasn't allowed into our house. Granny Warmington wouldn't let her, and Granny Kessler stayed in a little bed and breakfast down near the Railway Hotel in Enniskillen. We went down there every day, Mum and I, to visit her. And I just remember the two of them sitting crying. It was an upstairs room and Mum and her mother just crying, and I was playing with my toys on the floor. I didn't really understand it.

Granny Kessler had come all the way over from Austria to see her grandchildren for the first time since the war, to see her son-in-law for the first time. She didn't come to the wedding; maybe she wasn't allowed.[13]

Around this time the abuse turned more serious. Gertrude later told Charlie that Granny Warmington had threatened to use a knife on Granny Kessler. One day, when Charlie was in his first or second year at the Model primary school in Enniskillen, she acted on the threat:

I came home to find my grandmother had an arm around my mother's neck. Mum was facing me, Grandmother behind her with her arm around her neck and the kitchen knife in her lower ribs. I wasn't altogether sure what was going on. Mum was crying out to the old grandmother to let go of her, and she then did, and I went up to my bedroom to play with toys.

Mum told me later that it was something to do with Granny Kessler coming over and it was a threat. Mum told me that when I was in my forties, and she connected it with Granny Kessler's visit.

Granny Warmington had such hatred for Granny Kessler. But I also remember Mum crying her eyes out when Granny Warmington said to her, 'I have heard that you are a bastard. I have heard your Mum and Dad weren't married.' ... The whole of that very early life of mine is just overshadowed with this Irish grandmother, Granny Warmington, whom I called Nanny. Just constant references to Mum's Jewishness.

She called my mum 'Judas'; that was my mum's nickname. She fought with my mother and said my mother was poisoning her. She was just totally anti-Semitic ...[14]

In 1966 Charlie and Alan went with their parents to Vienna for the first time. They arrived on the same platform from which Gertrude had left in 1938, the last time she saw her father. 'Granny's big hug nearly killed me. She was a big lady. She ate a lot of fat, sauerkraut, bratwurst and Wiener schnitzel. I remember it hurt and she just cried. The whole thing was shrouded in tears.' The boys had a wonderful time, taking in the sights of the city, including St Stefan's Cathedral, the Prater amusement park with the Ferris wheel made famous in the film *The Third Man*, the Hofburg Palace, and the Opera House. But nobody talked about Leopold or the terrible times in Vienna. There were tears shared by Gertrude and Ernestine, but no explanations for Charlie or his brother Alan.

On that trip one incident occurred which Charlie, then aged sixteen, never forgot: 'I can only guess what was going on in the background at that moment. Mum went to leave and Granny put her arms around me and burst into tears and said, "Charlie, can I come and live with you?"' For him, such family trauma, not talked about, shadowed their lives. Sometimes it erupted into daily life with Gertrude, Charlie recalled. 'I remember the banging feet, the stamping. We would be watching television – it was always something to do with Germany or war history – and she banged the floor with her feet. Once she got up and left and went into the kitchen and she was crying uncontrollably, and that's only about fifteen years ago.'[15]

Later, Ernestine moved to a nursing home in Vienna, and lived there for several years before she died. Some years after Ernestine's death, Charlie took his mother back to Vienna. In one of the talks he has given about his family's experiences, Charlie told the story of that visit:

Once, I persuaded her back to the Kesslers' Viennese apartment – their family home before the Gestapo herded them into the ghetto. I had to, lovingly I hope, as gently as I could – but I had to push her up the stairs to the front door of the apartment. Her crying and grief worsened at every step towards the door. As I held her, weeping in anguish, I knocked the door of the apartment – but there was no one there to open the door. Perhaps it was a good thing, because I don't know if she could have coped with going inside. I desperately wanted to share her past with her. I sometimes regret trying to. I led her away from the door, and down the stairs out onto the street. 'The last time I was here,' she said, still weeping and pointing to the old paving stone that I was standing on, 'your grandfather was standing there. He was pushing a little wooden cart that he'd made, and in it was everything that we were allowed to bring to the ghetto, which wasn't very much.' As she spoke through her tears, the paving stone, for me, became a monument. It was Leopold's stone. Mum's anguished tears ruled out going to the ghetto. I begged her to even point towards its whereabouts so that I could go there myself later. She couldn't even point.[16]

Some years ago, Charlie met an Austrian journalist, Franziska Meinhardt, on a reporting assignment in Scotland. Over breakfast, they began talking and exchanged family stories. She asked Charlie a little about his family, then became tearful. '"Some of my family were Nazi sympathisers, including my grandparents," she said. I could see hurt in her eyes,'[17] Charlie remembered.

Franziska had moved to Bavaria, and as a university student in Munich she began a journey of discovery about the role certain members of her family played during the war. An exhibition in Munich in the mid-1990s, which highlighted Nazi war crimes, also deepened her interest.

Her grandfather, Franz Artmann, from the small town of Retz in lower Austria, had been an early Nazi supporter. As a member of the Wehrmacht, he had fought against partisans in Montenegro, Korcula, an island off the Dalmatian coast, and the Soviet Union, where he had a narrow escape, and made it back to Austria. He was awarded the War Service Cross, second class, with swords, in January 1943. After the war, he suffered psychological problems and nightmares, but never talked about what he had done. Franziska's great-uncle, Oscar Woehry, had joined the SS and she believes that he may have taken part in the massacre of 250 Hungarian Jews on a death march, in Eisenarz near his home town of Vordernberg in Styria, Austria, on 7 April 1945:

> I also remember I hadn't been able to talk to Oskar Woehry about his past on a day he visited my grandmother, after they hadn't been in touch for a long time. He was about ninety years old then, and I remember thinking about how I could bring up the topic. And I just didn't dare to do it.
>
> But when I met Charlie and he mentioned the Kindertransport, I felt his pain (even though he wasn't crying), imagined his grandparents' and mother's pain – all of which made me cry. I don't look for forgiveness for what my family did. I think there cannot be forgiveness – what would it mean? There can only be an awareness for the present, and what one can do so those times won't be repeated.[18]

In Vienna, after the war ended, the Allied authorities set up a legal process to investigate Nazis who had been active in Austria. Membership of the NSDAP (Nazi Party) between 1934 and 1938 had been illegal there and was still treated as such after the war. Former members, of whom there were several thousand in the city, now underwent a process that for some would last years.

Among them was Franz Pokorny, the Nazi schoolfriend of Otto Goldberger, who had let him escape from a holding centre on the night of 10 November 1938. Two thick files in Vienna's City and State Archives give an insight into his career, his personality and his evasions, typical of so many of his fellow Nazis after the war.

Pokorny never mentions his good deed to his Jewish schoolfriend Otto Goldberger in a Nazi holding centre. That would place him as a willing Nazi paramilitary and therefore convict him of involvement in Nazi activity as early as 1938. In a 19 July 1945 application for identity papers, he claimed only to have been a Nazi Party member between 1940 and 1945 and a block helper until 1943, and not to know his party number.

But another police report noted that, according to confidential information, Pokorny had been arrested during the illegal period (1934–38) and interned for a time in Wollersdorf detention camp.

It said that immediately after the Anschluss in March 1938, he was armed with a rifle and was on duty in civilian clothes in Vienna's tenth district. He oversaw the looting of a Jewish grocery firm, Lehrer and Hubler, and an adjoining Jewish-owned fashion shop. His brother-in-law Adolf Falkenburger and a Ludwig Hellman took active roles and the goods were driven away in a commercial vehicle. It added that Pokorny belonged to the SA for some time and wore its uniform.

Pokorny appears again in the police files on 19 April 1946, when he was questioned about his application for identity papers. A report noted that he was suspected of knowingly withholding details of his Nazi Party membership, which was a criminal offence.

Questioned in February 1947, Pokorny said he was from 1938 to 1946 a permanent employee at the telegraph office in Zollergasse. He said he was a member of the NSDAP from 1927 to 1929 and was detained for six weeks on political grounds in the winter of 1935. He said he had been automatically enrolled in the NSDAP, and regretted that he had not admitted this when he was applying for his identity papers. In this statement he still maintained that he was never a member of the SA or SS. He denied taking part in the looting of the Jewish shops or being seen with a rifle while on duty at the Favoriten Magistrates District Office in March 1938.

But a police witness report based on interviews with three residents of his Friesenplatz block of flats said that Pokorny was known there as a Nazi Party member who constantly wore party insignia. He greeted residents with 'Heil Hitler', argued for his political outlook against other house residents, and his windows were constantly draped with party slogans.

In March 1947 police interviewed a personnel officer in the telegraph office where Pokorny had worked during the war. He had been known as quiet and decent, and had not been involved in political activity. In 1946 he was removed from that office. On 28 August 1948, the police registry office for National Socialists noted that Pokorny had given incomplete and incorrect information about the details of his Nazi Party membership. The report says he omitted to say he was an 'old fighter', a Nazi member before the Anschluss in 1938, a member of the SA from

2 February 1934 until 1938, a block leader of his local branch from May 1939 onwards, and a cell leader – his membership number was 6.232.325.

He was convicted of Nazi Party membership during the period 1933–38, of being active in the National Socialist movement, and of being recognised as an 'old fighter' by the NSDAP. He appealed the verdict and the case dragged on until 1951, but Pokorny lost his appeal. His NSDAP record was in the hands of the Viennese authorities and showed his lengthy membership. Pokorny lived out his days in Vienna and is buried with his wife in the city's main cemetery.

Otto's parents, Hermann and Malwine, were not so lucky. Hermann, aged sixty-five, and Malvine, aged sixty, were deported from their last home at Komödiengasse 6, to Izbica in Poland on 12 May 1942 and perished there. They were among 4,000 Jewish men, women and children deported in four transports from Vienna's Aspangbahnhof between 9 April and 5 June 1942. The SS began deportations from Izbica to Belzec extermination camp in the summer of 1942. On 15 October 1942, 10,000 Jews were rounded up at Izbica station, of whom 5,000 were put on transports. During this selection, a massacre took place, in which roughly 500 people were shot. None of the 4,000 Austrian Jews deported to Izbica survived.[19]

After the European war ended in May 1945, Jewish refugees in Northern Ireland seeking to renew contact with their loved ones often faced obstacles at home and abroad. Among them were Zoltan Frankl and his wife, Anny Lewinter, who had escaped Vienna, and taken over the Newtownards factory after the Ministry of Commerce sacked Alfred Neumann in early 1939. Their company expanded and became a major employer in the town. The conflict had barely ended when Zoltan Frankl, who had helped his wife Anny's sisters emigrate from Vienna before the war, tried to rescue his relatives from behind the Iron Curtain. His father, Hermann, had died of natural causes during the war, and his mother Regina and sister Irene were living under the communist regime in Timișoara, Romania. Zoltan began sending food parcels to them and lobbying the Stormont authorities and the Home Office to have them admitted to Northern Ireland. A nine-year-long saga began.[20]

Margaret 'Peggy' Fink (*née* Loewenthal), daughter of a wealthy German family in Belfast, was a leading member of the Belfast Committee for Refugees from Germany and Austria. *(Photograph: Michelle Fink)*

Margaret 'Peggy' McNeill, in Friends' Ambulance uniform, joined female 'enemy aliens', most of them Jewish and from Germany and Austria, imprisoned in Armagh women's gaol after mass internment was introduced in May 1940. *(Photograph: Dr Tom McNeill)*

The Irish writer and essayist Hubert Butler worked with the Society of Friends in Vienna in 1938 to help Jews obtain visas to escape Nazi persecution. He was scathing about the refusal of the British and Irish governments to admit more Jewish refugees. *(Photograph: Hubert and Peggy Butler papers, TCD MS10304/657, The Board of Trinity College Dublin)*

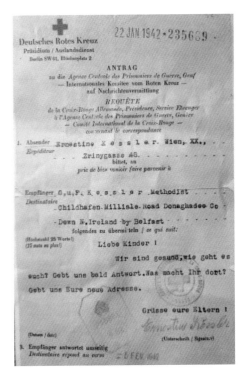

A Red Cross letter written by Ernestine Kessler from Vienna to her children, Gertrude and Fritz, in Northern Ireland. She puts a brave face on her and her husband, Leopold's, own grim circumstances, asks where the children are living, and begs them to write back soon. *(Photograph: Charlie Warmington)*

Otto Bermann had been interned by the Nazis for six months when his father Alfred wrote on his behalf to the Ministry of Commerce in 1938, but his application was refused. Otto survived Dachau and Buchenwald and made it to England, where he was interned for a period after his arrival in 1939. *(Photograph: The Deputy Keeper of the Records, Public Record Office of Northern Ireland, COM/17/3/8)*

Vienna,15th December 1938.

To the North Eire Trade Chamber

B e l f a s t

      In the name of my son, Otto Bermann,who has been impri-
soned in a concentrations-camp for six months as a consequence of the
persecution against the Jews, I beg you very much to be so kind to procure him a post anywhere and to render possible him to obtain the permit for this would be the only possibility to get him free.
      First at all,let me give,please,some particulars about him.
He is 29 1/2 years old,of unblemished character,very tall,
(194 cm) deriving of a respectable merchant family of Vienna,and perfectly healthy.He finished the higher Public Technical-School for textile-
industry,and has several year⁺s experience by working in large weaving-
mills at home and abroad commercial as well as a spooler,weaver,assitant-
of the weaver-master,and so on.
      For more⁺ than 4 1⁄2 years he was occupied in a weaving-
mill in Vienna(the Mother-mill is in the Czecho-Slovakia).Therefore he
is able to say,he has a firm grasp of his branche. Hor he is very skilful
and diligent.
      The unhappy,old parents of this⁺ young man beg you very
much to be so kind to grant their request and are waiting for your
kind answer.
              Yours very truly

             Alfred Bermann
           Vienna 9
        Liechtensteinstrasse 64.

The letter from Alfred Bermann pleading for entry to Northern Ireland for his son Otto Bermann, who had been in Dachau for six months in 1938. Alfred and his wife, Mathilde, were deported to Theresienstadt in July 1942, where he died in September. Soon afterwards Mathilde was deported to Treblinka and murdered. *(Photograph: The Deputy Keeper of the Records, Public Record Office of Northern Ireland, COM/17/3/8)*

Ernst Weiniger was captured by the Gestapo in Vienna and suffered torture in Berlin but, remarkably, was freed after being imprisoned for a year. He survived the war by living underground in Vienna. His brother Walter escaped to Northern Ireland and helped set up United Chrometanners in Shrigley, County Down. *(Photograph: David and Siobhan Weiniger)*

George Clare, who escaped Nazi Vienna and made it to Ireland. His parents, Ernst and Stella, also came to Dublin but returned to France. They were captured in 1942 and murdered in Auschwitz. George Clare wrote two classic memoirs about his experiences, and is pictured here after receiving an honorary doctorate from the University of Limerick. *(Photograph: Professor Gisela Holfter, University of Limerick)*

Otto Kisch applied for visas for himself, his wife, Hertha, and daughter Vera, aged eight, from Vienna, but they were refused entry. In January 1942 Otto was deported to a concentration camp at Jungfernhof near Riga, Latvia, and was murdered in March. Unusually, Hertha and Vera, who were deported with him, survived. *(Photograph: The Deputy Keeper of the Records, Public Record Office of Northern Ireland, COM/17/3/3)*

The wedding photograph of Gertrude and Arthur Chat. Gertrude wrote to Northern Ireland from Vienna in August 1938, requesting permits for herself, her husband, Arthur, and her daughter Edith, aged twenty-one, but they were refused entry. Gertrude and Arthur were deported together to Theresienstadt in July 1942. Arthur died there in December, and Gertrude was deported to Auschwitz a month later and murdered. Edith Chat was deported to Sobibor in June 1942 and did not survive. *(Photograph: Documentation Archive of the Austrian Resistance)*

Nicholas Vermes and his wife, Josephine Morrow, whom he met at the United Chrometanners factory in Shrigley, County Down. Nicholas had travelled from Hungary to Northern Ireland in February 1940, and later made a film with his daughter Vivienne about his war-time experiences. *(Photograph: Vivienne Vermes)*

In 1944 Nicholas' parents, Anushka and Eugene Vermes, were taken as forced labourers from Hungary to Berndorf, Austria. In January 1945, starving and fever-ridden, Anushka took three rotten potatoes from the kitchen where she worked. A female SS guard found them on her and ordered her to stand outside in the freezing cold. She died after a few hours. Eugene survived and came to London but committed suicide in 1957. *(Photograph: Vivienne Vermes)*

Leopold and Ernestine Kessler (left) were deported from Vienna to Modliborzyce in Poland in January 1941. Leopold perished in the Holocaust, but Ernestine, remarkably, survived by walking back to Vienna. *(Photograph: Charlie Warmington)*

Right: Leopold and Ernestine remembered in a Stein der Erinnerung (Stone of Memory) plaque outside their home in Vienna. *(Photograph: Franziska Meinhardt)*

Below: former BBC Radio Foyle Station Manager Charlie Warmington outside his grandparents' home in Vienna. *(Photograph: Franziska Meinhardt).*

Above: Leopold and Ernestine's daughter Gertrude Kessler came as a Kindertransport evacuee to Northern Ireland and later married Dr Theo Warmington, a key figure in the eradication of tuberculosis. She is pictured here with her son Charlie. *(Photograph: Charlie Warmington)*

Jewish evacuees were among 7,000 Gibraltar natives moved to Northern Ireland during the V-1 Blitz on London in July 1944. They were housed at a camp at Saintfield, County Down, but soon tired of their restricted living conditions and lobbied to return home. *(Photograph: Joe Gingell collection)*

Women, several of them Jewish evacuees from Gibraltar, at the Saintfield camp. They found life in the rudimentary Nissen huts and the damp Irish climate difficult and lobbied to be repatriated, but the last of them did not leave until 1947. *(Photograph: Joe Gingell collection)*

Zoltan wrote to Adrian Robinson, Secretary at the Ministry of Home Affairs, on 8 April 1949, saying that he had applied to the Home Office eighteen months before for permission to bring over his mother and sister, who was nearly sixty years old. The Home Office said it had no objection to the mother, but told him he could not bring over his sister as she was not a dependant. His mother, though, could not travel alone, since she was too elderly. A written note on the letter for A. J. Kelly at the Home Office in London, added: 'Dear Kelly, this bloody man makes to me the same proposition that had been turned down so recently. However, maybe things have eased up a little since?' Kelly replied: 'I am sorry you are being bothered a bit by Lewinter-Frankl.' The Frankl women could not come. Robinson wrote to Zoltan: 'I know these Home Office people well, and once they decide upon a policy of this kind, nothing on earth will shift them. So sorry.'

In a letter to Zoltan and Anny on 5 May 1950, Mrs Frankl and her daughter Irene said all the talk was of emigration. 'Any Jew who wishes can go to Palestine. Gold, silver, carpets, jewellery cannot be taken out, in a word everything valuable must be left behind and yet about eighty per cent of the Jews are going from here!' She thought about going to Palestine, then on to Northern Ireland, but one had to stay in Palestine for three to five years. Irene added that if they did go to Northern Ireland, the Frankls would have the burden of mother and her for the rest of their lives.

'The houses are being taken away again – I experienced that once in the Hitler era – but mine, up to the present, has not,' Regina wrote. 'How lovely it would be to be with you and to be able to share in the development of the children, but when and for whom do things in this life every go as one would like? God be with you, my dear ones.'

Zoltan continued to send food parcels to his mother and sister, but his mother died in January 1952. Finally, in November 1955 the Home Office relented and agreed to give Irene a visa if she could obtain an exit permit from the Romanian authorities. It was too late. Irene died in Romania. The Frankl-Lewinters had lost Anny's parents, Beila and Karl, murdered by the Nazis in Riga, Latvia, probably in January 1942, and tried for nine years and failed to get Zoltan's mother and sister out of Romania. They had created work for 850 workers during the war and employed many hundreds more later, but being a large employer and a 'de luxe British subject' was not enough to persuade the Home Office to allow in Zoltan's eighty-year-old widowed mother or his sister.

While that long saga dragged on, the Frankl-Lewinters built up the firm in Newtownards and Zoltan became a key figure in Northern Ireland's cultural life. 'The family got nothing out of Vienna,' recalled their daughter Vivienne Magee:

> The Nazis took their carpets, and everything they had. Everything was left behind, and they had to start from scratch. They used upturned wooden boxes as tables. My parents bought china at the market in Oxford Street in Belfast. Charlotte and Felicitas lived with them on Malone Road, and then lived in the house next door. Charlotte moved to London in 1950 and lived with Felicitas in Kensington Church Street. Felicitas played in concert halls such as the Wigmore Hall, and was a brilliant pianist.

Vivienne Magee remembered going to the Ards factory when she was nine. 'My parents had classical music playing in the factory so that employees could understand the quality of music. They had art on the walls, and beautiful furniture in the office, so the workers could appreciate beauty. Their door was always open. They were good employers.' Zoltan was a very close friend of the English painter Stanley Spencer, and many of the best Irish artists. 'Zoltan was a collector, not a dealer. Mummy sold the goods and Daddy bought the art. I think they were very grateful to Northern Ireland. They had such talent. They were always going to things, openings of exhibitions and so on. Mummy was very good as a speaker.'

Zoltan was the most significant private patron of modern painting in Northern Ireland throughout the 1940s and early 1950s when the Irish post-war movement developed. Among the artists he supported were Stanley Spencer, Gerard Dillon, Jack B. Yeats, Colin Middleton, Daniel O'Neill, Markey Robinson, George McCann, and the Ukrainian-born Paul Nietsche. Alice Berger Hammerschlag, a Jewish artist from Vienna, came to Northern Ireland in August 1938 and became a close friend of Charlotte Lewinter, Anny's sister. He also bought work by the next generation of painters, including Basil Blackshaw and T. P. Flanagan. Zoltan Frankl was organising exhibitions of the work of local artists as early as 1944, and his home became a salon for them. Vivienne Magee, surrounded by work by many of Ireland's greatest painters, recalled:

> I remember as a little girl coming down in my night dress sitting on the stairs, and the door was open to the kitchen, and listening to Paul Nietsche, the painter. He was sitting there, sometimes Stanley Spencer was there, and it was wonderful just listening to them. It must have been a very comfortable home for all artists because they were poor. They had no one to relate to. My father got on with all artists because at the end of the day they knew this man had an eye for making them money. Sometimes he would give an exhibition for them, and that was when they would sell to the public.

When the Council for the Encouragement of Music and the Arts, which would later become the Arts Council of Northern Ireland, organised its first tourist exhibition of Contemporary Ulster Paintings to be shown in Scotland in 1951, thirty-seven of the forty-one works in the show came from the Frankl collection.

Zoltan was also a close friend of the poet John Hewitt, who worked at the Belfast Museum and Art Gallery from 1930 to 1957, when he moved to Coventry to became Director of the Herbert Gallery after being passed over for promotion because of his socialist convictions. Vivienne Magee remembered Hewitt: "'Zoli, look at this painting, now that is something that might interest you,' Hewitt would say. And that is how the friendship began, and he would often go with my father and look at art and say, 'I think this one would be good.'"

Vivienne did sell one major painting from her collection. It was *The Whistle of the Jacket* by Jack B. Yeats, which went for £1,103,750 on 17 May 2001 at Christie's in London. It was bought by J. P. McManus, the billionaire Irish businessman. Today Vivienne's collection includes work by Stanley Spencer, Jack B. Yeats, Gerard Dillon, William Conor, Paul Henry, Colin Middleton, Daniel O'Neill, George Campbell, Felix Topolski and Paul Nietsche.

Zoltan died in 1961. Anny, Charlotte and Felicitas decided they could not keep on the factory and they sold it. In 1963, they opened two shops, Ulster Boutiques, in Belfast city centre. They prospered but when the Troubles started the shops were frequently badly damaged by IRA bombings. They finally decided to close down. Vivienne Magee recalled: 'As a child my parents never spoke to us about anything to do with the war. I remember one day, I must have been about eight or nine, I said to my father. "Why don't you tell us about your past?" He said: "No, we didn't ever want to because we don't want to upset you as a child, and it's better you don't know."'

Neither Zoltan nor Anny returned to Vienna, the city of Anny's 'happy, wonderful childhood', but after Zoltan's death in 1961, two of their daughters, Charlotte and Felicitas, did go back:

> They wanted to see again where they had lived, to find out more about their family. And it was so much of a stress for them. They were walking across a street and Charlotte took a stroke, and when Felicitas turned and called to her 'hurry up, come on', she was lying in the street. She didn't talk for about ten or eleven years before she died. She was taken to hospital in Vienna, then spent nearly a year at Hammersmith hospital.
>
> They never found the house where the family had lived in Vienna. They were very emotional people. My mother is rather like me. Her attitude was: 'It has happened. These things happen in life. Draw a blank over it. Look forward, never look back. It doesn't do you any good. To look backwards in life, it only makes you unhappy.' I can see that.
>
> Both had been engaged but the families of the men disapproved because they were Jewish and the engagements ended. Charlotte was engaged to a solicitor in Czechoslovakia. His family told him: 'No, you can't marry her, she is Jewish'. The same thing happened to Felicitas. She was very deeply in love with a conductor, a very handsome man.

Anny developed dementia and died in her home at 93 Malone Road, Belfast in 1999, aged ninety-one. Felicitas died in 1997, and Charlotte died in 2006. Vivienne Magee, daughter of Zoltan and Anny, summed up their philosophy:

> My parents' attitude to Northern Ireland was very positive, very thankful. But a lot of people have to thank them for giving them employment and for giving them beauty. How many people would do that nowadays? I find it such a privilege that people are still talking about the Lewinter-Frankls all these years later. I say to my children: 'Don't look backwards because it doesn't do any good in life. You have to look forwards and think, *'What can you do for people here?'*

22
'THERE'S CREAM IN
THE BOTTLE'

Once settled in Northern Ireland, Jewish refugee employers quickly set about building up businesses. When the war broke out, those who could turned their factories over to producing military clothing and equipment, including Kasriel Bloch's Ulster Laces factory in Portadown. During the war, the firm produced army regimental badges as well as guipure lace, using raw material imported on convoys from North America. This earned the firm hard currency, which allowed them to expand. George's uncle Jack Szajnik was a brilliant engineer who pioneered innovative production, and George's elder brother Richard was a dynamic leader.[1]

When the war ended, George studied engineering at Queen's University, Belfast, worked for a year with ICI in Scotland, and then returned to Portadown. The firm bought five Schiffli industrial embroidery machines in France, opened a second factory in the town, and in 1956 opened a third factory at Loughgall Road. They produced a 'very attractive lace' at high speed. The firm supplied lace trimmings to the ladies' underwear trade, but soon technical developments enabled this product to be developed cheaply in other parts of the United Kingdom and Europe. Ulster Laces switched to producing embroidered fabrics and sold them to other outlets, as well as making their own garments for sale.

They later developed a knitted crochet lace fabric and made it into cardigans. This was a great success and the Loughgall Road factory expanded three times, the family closing down the other two sites. At its peak in the late 1970s, it had 750 workers, making it one of the town's largest employers and producing more than one million garments a year, almost entirely for Marks and Spencer.

But in the early 1980s, Marks and Spencer began buying cheaper, hand-knitted products from the Far East, where labour costs were often a tenth or less of European ones. The Blochs could not compete and closed in 1984 after three years of difficult decisions, George remembered. 'It was the most traumatic period of my life. The human side, the relationships we had with our workforce, were very personal ... My brother Richard was one hell of a personality, a very competent, capable fellow. Richard had a nervous breakdown. Jack Shanik had a coronary.'[2]

Asked why Jewish immigrants prospered in Northern Ireland, George is wary of generalisations:

> It's like saying, 'Why did the Irish emigrants who went to America do so well?' You come to a strange environment, you don't have a background or support any more. People say Jewish people are very innovative and built up industries and do all sorts of things financially. People for some reason notice only that part of the Jewish community. It's like saying, 'there's cream in the bottle'. What about the milk down below, that huge percentage of the Jewish community who just eke out a living and find things as difficult as everybody else? Maybe historically it's because of Shakespeare [his portrayal of Shylock], and the resentment towards people who did well and weren't part of the indigenous community, that this has occurred. I don't think it is the case that Jews per se do well. And sometimes adversity spurs you on.[3]

George's experience of anti-Semitism in Poland on the eve of the Second World War proved extremely useful in handling one incident of sectarian bigotry in his Portadown factory. Around 1976, during one of the worst periods of the Troubles, a group of eleven Catholic women told the firm's personnel manager that they wanted to leave at the end of the week. Loyalists had 'got at them', and they just could no longer take it. George met them and described his boyhood experiences, where a group of older boys had assaulted him and stripped him in sub-zero temperatures on his way home from school. He told his mother he would never return, but she insisted he would: 'Whatever happens, you're going back to school today. Because if you don't, it will be impossible for the other Jewish boys in the school.' He told the women:

> That's my background. Now you know we don't ask questions, I don't know how many Catholics are working here, or Protestants. I haven't a clue. But if you leave, it's like loading a gun for somebody to fire again. So if I'm wrong and the working conditions are lousy, if the pay is lousy, if you're badly treated by management and so on, and you want to leave, I'd like to know about it. I'd like to correct it. But if it's what I suspect it is, I'd like you to think about it before you leave on Friday.[4]

The women changed their minds. 'I'm very glad they stayed. That's the only incident I can remember,' George said. In the small Jewish community in Northern Ireland, the Blochs were among the largest employers. George's second wife, Jacqui Herbert, was a daughter of Nathan Berwitz, the Belfast retailer who was a prime mover in setting up the Millisle farm. Berwitz owned several shops in Belfast, all of which were destroyed in the Luftwaffe blitz on the city in 1941. George was a close friend and a business associate of Billy and Ruth Kohner, whose parents, Franz and Edith, administered the farm. He believes any judgement of Stormont's action on refugees in 1938/39 should recognise that all governments were highly restrictive in their admissions policy:

> What people don't appreciate with today's open-door policies is that to get into Britain in those days, as a resident, money couldn't buy it. The Home Office controlled entry to the United Kingdom. You had to build up a big solid case with the Home Office and twist a few arms there in order to open the door for one or two people to come in. Before 1939, the immigration must have been in the single thousands. It was a different ball game altogether. I don't think the final decision rested with the Northern Ireland authorities.[5]

George Bloch lost all but three members of his extended family in the Holocaust.[6] His mother's brother Arek Szajnik travelled to Romania and sailed to France, where he joined the Polish Legion on the Maginot Line until it was overrun by the Germany army. He escaped to Switzerland, where he was interned for the rest of the war. Arek's wife Hala spent the war in the Warsaw Ghetto, lived through the Warsaw Uprising and was one of the tiny number of ghetto survivors liberated by the Russian army. Arek and Halina eventually settled in Northern Ireland. George's uncle Zamek Bloch served as a Jewish reserve cavalry officer in the Polish army. During the German invasion in 1939, a bomb killed a Polish officer close by. Zamek, fearing the Germans would kill him if he was captured with Jewish papers, took the dead man's identity papers and superimposed his own photo. He was taken as a prisoner of war to Germany and was liberated by the Russian army. His first wife and children perished in the Holocaust and Zamek migrated to Australia after the war, where he married. Another uncle of George Bloch, Henio, emigrated to Palestine with his wife Anka in 1934 and they had a large extended family. George's maternal grandfather, Hersch Szajnik, who had owned a successful textile business in Kalisz, Poland before the war, committed suicide in 1940.

George never returned to Danzig or eastern Europe: 'Why should I?' Like many Jewish immigrants, he felt he was well treated in Northern Ireland and did not personally encounter anti-Semitism. He died in January 2024, aged ninety-five.

While the Blochs built up their business in Portadown during the war, Franz Kohner and his wife Edith ran the Refugee Settlement Farm at Millilse until 1943. About 300 people, mostly under the age of seventeen, are believed to have passed through the farm between 1939 and 1948. Some Holocaust survivors also came to Millisle farm after the war and recuperated before moving on. Franz's mother Valerie Kohner wrote to her 'dearest ones' in the United Kingdom on 16 October 1941:

> From the first days of your lives, you were my happiness just as darling Edith has been since I first set eyes on her.

I re-read all your kind, lovely letters about the golden days of old, and those of Berterl and Putzerle and Dolf [Berta's husband], before putting them away. My heart ached so much when I did. Stay united, and stick together, then you'll be strong and no hardship will defeat you.

A thousand fond kisses to you all, and to my dear Kleiner [little ones] and Grösser [big ones]. I press you to my heart and am into all eternity your fervently loving, ever faithful Oma.[7]

Valerie Kohner wrote her last letter from a Prague holding centre to her relatives on the family farm at Bela in Czechoslovakia. In a postscript to it, she wrote: 'Perhaps I shall not see my golden children again. You know that my every thought has been of them and that I always prayed for their good fortune. I should be so happy if they could learn this from you. Tell them I do not cease to pray for them. All the best!'[8]

Franz Kohner learned of his mother Valerie's fate only after the war. Valerie Kohner was transported from the Masyryk railway station in Prague to Theresienstadt on 16 July 1942. She was deported to Treblinka on 22 October 1942 and murdered there.[9] Several of her relatives and friends were killed there too. In 1944, Franz and Rudi were still sending Red Cross food parcels to their mother in Theresienstadt, unaware that she had been killed two years before.

After leaving the farm, Franz first worked in a furniture shop owned by the Berwitz family in Belfast. He also studied for a law degree as an external student at the University of London, because his Czech qualifications were not recognised in the United Kingdom. Then he started making soft toys from ex-Army life-rafts, stuffing the toys full of kapok, a fibre filling. His daughter Ruth recalled:

He started with nothing, and made do with whatever he could get. I remember a little factory in Lower Donegall Street, in a two-up, two-down house. My mother was sewing then. Then he started to make clothes. He went to Harrods and sold them himself. He had no clothing background. Little by little he got things and gradually he made a success. Daddy started again three or four times and he made a success every time. He read and studied a lot. He had amazing ability. He was a very rare man. I'm just sorry more of my friends never met him because he was such a rare man, such a special man.[10]

His wife Edith had spent a year at a finishing school in Switzerland, had studied economics at Vienna University and had learned dressmaking and pattern-making skills, but she had never had a job and found herself needing clothes for her two children. From the United States her parents sent some pretty children's clothes. She soon found herself needing more.

Her son, Billy, said: 'My mother took them apart, copied them and made another set and people admired them. Gradually she set up a business in a house at 203 Clifton Street, with one sewing machine. They started making soft toys, but when she started making a few little dresses that people admired, then it became a business.'[11] In 1946 Franz founded Belart Ltd, which made children's clothes, at Northumberland Street, between the Falls and the Shankill roads. Billy remembered how the name came about:

My father was intensely proud of Belfast and what it had given him and done for him, and he decided to try to sell a few in Manchester to a firm called Kendal Milne, the Harrods of the North. But he was told by a buyer: 'Oh no, I won't see you, there's nothing of any quality comes out of Belfast, only shoddy stuff.' He was so incensed that at that point he determined he would only make the choicest, high-quality garments and he would combine the words 'Belfast' and 'artistic' into Belart. He got from Belfast Corporation permission to use the sea horse from its crest as the trade mark when we registered, and we used it all the way through.

He was very moved by the motto of Belfast, '*Pro Tanto Quid Retribuamus*' ['For so much, what shall we give back in return'], because they felt they had received so much from Belfast. They had received a lifeline, they had received a chance to be free. They wanted to give something back, to link the industrial endeavour with the name of Belfast and the emblem of Belfast. And they set about employing people on a very egalitarian basis. We had Catholic and Protestant working together and the rule in the business was there would be no emblems, there would be no demonstrations of any religious affiliation.

I always moved with equal ease through the Falls and the Shankill and I knew my staff very well and had been to their homes. Even in the worst of the Troubles within the business they were one family, one band. I had people who had lost brothers and husbands from shootings, one of my people had a brother who was inside for IRA activity. There were plenty of reasons for trouble, but within the firm they were like one solid band. The day the government said, 'You have to carry out a census to ensure your religious balance equates with your area,' my father refused for five years and the guys from the Department of Commerce begged him, 'Will you please fill in a form otherwise we are going to have to prosecute you.' And he said, 'I would not ask any of my employees their religion, that is their business,' because he had had enough experience of religious bigotry in central Europe and the destruction of a whole society.[12]

In August 1969 an Apprentice Boys march along Derry's walls sparked widespread rioting which developed into the Battle of the Bogside. The trouble spread to Belfast, and other towns, and the government mobilised the B Specials. 'Hundreds of houses were burned out, leaving thousands homeless, most of them Catholic. Ten people were killed and 154 suffered gunshot wounds before troops were deployed to replace police and B Specials in Belfast and Derry, to an initial Catholic welcome.'[13]

A number of Jewish families who had businesses straddling the religious divide in west Belfast were caught in the eye of the storm. The Kohner family's Belart Ltd factory had a floor across several buildings in the New Northern mill complex. Billy Kohner found himself in an extremely tense situation, and was the last to leave the factory:

They were ramming the gates at the entrance on the Falls as I left. I heard shooting flying over my head the night before, as I was on the roof, fire-watching. They had plenty of petrol bombs, I saw them carrying crates of petrol bombs. So I skipped out on the messenger boy's bike in the afternoon, because I didn't want a car about. 'Leave me the bike and I will get out through the side streets,' I told him. That night I saw the factory burn on television, and next morning we went in with hoses to try to contain the fire to prevent it spreading to another area. That entire building of the New Northern mill was destroyed in the blaze.

Billy, after completing a degree in economics at Queen's University, became managing director at the age of twenty-two and moved to a vacant site on Apollo Road in south Belfast. The factory doubled in size:

The fire was traumatic and terrible. But it gave us a huge opportunity. We were one of the early ones that were burnt out and the government was helpful and generous, and gave us grants and loans. We got a lot of support. That enabled the firm to grow and build.

I mean you think of Kristallnacht of course, but it wasn't anything like that. We weren't being attacked because we were Jewish. We were just in the wrong place at the wrong time. You have all those conflict lines between Falls and Shankill. The attack wasn't against us. We knew that. We were just unfortunate we were in that mill building. It was just an interface.

My father having suffered so much, this was the final straw and he only lived another year after that because it just wrecked him. He had lost everything, he had lost his profession, he had lost his home, he had lost his mother, he had lost his sister; then he had lost his first-born daughter Dinah, then he lost the firm he built up. It was just too much stress for a man to take, his heart gave out. He died aged seventy-two.

We expanded. We established export connections, bought another children's clothing company, took over as distributor of Levi's kids' jeans. My father was very much for building up the firm. Sister Ruth looked after the technical design and garment side, I looked after the business and sales side. Even though we disagreed strongly at times, it seemed to work.

At its peak under Billy Kohner, the firm employed 300 people, 180 in Newtownabbey and the rest in England, where they had staff in more than twenty retail outlets.

Once again, the family were in the eye of the storm, however. 'Some unsavoury individuals resettled in the area,' recalled Billy. 'There was one awful murder in a house at Longlands, which was subsequently knocked down. It was just outside our gates.' Billy helped found the Longlands Residents' Association, was its first chairman and tried to get a community centre for the area. As the Troubles intensified, Billy sensed polarisation growing among the Longlands residents:

> I could understand it, I could feel the threat they were under from the people who were coming across from the White City area and throwing stones. It was difficult at times to keep a feeling of common sense and harmony going in the premises … So the whole area just deteriorated and in the end we closed in 2001. We started to sell off the businesses in 1999. I made very few actually redundant, I gave them time to get other jobs. I sold the Belart brand to an English firm, and the retail business to another firm in England, which didn't work out. It ran down from 180 workers to 50 at the end.

Billy Kohner was philosophical about the sale of the family business, and delighted at his mother Edith's support: 'I remember when I drove down to tell her my decision to close the place, my mother, who had worked relentlessly to set it up, she was the technical brains behind it, she took it completely in her stride. She said, "Everything has its time. If you decide that's what you're doing that's fine with me." And she was wonderfully supportive. My sister and I ran it for thirty years.'

Since then Billy Kohner has rehabilitated small family terrace houses – he rented many to refugees from eastern Europe and north Africa, who could not find accommodation elsewhere.

Franz Kohner had a gift for friendship. Among his closest friends was RUC Inspector Bill Moffatt, who was in charge of the RUC Enemy Aliens Unit and highly sympathetic to the Jewish refugees. He later became RUC Deputy Inspector-General. Ruth remembered him with great affection: 'He was a lovely, lovely man. I think of him as Uncle Bill. He was the most quiet, big gentleman. But he knew then that there was trouble ahead … He had a big heart and a big soul and he was a wise man. He was wonderful.'

The Kohners lived off the Malone Road in leafy south Belfast and became close friends with Peggy Fink, née Loewenthal, who played a central role in the BCGR. Ruth recalled her warmly: 'Peggy was our closest friend. She told us stories about her work with Egon, her husband, with refugees in Europe after the wars … She was another amazing person. She worked incredibly hard for everybody. I visited her at Cambridge near her hundredth birthday.'

Ruth's mother, Edith, was a close friend of Helen Lewis, a Czech woman, and her second husband, Harry. Helen became one of Northern Ireland's greatest dance teachers and choreographers. She was from Trutnov in Czechoslovakia, and had attended university in Prague and married her first husband, Paul Hermann, a Czech Jew, in 1938.[14] They were deported to Theresienstadt in 1942 and in 1944 to Auschwitz, where they were separated. Helen survived two 'selections' by Dr Josef Mengele, but Paul Hermann died on a forced march in 1945, shortly before the war ended. Helen was transferred to Stutthof, a concentration camp in northern Poland. After the war, she returned to Prague, where she found out that her husband had died and that her mother had been deported to Sobibor in early 1942 and had perished there. In the summer of 1947, she married Harry Lewis, a Czech with British nationality, in Prague and that October they moved to Belfast. Helen wrote a memoir of her life, *A Time to Speak*, and gave interviews about her experiences. Harry Lewis became involved in the linen business. She became a very close friend of the artist Alice Berger Hammerschlag.

The Kohner family suffered another blow when Dinah Kohner, the first-born child of Franz and Edith, died at the age of twenty-eight. She had studied medicine at Queen's University and became an outstanding doctor. She died in Jamaica on 12 September 1964 from injuries received in an aeroplane crash in southern Ecuador. She had been working successfully there to combat the very high infant mortality rate.

While Ruth did not attend synagogue, she values greatly the Bible stories her father taught her:

> But they were explained to us and they were not meant to be taken 'as a Gospel'. My father taught me to understand that stories are meant to teach you about something as opposed to saying that they are the absolute truth ... I am so amazed that religion is spoiling ethics for people, and making them concentrate on the stupid laws instead of concentrating on the real ethics of it. I was brought up to understand that everybody has their own opinions and their laws and there are different religions, and I don't think anybody's is more right than anybody else's.[15]

She remembers one rabbi in particular who visited her mother when she was in a nursing home at the end of her life: 'She had Christmas cards and a little Menorah on the table. I was busy hanging up Christmas cards, but he took it all in his stride. He quite accepted the fact that we all did Christmas. Free thinking was the way we were brought up. I am happy with it.'[16]

Billy Kohner believes his parents' resilience in the face of tragedy was the key to their success and that of other Jewish immigrants:

> Mother came from a fairly lavish lifestyle. She adjusted instantly to live in a cow byre with an orange box for a table. She just made the best of it always. To her the glass was always half-full, never half-empty, although she went through the pain of losing aunts and uncles and many people. But she coped with loss and stress amazingly, she was an incredibly positive person. And she coped with my father, which wasn't easy, because he was quite emotional and tempestuous and depressive at times and manic at others. It wasn't easy living with him, but he was a kind of larger-than-life inspirational guy who lived always as he felt. She, I'm sure, was the one

who held the family together when everything was collapsing in the old country. She was practical to the core. In Belfast, she ran the books and the business.

He would go off and buy war surplus stuff and imagine what to make of it. He had great ideas and a salesman's gift of the gab, but when it came to running the business she was the one. She was always constructive to the very end. Even when she moved into a nursing home, she viewed it as an opportunity for a different lifestyle.[17]

Edith died aged ninety-five in 2007. 'She had been a widow longer than she was married, about thirty-five years,' says Billy. 'She coped amazingly well, she had a great spirit, so many of the people who came had it.' It was a quality that was vital to the success of Jewish refugees in Northern Ireland, he believes:

It's this enormous willingness to rebuild, to create, to generate a new business and industry, and then to be able to cope with the loss again of the business. My parents had so many losses in their lives and yet went on. I talk sometimes to school kids as part of Holocaust Memorial Day and I try to explain to them, there are two things that kept my parents and a probably a lot of the Jewish families going. One was education, the willingness to absorb other languages ... My father spoke several languages, studied philosophy and Irish history, and had this constant desire for education, to increase one's ability, as you never knew what turns up as good. My mother picked up pattern-making in finishing school, and suddenly produced a business which employed a lot of people.

That's one element. The other is in looking forward and not back. Because if all the Jews who came out of that horrendous situation had spent their lives curled up on the sofa bemoaning their losses, they would never have created what they did create. My parents didn't want to discuss those terrible days, like the day they found out my father's mother had been killed. When her last letter came, they knew what was happening. They didn't want to discuss that. They didn't want to touch on that.

They raised me in a manner that was to leave me unfettered by the past. Not every family behaves like that. Some are very steeped in the historic issues. My father sent me off to Belfast schools and kept me just like a local person. It was up to me if I wanted to go to church services with scouts or the school. We had to go to Sunday church service, so he asked me which one I wanted to go to and I picked Methodist as it was the closest walk to the school, and had a fairly uncomplicated service. That was fine and I joined in the morning prayers and services, all the rest of it and grew up having a very Northern Irish existence. That was a gift to me in a way, that was a gift to avoid if possible burdening me with the combination of the pain and the difference and the guilt and everything about the past that could be limiting or hampering. And I think that was the attitude of quite a lot of people coming over to regenerate. Because don't forget the Jews as a nation, as a people, have moved about and been expelled from so many places, when you look at Spain or middle Europe, I don't know whether it's engrained in their character, but they have the ability to restart and make the best of things.[18]

Many of the refugee families who came did not give up their faith, but, like the Kohners, were not strictly observant. The close friends the family made also helped them stay, Billy believes:

They stayed because they were open to making friendships with people they met on the farm. Billy Moffatt became incredibly close. He was like an uncle to me. I am called Billy after him. He gave my father lots of room to manoeuvre and move about. He was supportive and he was kind. More than that, my father and he had a kind of philosophical understanding that was more than mere friendship. It was a friendship that lasted until he died. It was quite significant.

Peggy Loewenthal was very close to me, was like an extra mother to me. My parents made friends with a local doctor in Millisle. They made friends with a lot of people and there was no valid reason for them to go anywhere else. My parents loved the Mournes … it was very like the Riesengebirge in the Sudetenland of Czechoslovakia. Our father rented a tiny cottage in the Mournes and then bought a house near Maggie's Leap. I sold it only in 2016, I couldn't part with it till then.

My father said the people here are enormously generous-spirited, welcoming and accommodating. The warmth and generosity of the Northern Ireland people as individuals is amazing. It is unfortunate what happens when they get into stereotyped political groups. Franz kept contact with two or three Millisle farm children, but almost all left to go to the USA, England and continental Europe. They were individual, anchorless people, they didn't have strength of a family, they may have subsequently discovered a relation elsewhere who may have survived. When they left the farm, they had learnt some farming, but had no overwhelming reason to stay.[19]

Billy was close to the late Walter Kammerling and his wife Herta, Kindertransport refugees from Vienna, and later visited the Millisle farm with Walter. His father's row there with Rabbi Shachter pushed him outside the community, he believes. 'My father felt incensed, I'm sure he felt humiliated. But it certainly set him apart.' He is friendly with a few older members of the Jewish community, but there are many he does not know. 'And my father used to say he felt closer to God in Tollamore Forest Park, Newcastle, County Down, in a wood looking at the grandeur of nature than he did in a shul or synagogue. It's possible to feel Jewish without being a practising Jew.'[20] While Billy doesn't know Jewish prayers, he has a sense of belonging to the Jewish tradition:

The Friday evening meal was always special. And my father would say a brief blessing. It was not formalised but recognised. My father felt at odds with the strict orthodox attitude of the Belfast community. Maybe that is another reason why a lot went away. There was such acceptance of Jews coming from middle Europe at the time of the war and such help from the Jewish community, there is no doubt that a huge amount was done. But I think my father felt as close to many of the people he met in just ordinary everyday life and I don't recall in my early days a hugely Jewish social life. I have Jewish friends, would know them socially. When I go to their houses, two-thirds of the guests are Jewish. My father was as likely to have his local postman as guest as anybody else. He had a totally egalitarian attitude, and maybe that was enormously helpful in those early post-war years.

The farm was an enormous opportunity for those stateless, orphaned individuals and for my family. So many came to the United Kingdom and were fostered by individual families. My father was a great devotee of the outdoors and physical exercise, and used to take them swimming on the beach in all weathers. I remember going in with him when I couldn't see the sea, because of the fog and the rain lashing down. But the farm gave an opportunity for outdoor life, for creative living, for food production, for being a cohesive bunch, for mutual support. Those were kids who could have been a complete catastrophe. You take somebody out of their homeland, out of their country, out of their school, their parents probably killed in the Holocaust, and you stick them in a foreign state, it sounds like a recipe for disaster, yet so many became successful and went on to do good things. So there must have been a great deal positive about that project.

The scheme was a shining light. But you have to remember that for the 10,000 who came to Britain, for every 1 child there were 99 who died in the gas chambers. So for the 10,000 it was a blessing, it was wonderful, it was our salvation, but there were so many more because it is estimated that roughly a million children were killed in the Holocaust.[21]

Some Jewish refugees from Vienna who arrived just before the Second World War to work for other exiles started their own businesses, which thrived. After working with the Utitzes at United Chrometanners in

Shrigley, Walter Weiniger set up a knitwear business, Jersella Limited, at Rydalmere Street, off the Donegall Road in Belfast. During the war, the factory made material for barrage balloons. In 1968 they moved to Lyle Hill, near Mallusk, on the northern outskirts of Belfast. At its peak it had about seventy workers, but at Lyle Hill it had only about ten or twenty, and it closed in the early 1970s.[22]

The Weinigers lived at Annadale Avenue, an affluent part of south Belfast, and Walter brought servants over from Vienna to run the house. When he retired, he bought a seventy-acre farm with a cottage at Lyle Hill. It had cattle, pigs and chickens, and he employed a man to run it. Richard Weiniger, who had been born in Belfast in 1940, the youngest child of Walter and his wife Mary Meyer, says his parents spoke German at home, and he became fluent when he was a child. He also went to Germany for a year to work in the clothing industry – six months in Hamburg and six months in Stuttgart. His parents spoke very little about their experiences in Vienna before the war:

> I'm not surprised. They must have gone through hell on earth. Father was a very quiet man. He left Vienna before Mother, then she flew out with her two children, Michael and Gina. My theory is that it must have been very unpleasant, quite horrifying. We used to go once a year to visit my grandfather and uncle, Salomon and Ernst, in Vienna. Ernst talked a little about what he had been through and showed his identity cards. His wife Grete was 'a hard nut'. She idolised him. She felt very grateful to him during the war. He was able to help her.
>
> Ernst was very well off, and quite nice. He used to bring drink and smoke with us in our apartment and Grete would get annoyed because she said he had a bad heart. He had a lot of health problems, including diabetes. He had a very nice lifestyle. A barber shaved him every day, a maid cleaned the house, and somebody looked after his meals. He was an antiques seller and interior designer. His home was full of antiques, and people would pay him to design and furnish their homes.[23]

On their trips to Vienna, Richard remembers two British soldiers boarding the airport bus and travelling through the Russian sector. 'It was quite nerve-racking,' he said. At home Walter was quiet and very strict. Children were not allowed to talk during meal times. 'We had to dress formally. Mother wore evening dress and father a dinner jacket. A maid served the food. That's the way they were brought up.' Richard got on well with his parents, and remembers them as being quite formal. Once when they were in Vienna, Walter told him, 'When you meet this lady, you have to kiss her hand.' When the firm closed, Walter sold part of the farm and moved back to Salzburg:

> He went back thinking it was 1938. There was something about Austria made him go back. He had to get it out of his system. He thought it was going to be the way it used to be. He said, 'they're as big crooks as ever!' Ernst also had an apartment in Salzburg. Walter wasn't happy there. He decided to come back. It was a pipe dream. The world had moved on.
>
> Walter didn't mix much in Northern Ireland. He felt a lot of people looked down on him, perhaps because of his Austrian background. One thing he did enjoy was hunting on horses. But people didn't go out of their way to make friends with him. He didn't feel he was accepted.[24]

Richard experienced some anti-German prejudice when he was at primary school. 'Some pupils would shout "Sieg Heil!" and make Nazi salutes. I just thought it was bloody stupid,' he said. At home, his mother Mary was twelve years younger than Walter and more outgoing. 'She was conscious of being illegitimate, though we only found that out later. Her father and mother were well off. She never had to work in her life.'[25]

Mary went to a posh finishing school, which Hedy Lamarr, the Viennese-born actor, had also attended. Though Mary had never worked, she came up with an innovative idea of producing knitwear out of the raw material, and looked after the 'making up' end of things. Michael ran the clothing-making section, and Gina was the designer. They had 'a very talented Polish technician, Ted Nabokowski', a former RAF airman, who looked after the knitting machines. He stayed with them for over thirty years.

Mary had been married to a Paul Brandl in Vienna when she was very young. But the marriage had failed, and Paul had gone to London. They were divorced and she married Walter in Vienna in a civil ceremony. It was only when Paul Brandl died in the late 1940s that the couple had a Catholic church blessing of the marriage. Walter became a Catholic convert after Mary died. 'He was deeply impressed by the Latin Mass' remembers Richard. Mary was raised in a Jewish environment; she was highly critical of the Catholic church in Austria, and would recall when Cardinal Innitzer, the Austrian primate, gave the 'Heil Hitler salute' on meeting the Führer during his triumphal visit to Vienna after the Anschluss in March 1938.

Richard visited the synagogue in Belfast when young but did not take part in services, though Walter's family had been observant Jews in Vienna. Mary Meyer had shares in London and Walter may have been able to access them when he arrived from Vienna in 1938. He also appears to have been able to move some of his family property out of Vienna before the Anschluss, and long after the war received restitution from the Austrian government for land confiscated by the Nazis.

In Northern Ireland, Mary became an alcoholic and died at the age of forty-two. Her son Richard believes the trauma of her own experiences and her consciousness of her illegitimacy contributed to her early death. Walter married Theresa Barrett, who had been a nanny to the children, four years after Mary died. It was a happy marriage:

> Theresa more or less brought me up. We all got on well with her. She did everything for me. My own mother was not physically affectionate, but Theresa was. Mary always said she hadn't a maternal instinct. Nanny, as we called Theresa, was great craic. She was good to us, very friendly. Walter and she would go to events and she was beautifully dressed. He could show her off.[26]

Theresa, a Dubliner, had also been married before, but had divorced and married Walter in a civil ceremony in 1959, which was followed in 1966 by a Catholic church solemnisation when Theresa's first husband died.

The family went skiing every year in Austria, and Michael and Gina were talented skiers. Once in the heavy winter of 1963, Walter skied from his Lylehill home to the firm at Mallusk, to the amazement of passers-by. Walter was visiting Ernst in Vienna once when the latter became seriously ill. He underwent an operation and had three-quarters of his stomach removed. After that he ate little and often. The illness was not uncommon among Viennese Holocaust survivors. Grete died in January 1971 and Ernst died in October 1978, of a heart attack at home in Vienna. Walter died suddenly the same way, in the family kitchen, in October 1984. Theresa died in August 1993.

Richard had four sons, and three became businessmen in the catering trade in Northern Ireland. David, one of his sons, asked his advice on a career, and Richard replied, 'Everybody has to eat,' which led David into the restaurant trade. One became a specialist in diabetic nursing. All worked in the family factory when they were young. 'They all had to earn money,' Richard says.

Like many refugee exiles, Paul Sochor's parents Zdenek and Eliska (Elizabeth) barely spoke about the family's grim experiences under the Nazis in Czechoslovakia. They concentrated on building up their textile printing works, employing both Catholics and Protestants. When the Troubles broke out in 1969, their factory was caught in the middle. It was only yards from Bombay Street, which was attacked and burned by loyalists on 15 August 1969. Fierce rioting and shooting followed. Paul remembered Catholic men coming to the factory and asking for cloth for bandages. Barricades were erected and he was not allowed to bring his car into the area, so he parked it at the nearby Royal Victoria Hospital and walked to work, past windows where an occasional curtain twitched as he passed, a local checking out the pedestrian. He had to negotiate the passage of essential deliveries of dye into the factory with the British army and at times the local IRA.

On another occasion an IRA gang, dressed as priests, robbed the Munster and Leinster Bank on the Falls Road, where he was a customer. The bank closed a short time later and moved its operation to a Belfast city centre branch. (Once Paul noticed that one of his former employees, not long released from internment, was working as a security man at the bank.) The local nationalist MP for West Belfast, Gerry Fitt, sometimes met Paul, encouraging the family to keep the factory open despite the Troubles.[27]

One of his cousins, Blanka Suehiro, came to Belfast from communist-controlled Czechoslovakia in 1969 to study at Belfast's art college. She stayed with him, his wife Jenny and daughter Mandy in their Malone Road home. In 1972 she was badly injured in a Provisional IRA bomb attack in Donegall Street which killed seven people. She had been walking down the street to collect materials for a project she was working on when there was a security alert. In the confusion that followed, Ms Suehiro and others unwittingly ran towards the bomb. She suffered severe leg injuries and surgeons at one stage considered amputation, but Jenny pleaded with them to consider different treatment. In the following year, doctors managed to save her legs using pioneering skin-grafting techniques. She left Northern Ireland for Canada in 1975 but never forgot the British soldier who gave her first aid immediately after the explosion. In the summer of 2019, she got a message to the former member of the Parachute regiment, forty-seven years after the blast which almost killed her, to thank him for helping her.

Paul Sochor moved to premises at Whitehouse, north of Belfast, and brought some of his 'excellent' workers from Waterford Street. But the factory was set on fire, destroying the vital recipes used in dyeing cloth. He got the factory going again, and it thrived so that he eventually moved to bigger premises at Dunmurry, south of Belfast. He sought business north and south of the border. On one occasion he obtained an order from a firm at Balbriggan, County Dublin, owned by a friend, Charles Gallen. There was a condition. It was for an Irish tricolour tea towel, which had a healthy market in the Republic of Ireland, but was not much in demand in Northern Ireland, least of all during the Troubles. 'If you print the tricolour tea-towel up in Dunmurry for us, you're in.' It was the start of a beautiful friendship.

Another customer from the Republic of Ireland presented them with a major order. Dunnes Stores contracted for 30,000 papal flags in advance of Pope John Paul II's visit to Ireland in 1979. The Sochors bought cotton cloth from Lancashire and made the flags, which only needed to be hemmed. The firm which usually did the hemming agreed to do the work. A lorry delivered them to the factory, which was in the heart of the loyalist Shankill road. Next morning Paul took a phone call from the owner. 'Get these flags out of this place quick, because we've been told that if we start hemming them, we're going to get burned down,' the owner said. Paul had the flags brought back to Dunmurry. He knew one other firm which did hemming. It was in the heart of the loyalist Newtownards Road. He explained his problem to the owner. 'Paul, the only thing you can do is, when it's dark tonight or tomorrow night, bring them up to me. I've arranged for two or three girls to take them home, and hem them in their kitchens.' Paul delivered them and they were taken home by the stitchers. While one of the women was hemming the papal flags in the kitchen, there was a knock on the front door. She opened up to a man who said to her: 'I'm here collecting signatures to "Keep the Pope Out". Will you please sign this for me?' She did and went back to hemming the papal flags. The 30,000 flags were finished, and proved extremely popular. 'We could have made an absolute fortune because people were coming to the factory when they heard we were making the flags. They had bundles of notes and said, "We will take whatever you have, and there's the money." We could have done a hundred thousand of them.'

Paul Sochor said there were no sectarian troubles among the workforce. 'We had no problem over what we did in the factory, because we never discussed religion. We couldn't be bothered'. His firm had extensive contracts with companies in the Czech Republic. Men's suits were made there and sold on to retail outlets by the Sochor firm. At one point, they were importing 4,500 suits a week for sale in the United Kingdom. Once, two Czech workers parked their lorry packed with suits for the night near the M1 in west Belfast. Next morning, they found that the local IRA had broken into the lorry and stolen 400 suits, which were sold on in Manchester.

Paul found out later that some of his staff used unorthodox sales methods. The factory stocked 'seconds' and certain customers would offer bundles of money for them to two male members of staff, then leave when the deal was agreed. 'Half an hour later there would be a phone call to one of these two guys, saying "We're down at the Grand Central Hotel and the girls are here now, so come on down." They had dancing girls in the room. Sometimes my father would give the men money for their work trips to England, because we did a lot of dress materials for English customers, who were nearly all Jewish. They had their expenses used before they had left Belfast. It was unbelievable what used to happen.' The staff were highly talented, and he brought some to Czech factories to train their workers in textile printing. Like many clothing firms in Northern Ireland, the Czech factories Paul did business with have now closed, casualties of Chinese domination of the market. The Sochor factory has now closed too, but Paul continued to work as an import agent into his nineties. The family lost everything in Czechoslovakia, first to the Nazis, and later to the Communist authorities. The factory in Dvur Kralove was demolished but the striking modernist Sochor family home is now a school and a listed building. Despite concerted attempts, the family have never received a penny in compensation for the loss of their Czech business or home.

Another Czech family, Jan Pick, his wife Elizabeth and their two-year-old son Hubert, who had a factory close to the Sochors in Dvur Kralove, also managed to escape from Czechoslovakia to the UK after the German occupation in March 1939. Jan joined the RAF in 1940, becoming an officer/photographer.[28] According to Paul Sochor, whose family were probably their initial contacts, the Picks travelled to Northern Ireland after the war and went first to Enniskillen, County Fermanagh in the hope of setting up a workshop there. But when they arrived they were told that Jewish people weren't wanted, so they headed back on the bus for Belfast and stopped at the Valley Hotel in Fivemiletown, a County Tyrone village sixteen miles from Enniskillen. They asked if they could stay, and were told, 'You're very welcome here and we will give you a room and you can put two or three sewing machines in to get you started.' The company started a stitching business and worked closely with the Bloch company, Ulster Laces, supplying Marks and Spencer. At one stage, they employed upwards of 100 people. When Zdenek and Eliska Sochor retired to a flat on Lake Geneva, the Picks flew to visit them, and kept the trip a secret from them. But Jan collapsed and died on an escalator on arrival at Geneva airport. Elizabeth rented a flat near the Sochors, while Hubert first emigrated to France and then the USA.

The Sochors sold their Newtownards factory to the Mladic family. A son, Zdenek Mladic, took over the running of the family firm, and when the Czechs invented a new loom which wove cloth three times faster than Western machines, he told them that he had contacts throughout the world and managed to win the agency a contract to sell them outside Czechoslovakia. 'He made a million pounds in eighteen months,' said Paul Sochor. 'He did very well.' When Zdenek Mladic died, a choir was flown in from Prague to sing at his funeral in the Jesuit church at Farm Street, London. The Crepe Weavers factory is, like many of the premises where the Czech exiles started their business, now demolished.

Paul Sochor and his wife Jenny were invited to the Czech Republic as guests of honour at the centenary celebration for the company his family had set up. Nationalised by the Communist regime, it was now known as Tiba. A female Czech TV reporter asked him in Czech one question in front of 300 workers, 'What do you think of Czech women?' Paul replied: 'When I first came here in 1990, they were all drab, their clothes were terrible, they had terrible make-up and they never smiled. I stopped for a moment, then said, "and now they are all lovely". Everybody got up and applauded.' The Czech government also presented him with a posthumous medal, the Czechoslovak Military Cross, in honour of his Uncle Pavel's bravery. It is one of the family's most prized possessions.[29]

One young Polish Jew who came to Belfast in the wave of eastern European immigration in the early twentieth century founded a family business in Belfast which created significant employment for a century.

Isaac Schwartz was born in the city of Kraznystaw, in the Lublin area of eastern Poland, 'the great centre of Judaism in the Diaspora'. Aged eighteen, he travelled from Warsaw via Hamburg to Hull with little money, a few clothes and a lot of hope. Before he was allowed entry, he had to prove he was not destitute by showing that he had five pounds in cash. He couldn't and had to return to Hamburg. He was helped by a charity which gave him the five pounds travelling expenses and a new suit. He landed in Liverpool but, with few prospects, he decided to head to Belfast, which was booming because of the growth of the shipbuilding, engineering and linen industries.

At first he worked as a pedlar. He married and tried to convince his new wife Sarah to return with him to Liverpool. She tried to dissuade him, but he went to Liverpool himself. He did not prosper there and returned to Belfast.[30]

He opened a second-hand furniture business, and soon branched out into retail, opening stores in Sandy Row, Belfast, east Belfast and Carrickfergus, trading under the name of Black and Sons. The business thrived, and he also set up an agency for pianos and ran a musical instrument business, Crymble's, which became a household name in the city. He brought his parents, brothers and sisters to Belfast, but all except one brother went to America. After the Anschluss in March 1938 he succeeded in organising the emigration of his wife Sarah's extended family from Austria.

Isaac was a lifelong supporter of a Jewish homeland, and had been a regular visitor to Palestine since 1925. On one occasion, Leib Jaffe, a member of the Keren-Hayesod (United Israel Appeal), a support organisation for Jewish causes, visited Belfast and appealed for an immediate £500, which the local Jewish community could later collect from its members. Isaac Black gave him a cheque for the amount of money. He became the major benefactor for a Jewish settlement at Kfar Hasidim, which had a large number of Polish Jewish settlers, and financed the completion of a Mikveh, or ritual bath. A plaque on the wall of the building commemorates the 'rabbinical and orthodox Isaac Black, from Belfast, England [sic], 1932'.

In 1930 he bought land and planted it to grow oranges and grapefruit. Isaac continued to visit Palestine even after war broke out in 1939, leaving it for the last time on 2 May 1940. In 1947 he visited his parents and siblings in the United States, whom he had not seen in forty years. He fell ill with chronic asthma and, after two months in a convalescent home, died there.

Two of his sons, Robert and Louis, bought a furniture firm, Gilpin's, and traded under that name. The brothers opened several stores and in the 1960s employed upwards of 100 staff. Louis Black died in 1964 and Robert in 1980. Their younger brother, Michael, current president of the Jewish community in Belfast, entered the firm in 1971, just as the Troubles were worsening.

The family business, Gilpin's, had its premises bombed four times by the IRA in the 1970s and a member of staff was killed in a loyalist feud. Michael Green, a dispatch manager aged forty-two, was shot as he arrived for work at the Gilpin's Furniture store on Sandy Row on 15 August 2005. Green, a father of three, who lived at Ballysillan Avenue, Belfast, was shot at close range by a gunman on a stolen motorcycle as he got off his motorbike outside the shop. Green's family strongly denied that he had any paramilitary links. The Loyalist Volunteer Force (LVF) blamed the Ulster Volunteer Force (UVF) for the killing, but an LVF source denied that Mr Green was one of its members. Three other men died in the feud between the loyalist paramilitary groupings.

Michael Black has vivid memories of the IRA bombing attacks on the family furniture shops in the mid-1970s:

> Two men, one armed with a handgun, the other carrying a bomb, held up the Sandy Row premises. My brother Tony approached them, and the IRA man priming the bomb told his gunman accomplice, 'Shoot him, if he gets any closer.' He didn't get any closer. So we cleared the building, and then it blew up. That was a big bomb and did a lot of damage. Nobody was hurt. On other occasions incendiary devices were left. They used to come in with a cassette device and slip it down the back of a sofa. We lost contents, but were able to put the places back together again. We had a place on the Woodstock Road in east Belfast and that was badly burned. Once we had a device left in our Carrickfergus shop. A woman brought in a pram, but the device was spotted. The police were alerted and the woman arrested. That was in the early 80s.[31]

On another occasion the IRA left a bomb at Crymble's music shop, which was then in Dublin Road, in the ground floor of a building owned by the Orange Order:

> The police told us we were a ticking time bomb, so to speak. We put in panic buttons and so on, but the day came when the IRA came in with a bomb. The staff panicked and ran out.

The police stopped traffic on the street and a policeman came up past the shop. The secretary of the Grand Orange Lodge of Ireland, wondering why it had all gone quiet, looked out of an upstairs window and asked what was going on. The policeman shouted up he was sitting on top of a bomb, literally. Minutes went by before the secretary appeared. He had taken the time to screw a painting of King William of Orange on his horse off the wall, and was walking up the street with it under his arm when the building blew up. He was a bit lucky.[32]

Jewish refugees from Vienna who set up businesses in Northern Ireland enjoyed a good reputation as fair employers who recruited solely on grounds of merit, not religious or political affiliation. In general, they avoided partisan political activity and their commitment to progressive work practices also helped earn them a good name.

23

'SO LUCKY YOU WERE BORN JEWISH'

The Jewish community in Northern Ireland knew from bitter personal experience what a victory for Nazism would mean. After war was declared, several members of the community joined the British armed forces. Those too young to join vividly recalled the apprehension they felt. Ronnie Appleton, who became Chief Crown Prosecutor during the Troubles, and was later president of the Belfast Jewish community for twenty-five years, retiring at the age of ninety, was a teenager and expected the German bombers to come over the next day.

Most of his friends were Protestant, as he went to a voluntary grammar school, but he also had Catholic pals. He joined the Air Training Corps at Belfast High School – Spitfire pilots were his idols. When the war ended, he was recording secretary to the community and joined its debating society. He was seventeen when he made an impassioned speech about the Holocaust at the Jewish Institute: 'It was about how terrible it was and how we must always remember. I talked about it whenever I got a chance to make it public. People in Northern Ireland did not want to believe it.'[1]

Later, on a visit to Israel, Ronnie met Shoshana Schmidt, whose parents had left Vienna for Palestine in the late 1930s. Her father was from Poland and her mother, Ruth Cohen, from Vienna. Her father didn't want his children to be called 'dirty Jews', she recalled:

> They were pioneers. They came to Israel to help build the country. They never saw their families again. They didn't know they would never see their families again. I couldn't

ask my parents what happened. I had no grandparents. My mother would start to cry. It was a taboo subject. For many years most people didn't talk about it. Even couples did not know that their partners had families killed in the Holocaust. It was too horrible. After fifty years suddenly it was like you opened the flood gates, now everybody has a story, and it's all coming out. Holocaust Memorial Trust events helped. Once people started talking about it, they couldn't stop. I never really spoke about it to my parents.[2]

Four of the Cohen children survived: Ruth, Shoshana's mother, her younger sister Hannah, her brother Paul, a graphic artist, and Jonas, who became a pilot in the Israeli air force and was killed in the war which marked the establishment of Israel in 1948. Shoshana and Ronnie settled in Belfast, and one of their daughters, Talia, went to an Ulster grammar school and had a strictly evangelical religious education teacher. She was the only Jewish girl in the school; one best friend was Catholic and one was Protestant:

The religion teacher was dreadful. 'Unless you are a born-again Christian, you're going to Hell,' he said. I remember Ronnie and I going up to him and saying to him. 'Look, teach them comparative religion, but don't tell them that their religion is wrong.' Once he said: 'You Jews don't even eat with non-Jews, you eat with the rats from the sewer.' The class erupted, because the week before was our daughter Talia's birthday and I had a dinner party for all her friends and they said, 'We all ate in Talia's house.' He would come out with dreadful things. Luckily, we had just one child there.[3]

But, overall, the family had very good experiences in Northern Ireland and encountered no other expressions of anti-Semitism. Shoshana was for more than twenty years joint co-chair of the local Council of Christians and Jews. People even came up to her and said: 'Oh, you're so lucky you were born Jewish.' 'I look at them and think, *How can you say that to me!*'[4]

Shoshana's maternal grandmother, Rosalie Streicher, and her husband, Josef Cohn, wrote to their children, pleading with them to get them out of Vienna. Shoshana's mother, Ruth Schmidt, had obtained visas and tickets for her parents at the last hour but it was to no avail. Rosalie's last letter finished: 'It's too late anyway, they're coming for us.' Shoshana's grandfather, Josef Cohn, had been a rabbi to Emperor Franz Joseph; he was very learned and highly regarded. 'I'll consult my Rabbi,' he used to say. Shoshana's parents didn't know what happened to their own parents until after the war.

Shoshana vividly recalled one particular incident: 'I remember children were calling their grandmothers "Granny", and I said to my mother, "Do you mind if for a while I call you 'Granny'" because I missed not having grandparents, and she said: "Never, ever, ask me that again."'[5] Two aunts and an uncle of Shoshana's mother did not survive.

In Northern Ireland, where Ronnie and Shoshana settled, there were occasional tensions between the learned but very strict Rabbi Jacob Shachter and some of the more cosmopolitan and less orthodox migrants who came, recalls Shoshana:

> Rabbi Shachter felt that Franz and Edith Kohner weren't observant enough. Not only that, a lot of Jewish families here were alienated because this community was big and if they weren't strict or if there was intermarriage outside the Jewish faith, they were sort of sidelined and regrettably we lost a lot of them and their children. The Jewish community was very strict in those days but those who came from Germany, and other places such as Vienna were not, including the Kohners, and they didn't get on with the Rabbi. He was strict, and aloof. He was very highly respected but not liked by some. He fell out with Franz Kohner. Franz was doing things on the farm on the Sabbath which Rabbi Shachter felt he should not have been, and the Rabbi more or less told him.[6]

Shachter was one of three rabbis, including the Chief Rabbi of Tel Aviv, who officiated at Shoshana and Ronnie's wedding. Ronnie phoned Shachter after the Chief Rabbi of Tel Aviv was booked and asked him if he would assist. 'Assist? I will marry you!' He said he knew Ronnie before he was born. Shoshana jokes: 'A marriage with three Rabbis. That's why our marriage has lasted fifty-six years!'[7]

Ronnie said Jews in Northern Ireland had generally an excellent relationship with the Christian community. There was no pogrom, as there had been in Limerick in 1904 and in parts of England. He experienced no anti-Semitism at school in Belfast. Jews simply left the class during religion instruction and went to Hebrew school at another time.

Ronnie is proud of the contribution the Jewish refugees made to life in Northern Ireland: 'So many of the children of refugees made their names and did wonderful things for Britain. Those people who came here started factories and made a big contribution to the commercial life of Northern Ireland by giving employment to lots of people. We always got on well and I don't remember any anti-Semitism.'[8] Shoshana believes she knows why:

> I think a lot of it has to do with the fact that there was no Jewish school here. Ronnie went to school with Protestants and some of his Jewish friends went to Catholic schools, and they all intermingled ... If there had been a Jewish school the Catholics and Protestants would not have met Jews and so would have thought, *I wonder what they're teaching them behind those walls.* I think that is the different thing about Northern Ireland, that there was no Jewish school, whereas in a lot of places in England there was. There were no ghettos here.

The Jewish population of Northern Ireland was around 1,500 in the 1960s, but declined inexorably after that. Many Jewish students used to go to Queen's University, Belfast, but started going to other places in the United Kingdom, then marrying and staying away. The Troubles also caused people to leave. Local Jews went to places where there were bigger Jewish communities, such as London and Manchester. Smaller communities got smaller. Today the community in Belfast numbers 59, with 439 people in Northern Ireland who identify as Jewish.[9]

Could Northern Ireland and the United Kingdom have let more Jews in before and during the war? The Appletons are adamant that they should have done so:

> The whole world should have allowed more people in. They had a conference at Evian of the countries of the world and decided they weren't letting people in. If there had been an Israel in those days, the Jews could have been saved from Germany and Europe. The world was to blame for not allowing the Jewish people out. The British stopped ships landing at Haifa. Some people were sent right back to Germany, others to camps in Cyprus.[10]

Around 730 names are mentioned in the 300 or so letters from Jewish refugees to the Ministry of Commerce from 1938 to 1940, almost all from Vienna, with a few from Hungary, Czechoslovakia, France, Germany and Switzerland. A small number of the letters, from applicants deemed most suitable, led to correspondence with the ministry, usually about conditions of entry and available assistance. It is impossible to say exactly how many applicants were admitted under the New Industries (Development) Scheme. The ministry files do not give a figure, but the total was probably 100–150. A few who had been granted visas did not come, either because they went to other places, or were unable to emigrate owing to Nazi obstruction. Alfred Neumann claimed to have brought seventy Jews from Vienna to Northern Ireland. His brother Julius claimed that Alfred had rescued forty as well as another fifty-five taken elsewhere in the United Kingdom.

The majority of refugees admitted under the scheme came to Belfast and Derry. Some individuals and couples were admitted outside the New Industries Scheme, usually with the assistance of the Belfast Jewish community and of the refugee support groups in both cities. It was difficult to get into Northern Ireland without local backing. About 300 people, mainly children and teenagers, and also including some Holocaust survivors after the war, went to the Refugee Settlement Farm at Millisle.

‘So lucky you were born Jewish’

In November 1942, the last meeting of Youth Aliyah, the Zionist Youth Movement, was held in the city. Martin Vögel, the leader of its Viennese groups, described the plight of Austrian Jewry:

> We are living through a most grievous and severe destiny; humiliation of the worst kind, arrests, forced evacuations, suicides, loss of all that has been gathered together by the work of man through generations, separations from our dearest relatives, news of the death of far-off friends and relatives, without being able to assist them, without having an idea of how it all happened ...[11]

Vienna's Jews, even with exit visas, were at serious risk until they got out of Austria. Some obtained visas but were unable to emigrate, while others made it to then unoccupied countries such as France but were later captured and sent to the gas chambers. Historian Herbert Rosenkranz wrote:

> From October 20, 1939 to September 1, 1944, 71 transports of 15,344 men and 28,077 women, 43,421 in all, had been deported to Nisko, Opole, Kielce, Modliborzyce, Lagow-Apatow, Lódz, Riga, Minsk, Izbica, Wlodawa, Theresienstadt and Auschwitz. Only 1,747 of the deportees survived to return to Vienna.
>
> A further 17,779 Austrian Jewish emigrants in 15 Nazi-occupied European countries (not including those parts of the countries occupied by the Nazis, countries allied to them or the camps in the Far East) were also killed by the Nazis. To them must be added those who died of hunger and illness in Austria, making a total of one-third of Austria's Jewish population killed during the seven years of the Nazi regime in the 'Ostmark'.[12]

At least 125 of those who applied to come to Northern Ireland via the New Industries Scheme and were rejected were murdered by the Nazis. These were applicants and often their dependents, and included single men and women, parents with children, extended family groups, and many grandparents. Most had no previous connection with Northern Ireland, though a few sought to join relatives already in the North. The majority of the murdered are named in the letters, but the identities of others unnamed, almost all relatives, have been established because they appear along with the applicants in the DÖW in Vienna. These can be established by comparing family names, shared addresses and dates of birth. The greatest sources of information are the passenger lists of those deported to the Nazi extermination centres of eastern Europe. These reveal the final journeys and shared fates of the rejected and their loved ones.

24
PILGRIMAGE OF MEMORY

The children of Holocaust survivors in Northern Ireland must live with the crimes and trauma inflicted on their families. Their parents often were unwilling to speak in detail about what had happened to their closest relatives in Vienna, many of whom the Nazis had murdered. Their children often continue the quest to add to the few details they have learned. Vienna, a city where their families were persecuted and from where so many were sent to their deaths, is for some a place of searching. Their yearning to find out more is also a declaration of resistance against the oblivion to which the Nazis sought to assign their loved ones.

Charlie Warmington is one of those who has returned to Vienna, and feels compelled to find out more. He first visited it in the 1960s with his mother Gertrude, father Theo and brother Alan. When they started to go to Vienna, Gertrude was still carrying the trauma and anger over what the Nazis had done to her father, Leopold, and her relatives when she was a teenager. But a chance encounter on holiday set her on a journey which helped her come to terms with the grief and rage she felt. The Warmingtons were in Kilkee, County Clare in 1967 and were strolling along the promenade when Gertrude heard a middle-aged couple speaking German. She introduced herself and Charlie, and talked about her family background in Vienna. It turned out that the man, Fritz Schöll, had been a conscripted German soldier posted to Vienna during the war, and was holidaying in the area with his wife Irmgard. They shook hands, Charlie recalled:

That handshake, that look in his eye, I just can't find the
words to describe. He looked at me and it didn't last, it was
only a few seconds, but it was a most unusual situation.
He must have known a good deal of Mum's story by then,
and all I knew was he had been a German soldier. Maybe
I was imagining it, it was just that look in his eye, it was
sadness. It was phenomenal. It brought to mind those lines
of Wordsworth from the poem 'Intimations of Immortality':
'Thoughts that do often lie too deep for tears.'[1]

When she met Fritz, Gertrude was still furious about the German
takeover of her home country nearly thirty years before. Charlie
remembered her pointing to a change the Nazi authorities had made
to Austria's name on a school report she received:

The address had been changed from Wien Österreich to
Wien Deutschland in 1938. Mum got really het up again
and said, 'How dare they write that on my report. That
was in Vienna, in Austria! My Austria!' When I met Fritz,
I remember thinking, 'This man could have wiped out the
Kesslers and I would never have been born. But here he is
being introduced to the son.' Fritz told me that Jewish people
called on his parents, who gave them food, and asked the Jews
for something in return. This was in Germany, and it could
have been before the war. I sense this was qualified sympathy.
His father didn't take them in. Good God, it was more than
his life was worth, I suppose.[2]

Gertrude now had to confront a most difficult decision. She had
refused to teach German to Charlie and had told him: 'I hated the
Germans.' She had even told him she would kill if she could:

Mum said it was one of the most difficult things she had ever
done. She said: 'You have to forgive. I had so much hatred in
my heart, I had to get rid of it. As a Christian, I have to love
Fritz.' It was sort of bitter sweet. It seems that from what Mum
told me, that they probably knew that Fritz was sympathetic.

He claimed he never knew about the concentration camps. I believed him. He was a lovely, lovely man, quite a devout Christian, but not madly evangelical.

All I saw was huge friendship, very unusual friendship. This friendship between Mum and Fritz and Irmgard and my father was powered by this whole story. My parents were regular visitors to Fritz and Irmgard in Germany. They toured Ireland and Germany together.

On a hot sunny afternoon on 25 June 2019, the author accompanied Charlie and his friend Franziska Meinhardt to his family's old home at Streffleurgasse 4, in the Brigittenau district of Vienna. He had come to honour the memory of his murdered grandfather Leopold Kessler, and his grandmother Ernestine, née Schrekinger, who miraculously survived deportation to Poland. He was among a small group of relatives who had made the journey to attend the unveiling of a number of memorial plaques to Holocaust victims at their former homes in Vienna. The event had been organised by the Stones of Remembrance organisation (Verein Steine der Erinnerung).

Charlie told the small group of relatives he was just learning to cope with the story of his mother, Gertrude Kessler, a Kindertransport refugee who came to Northern Ireland in 1938. He had been to Vienna a few times, but he knew very little of her story. The last time he had been to that spot was in the late 1980s when he brought her back to the flat. They went inside the building, and Gertrude began to cry. No one was in the flat that the family had been forced out of fifty years before, so they left. Outside Gertrude pointed to the spot where her father had gathered all the possessions in a little cart before heading off to the Jewish ghetto:

And I said, 'take me to the ghetto', and she started crying again and I said, 'point in the direction of the ghetto' and she couldn't even point, she couldn't give any directions. A common story, I'm sure, but coming from Northern Ireland with my mother and knowing so little, it really has overtaken my life. In the previous couple of weeks before that visit, there had been an anniversary of the Wall Street crash and to explain what it was like in the ghetto, she said, 'Charlie, do you remember the story you did last week, about people jumping out of windows?' And she said, 'Well, in the ghetto where we were all playing in the street, when the Gestapo came, the parents more than occasionally jumped out of the window, rather than be taken away.'

There is a host more stories I could talk about. Mum and I had an unwritten agreement: even though I was a journalist, I wouldn't really push it – I tried, but we came to an agreement. I had enough to fill a column, about a thousand words, which I did many times over, but it was the same story. But then I met Franziska Meinhardt in Scotland, we were both working on a story, and it was Franziska who told me, three or four years ago, about the Stones of Remembrance.

And you'll never understand what it was like to say you're a friend of the Kesslers, because Mum never said a word. I met my Granny, I came over here, we had a lovely time, many times. I never knew anything, I never even thought to ask about Leopold. There is a photograph in the house, I didn't even see a photograph of Leopold until a Jewish friend in Belfast sent me a photocopy of his picture in Yad Vashem [the World Holocaust Remembrance Centre]. My mother had gone over in 1996 to leave his picture and his details in, but hadn't told me. I got the picture sent to me by email.

One day she did say that my grandfather was called Leopold. Something woke up; I had the name to go on. My mother died three years ago next month, and maybe next time, I'll be able to tell you Leopold's story properly because I certainly don't want to go to my grave like my mum did, without knowing anything or, if she did, she certainly didn't tell me.[3]

Charlie thanked the organisers and the Documentation Archive of Austrian Resistance, and the little group who stood in the hot Vienna sunshine listening to his family story:

I'm just so proud to be part of this wonderful family. I love Vienna, I've loved it ever since I came here in the sixties, but I didn't know this side of our story. Every one of you are so close to me and I didn't even know you existed. I didn't honestly know I would make it today. This has been too emotional, and I thought I wasn't going to get over it. Thank you so much and I'm sorry I have rambled on. In Ireland we would say '*Sláinte*' but I guess in these circumstances I have to say '*Shalom*'.[4]

As the group listened to other speeches, Charlie returned once again to the flat where he had taken his mother more than thirty years before. He rapped on the door but again no one was in. He returned to the sunny street, and exchanged stories with other relatives about their families. They talked about discovering precious details about their loved ones, about survival, and about the lives the families had led abroad in England, the United States and Northern Ireland. The Brigittenau district had been a thriving area with a significant Jewish population until 1938, when they were evicted from their homes, and moved to the Leopoldstadt ghetto district. Now in several districts in Vienna, the beautiful metal plates on the pavement and the walls recall the fate of hundreds of the 65,000 Viennese Jews murdered in the Holocaust. Relatives paused in silent homage at the memorials to their loved ones, who lived in these houses before they were evicted and deported to their deaths.

EPILOGUE

It is eighty-six years since several hundred Viennese Jews tried to escape Nazi persecution by applying to come to Northern Ireland through the New Industries (Development) Act, in the vast majority of cases without success. Another 550 or so Jewish people, the majority from Vienna, contacted the Jewish community directly and a small number were admitted. Within six years, by the end of 1944, a third of Vienna's Jewish community had been murdered, around 65,000 men, women and children. Of the 730 or so people mentioned in the letters sent by roughly 300 applicants in the PRONI files, at least 125 were killed in the Holocaust. For every Jewish person from Vienna admitted to Northern Ireland under the Stormont scheme, at least one of those refused entry was murdered by the Nazis in the Holocaust. The 120,000 who were forced to migrate, and the 2,142 who survived the Nazi persecution in the city, lost everything: homes, careers, property, businesses, savings, possessions. Above all, in many, many cases, they lost loved ones.

As we have seen from the PRONI letters, the DÖW archive, and the personal interviews with local Holocaust survivors, among the tiny number of people who came to Northern Ireland, there was hardly an individual or family who did not lose close relatives, including parents, brothers, sisters, grandparents, cousins, aunts, uncles, nieces and nephews, as well as friends, work colleagues, fellow synagogue or club members, school pals, neighbours, housemates, lovers.

Reading their letters is a moving and chastening experience. Usually, the writers give brief career synopses, with accompanying requests for a visa and work permit. They have lost their jobs, but they could create work for local people in Northern Ireland. They have lost their money, but they would not be a burden on the taxpayer. They would work tirelessly in whatever job they found themselves. They would bring honour and success to the country. They rarely go into detail about the frightening realities of their lives under Nazi rule, but occasionally they make a personal, direct appeal for admission. They have a son or husband in a concentration camp, their ageing parents are not well, they are penniless and are banned from working. They hope for a 'a good deed for humanity', as one applicant described it, a gesture of solidarity with the persecuted and powerless.

We read their letters with the benefit of hindsight. We know the fate of the applicants, but they didn't when they wrote the letters. We can survey the scene, while they were trapped in it. We can track their histories, however briefly, in archives or websites. These official records, and the letters of the Vienna applicants, help keep their memories alive. It is a valuable albeit sparse record – names, dates, final addresses, journeys, fates. It gives, however fleetingly, a precious sense of the rich and irreplaceable experience of the individuals named in them, the unique presence that every person contributes to the world, the formative moments of their lives, the births, deaths and marriages, the personal landmarks that make a life.

The civil servants tasked with appraising the applications for the Ministry of Commerce had to decide which met the criteria of the New Industries (Development) Act. They had to back those individuals they felt could create employment, or could train others in companies chosen for aid under the scheme. Today, with our knowledge of the Holocaust, it seems an unbearable decision to make, but at the time it must have seemed less so. We can only speculate about how easy or difficult individual civil servants found their task.

For us, the choice seems simple. These people were living in appalling circumstances and if any group of human beings ever deserved rescue, they did. The local media had covered the brutality and wickedness of Nazi rule in Austria, and no one could be ignorant of the injustices and dangers that Jews there were experiencing. But the governments of all free nations, including the United Kingdom, Ireland and the United States, imposed extremely tight admission policies, which tied the hands of civil servants, even if they had wanted to adopt a more liberal attitude. They were obliged to work within these guidelines. Occasionally, some civil servants expressed frustration and irritation at the persistence of Jewish émigrés who lobby on behalf of relatives in Vienna, and their bureaucratic conformism sounds callous. Of course, we are much more knowledgeable now about conditions in occupied Europe than they were, but reading their dogged determination to reject tiny numbers of people if they did not meet the strict criteria is disheartening and disquieting.

No one can read the letters in PRONI now without feeling pity and rage at what was happening in Vienna, and in the corridors of power where different decisions could have been made. The voices of the innocent, their dignity and nobility in the face of terror, speak to us across time and space. Reading their applications, it is impossible not to feel the grave injustice done to them by the states who shut their doors and the governments that closed their hearts to their terrible predicament. So much more needed to be done and, with goodwill, so much more could have been done. What is past is past, and unhistorical ideas of mass rescue are easy to dismiss as pointless. Yet the imagination refuses to be silenced. Would a mass appeal to the people of Northern Ireland, and Ireland, to the churches, to sporting and charity organisations, to political parties, not have found an echo? Could the better angels of our nature not have found their voice, and opened their homes to these dispossessed and despised men and women? The realist says 'no, not possible', but the idealist cannot be silenced, and says 'yes'.

The letters are the utterances of the powerless, and give individual presences to the anonymous thousands from Vienna who were killed. In them we hear the voices of people like us, members of a once great community, remarkable in its talent and variety. The streets and palaces and landmarks of modern Vienna recall its glorious past, but it is a shadow of its former self.

On a summer's day, the visitor can take in the sights in the sunshine which bathes the city. Tourists flock to its Habsburg palaces, art galleries and museums, St Stefan's Cathedral, the Opera House and the Ring, the Ferris wheel in the Prater, the cafés once humming with debate and gossip. But in one sense, this Vienna is a ghost town, for its brightest and best were driven out of it, to the emigrant ships and the deportation trains. Its real history, the history of its darkest seven years between 1938 and 1945, is presaged in the PRONI letters.

In them the streets all have names, and the names are signposts to who lived in them, who were forced to leave or were taken away: Nussdorfer Strasse, where George Clare witnessed a friendly neighbourhood policeman assaulting a Jewish man on the night of the Anschluss; Rögergasse, where Otto Goldberger was taken from his shirt factory to a makeshift holding centre; Streffleurgasse, from where Leopold Kessler went to Theresienstadt, then to his death at Treblinka; Grosse Mohrengasse, the last address of Max Kammerling before he was sent to Theresienstadt and then Auschwitz; Rossauer Lände, where Alfred Neumann lived before his short sojourn in the United Kingdom, his internment as an 'enemy alien' and his early death in the cold waters of the North Atlantic; and the Aspangbahnhof, from where 47,035 Jewish men and women were deported on 47 transports between 1939 and 1942, and just 1,073 survived. The station has now gone, and in Platz der Opfer der Deportation (Victims of the Deportation Square) the murdered are remembered in a thirty-metre-long memorial, concrete railway tracks ending with a dark concrete block symbolising the risk of forgetting.

I became familiar with dozens of the city's street names, particularly those in Leopoldstadt, the inner-city area which became a Jewish ghetto, when I read the hundreds of letters from Jews preserved at PRONI. They stay in the memory: Taborstrasse, Grosse Mohrengasse, Singerstrasse, Dorotheengasse, Kleine Sperlgasse, Grünentorgasse. Vienna's wide boulevards recall the capital of an empire which once numbered 50 million inhabitants. It was bombed during the war but never suffered the extensive and deadly Allied air raids which flattened German cities; neither, unlike Berlin, did it undergo the devastating damage of all-out Red Army siege and capture. Its palaces and government buildings, its apartment buildings and theatres, were restored to their former splendour. But to travel around the city, knowing its hateful past, is a melancholy and at times unsettling experience. It is a beautiful place but it lost its soul when the Nazis marched into Vienna on 12 March 1938. Occasionally one sees a plaque on a wall or a street named after a notable person who became a victim of the Nazis, or brought intellectual distinction and helped garner its reputation as one of the world's creative powerhouses: Jura-Soyfer-Gasse, which recalls the young poet who died in Buchenwald, or Egon-Friedell-Gasse, the writer who jumped to his death when the Gestapo came for him. In Kleine Sperlgasse you can buy food at a Jewish deli. I saw Orthodox Jewish men with their trademark black coats and Homburg hats, and was surprised that a small remnant of the city's once thriving Jewish population had a presence in the city.

One evening, I had a beer outside a café in Karmeliterplatz, a picturesque square off Taborstrasse, one of the main thoroughfares in Leopoldstadt. It was a pleasant warm evening in Vienna, which keeps the heat of the day in summer. Sitting at a table, one can watch the passers-by, and feel that one is in a cosmopolitan, civilised city, and that this is how life can be lived on a fine evening. In 1942, Gertrude Bunzlau, a forty-year-old single woman, was living in an apartment building at Karmeliterplatz 1. Four years earlier, she had written to the Ministry of Commerce seeking entry to Northern Ireland. She had been producing knitwear and other articles for eight years, and could train people in all kinds of work. Her application was rejected with the usual one-word note 'Regret' in pencil. Trapped in Vienna, she had been evicted from her home at Hollandstrasse 10 and housed at Karmeliterplatz, sharing a crowded apartment building with other Jews who had been similarly treated. Gertrude was deported to Theresienstadt on 13 August 1942 and died there on 11 September 1942. She was probably deported from the next street, Kleine Sperlgasse. Jews were gathered there in a collection centre before being taken to the Aspangbahnhof and transported to the east. The past is another country, but in Vienna it is only a street or a house or a name away. Once one is aware of this shameful part of its history, one can never quite forget it.

In Vienna, metal plaques on the footpaths and at the entrances to some buildings bear the names of Holocaust victims and the dates on which they were sent to their deaths. The fierce thunderstorms which come and go rapidly in summer wash away pavement dust, and the polished metal plaques shine like gold in the clear air.

APPENDIX

The following paragraphs detail the fate of those who applied to Northern Ireland via the New Industries Scheme, but were rejected and murdered in the Holocaust. Most of their personal backgrounds in their letters to PRONI are given in Chapters 5 and 9, which describe the applications sent after the *Zionistische Rundschau* briefly publicised the scheme in August 1938, and the Kristallnacht pogrom in November 1938 respectively. More information can be found on the website of the Documentation Archive of Austrian Resistance, at DÖW.at.

Alfred Bermann, aged sixty-seven and his wife Mathilde, aged sixty-four, were deported from Springergasse 27, to Theresienstadt on 14 July 1942. Alfred died there on 5 September 1942. Mathilde was deported to Treblinka on 21 September 1942 and murdered there. They wrote to PRONI on behalf of their son Otto, who had then been in a concentration camp for six months. He survived the war and applied for compensation from the Austrian government. He died in Canada on 27 July 1964.[1]

Henriette (Hinda) Wollisch, aged sixty-eight, of Liechtensteinstrasse 73, was deported to Theresienstadt on 24 September 1942 and from there to Auschwitz on 16 May 1944, where she was murdered. Her son Alfred, on whose behalf she had written to the Ministry of Commerce when he was in a concentration camp in 1938, appears to have survived.

Hedwig Neufeld, aged forty-one, and her son Erich, aged thirteen, of Czerningasse 9, were deported to the Lödz ghetto in Poland, renamed Litzmannstadt by the Nazis, on 19 October 1941. They perished there. Hedwig's daughter Anny, aged five, and husband Dr Heinrich Neufeld are not listed in the DÖW archive, so it is probable that they survived the war.

Fanny Bäck, aged fifty-six, of Ferstelgasse 5, had a millinery company and also produced knitwear and leather goods. She was deported to Izbica in the Lublin district of south-east Poland on 9 April 1942, and perished there.

Otto Kisch, aged fifty-three, was deported from Sterngasse 11, Vienna to Riga, Latvia on 1 January 1942 and moved to a concentration camp at Jungfernhof about four kilometres away. Otto was murdered on 26 March 1942. Unusually, his wife Hertha, aged forty-five, and daughter Vera, aged twelve, who were deported to Riga with him, survived. After the war, Hertha applied from New York for compensation to the Austrian government and mentions Vera.[2]

Nearly 4,000 Jews from Vienna, Nuremberg, Stuttgart and Hamburg were transported to the Jungfernhof camp from late November 1941 onwards. The camp's commandant, Rudolf Seck, sometimes executed prisoners himself. According to testimony from witnesses at his trial in the 1950s, he shot one prisoner for showing up a few minutes late to roll call and another because he'd forgotten his braces and was holding up his pants with his hands. In March 1942, the Nazis carried out what became known as the Dünamünde Action. Some 1,800 prisoners from Jungfernhof and another 3,000 from the Riga ghetto were taken by truck into the Bikernieki forest and executed. Only 148 of the Jews taken to the camp were still living at the end of the war.

Hedwig Swoboda, aged forty-two, who had her own tie-making business, had applied for visas for her daughter Helene, aged eighteen, and craftsman Otto Urbach, aged forty-four, formerly of Deinhardtsteingasse 11, and his unnamed seven-year-old child. The Swobodas appear to have survived the war, but Otto Urbach, then aged forty-eight, was captured in France and deported from Drancy, Paris on 19 August 1942 to Auschwitz, where he perished. His child appears to have survived.

One of the youngest applicants, Helene Gutter, aged twenty, who lived at Darwingasse 4, was not admitted, but appears to have survived. However, a Helene Gutter, aged forty-four, with a last address at Malzgasse 2, was arrested by the Gestapo on 22 March 1944, deported to Auschwitz on 4 July 1944 and murdered there. In an extract from the daily Gestapo Vienna report on the DÖW website, she is described as a seamstress, stateless and single: 'Gutter, who has two children outside marriage who qualified as mixed race of the first degree, despite the obligation to register her identity, did not comply and did not use the additional name "Sara". On account of these, she was taken into protective custody.' 'Protective custody' was a Nazi euphemism for detention without trial. Helene was held for three months before being transported to Auschwitz. It is possible she was related to the young Helene who applied unsuccessfully to come to Northern Ireland.

Fritz Jökl, aged sixty-six, married with two sons, who wanted to set up a feather bed-making factory in Northern Ireland, was refused, and died in Vienna on 10 January 1940 in unknown circumstances. A second Fritz Jökl, aged seventeen, Johann (Schani) Jökl, aged sixty-seven, and Stefanie Jökl, aged fifty-seven, were deported together from Grosse Stadtgutstrasse 20, to Lödz (Litzmannstadt) on 23 October 1941. All three perished there: Stefanie on 8 February 1942, Johann on 5 April 1942, and Fritz on a date unknown.

Several other applicants recommended by Alfred Neumann were also unable to escape Vienna. One was Max Neumann (no relation), aged fifty-six, of Novaragasse 40, a leather goods manufacturer. He sought a permit for himself and his wife Dobe, aged fifty-five. Max and Dobe were deported from Vienna to Maly Trostinec near Minsk in Belarus on 17 August 1942 and killed there four days later.

Friedrich and Jacques Schafranek, of Werdertorgasse 17, each wrote in German in the autumn of 1938 seeking to set up a joinery works. Several Schafranek brothers ran a firm in Vienna. The Ministry of Commerce expressed interest, but they were not admitted to Northern Ireland. Friedrich appears to have survived the war, and there is no record of a Jacques Schafranek in the DÖW archive. Adolf Schafranek, aged fifty-two, and of the same address, was deported to an unknown camp in Yugoslavia and died there.

A Jakob Schafranek is listed along with three other Schafraneks who were deported together from Vienna on April 1942 to Izbica and murdered there. Jakob, aged forty-nine, and Rosa, aged fifty, both of Untere Donaustrasse 39, travelled with Stella Schafranek, aged forty-five, and Rudolf Schafranek, aged sixty-one, of Obere Donaustrasse.

A second Rudolf Schafranek, aged forty-four, of Liechtenstein-strasse 119, was deported from Vienna to Theresienstadt on 9 October 1942, to Auschwitz on 29 September 1944 and to Dachau on 10 October 1944. He died there on 4 April 1945, just over three weeks before the camp's liberation, after surviving two and a half years in three deadly camps. Leopold Schafranek, aged seventy, and Johanna Schafranek, aged sixty- five, perhaps Rudolf's parents, were deported from Liechtensteinstrasse 119/23 to Theresienstadt on 13 August 1942 and to Treblinka on 29 September 1942. Isidor Schafranek, aged sixty, and Gisela Schafranek, aged fifty-one, of Kolingasse 13, were deported from Vienna to Maly Trostinec on 31 August 1942 and were murdered there on 4 September 1942.

Fritz Mieser, aged fifty-one, of Liechtensteinstrasse 119, was deported to Maly Trostinec on 27 May 1942 and murdered there on 1 June 1942. Of the 8,700 Austrian Jews, 8,500 from Vienna, transported to Maly Trostinec, there were only 17 known survivors. The victims were killed either by shooting at mass graves or by gassing.

Both Wilhelm Wohlfeiler, aged forty-eight, of Untere Viaduktgasse 11, and Leopold Wohlfeiler, aged fifty, of Lerchenfelder Strasse 124, were deported from Vienna to Nisko in Poland on 20 October 1939 and did not survive. Emanuel Wohlfeiler, aged fifty-four, of Lerchenfelder Strasse 146, probably their elder brother, died in Vienna on 20 August 1938, in unknown circumstances.

Heinrich Molnar, aged sixty, was deported from his flat at Köllnerhofgasse 6 to Maly Trostinec on 20 May 1942 and was killed there six days later. There is no record of his wife or mother.

Hans Berger, aged forty-seven, and his wife, Regine Berger, were deported from their Heinrichsgasse home to Minsk on 28 November 1941 and murdered there. The fate of Hans's mother is unknown.

Manele Bohm was deported to Dachau on 16 November 1938. He was later released but was deported from his final home at Klosterneuburger Strasse 60 to Buchenwald on 2 October 1939. He died there on 28 April 1941. His fellow applicant Gottlieb Mendel appears to have survived the Holocaust.

Leo Friedmann, aged forty-five, a maker of buttons and buckles, had sought visas for himself, his wife Gertrude, aged thirty-eight, and their son Kurt, aged four. The couple had been born in Czechoslovakia but were all now naturalised German subjects. Friedmann also mentions a couple, Erwin and Regine Pollak, who had been living at Praterstrasse 52. All five were refused visas.

The Friedmanns, then living at Grünentorgasse 24, were deported from Vienna to Auschwitz on 17 July 1942 and murdered there. The Pollaks appear to have survived because they are not named in the DÖW death list.

Ernst Löbl, aged forty-one, was deported from his final home at Haidgasse 109 to Modliborzyce in Poland on 5 March 1941, along with his wife Renee, aged thirty-six, and his mother Reisi Löbl, aged seventy-four. All three perished there.

Another couple called Löbl, Fritz and Gisela, aged respectively forty-seven and forty-nine, were transported from Vienna to Theresienstadt on 1 October 1942. Fritz was deported to Auschwitz on 28 September 1944, and Gisela on 4 October 1944. Both were murdered there.

Grete Schubert and Aladar Tausig survived the Holocaust, but Alfred Schubert, then aged seventy-six, and his younger brother Siegfried Schubert, aged seventy-three, were deported from their home at Praterstrasse 38 to Theresienstadt on 14 July 1942, and perished there, Siegfried on 25 January 1943 and Alfred on 1 March 1943. Franziska Tausig, aged fifty-nine, and Erwin Tausig, aged thirty-six, were deported together from Grosse Stadtgutgasse 7, to Lödz on 23 October 1941 and perished there.

Simon Kleinberger, aged fifty-two, and his wife Berta, aged fifty-six, were deported from Weissgerberlände 40, on 26 February 1941 to Opole in Poland and died there. Their son appears to have survived the war.

Ignaz Rothmann, aged thirty-five, was deported on 10 October 1939 from Vienna to Nisko and did not survive. The fate of his unnamed female co-applicant is unknown.

Frieda Schablin, aged forty-two, of Pulvertumgasse 7, escaped to France, but was deported from Drancy, Paris on 4 November 1942 to Auschwitz and perished there. Her husband, Ernst, appears to have survived.

Dr Leo Adler, aged seventy-two, and Johanna Adler, aged fifty-nine, of Mosergasse 11, were deported to Kaunas in Lithuania on 23 November 1941 and was murdered there on 29 November 1941. It is not known for certain what became of their son Rudolf. A Rudolf Adler, aged thirty-eight, and Stefanie Adler, aged forty, were deported together from Novaragasse 48 on the same train and it is possible they may have been related to Leo and Johanna.

Friederike Altstädter, aged forty-one, her husband Alexander, aged thirty-eight, and daughter Vilma, aged thirteen, formerly of Bräunerstrasse, Vienna, were deported from Prague to Lödz on 16 October 1941. Friederike died there on 14 May 1942 and her husband and daughter died there on dates unknown.

Elsa Abeles, aged fifty-one, and Samuel Abeles, aged sixty-five, were deported from Alserbachstrasse 33 to Izbica on 5 June 1942 and did not survive. They are listed as numbers 1 and 2 on the 25th 'migration transport' from Vienna, a euphemism for the deportation trains.

They were among 4,000 Jewish men, women and children deported on four transports from Vienna's Aspangbahnhof to Izbica in Poland between 9 April and 5 June 1942. Izbica originally had a population of 6,000 people, of whom 90 per cent were Jewish, but with deportations from other parts of Poland, Czechoslovakia, Austria and Germany, the number of Jewish inhabitants increased to 12,000. To make room for the new arrivals, the Nazis deported around 2,200 of the original inhabitants to Belzec extermination camp on 24 March 1942. It is not known if the Abeles were among the 10,000 Jews taken to the Izbica railway station on 15 October 1942, of whom 5,000 were deported to Belzec, or among the 500 people the SS massacred during this operation.

Josef Haber, aged sixty, his wife Zofia Haber, aged forty-seven, and their son Friedrich, aged sixteen, all of Malzgasse 12, were deported on 31 August 1942 to Maly Trostinec and were killed there on 4 September. The Boths, who applied with them, were not deported and appear to have survived.

Rudolf Berger, aged fifty-three, was deported with his wife Julie Berger, aged fifty-six, from Otto-Bauer-Gasse 24, to Minsk on 28 November 1941 and did not survive.

Gertrude Bunzlau, aged forty, of Karmaliterplatz 1, was deported to Theresienstadt on 13 August 1942 and died there on 11 September 1942.

Elisabeth Fränkel, aged twenty-one, was deported with Pessel Fränkel, aged fifty-three, almost certainly her mother, from a flat at Bläuerlegasse 24 to Litzmannstadt (Lödz) on 2 November 1941 and perished there. Rudolf Fuchs, aged fifty-two, of

Appendix

Breitenfurterstrasse 34, Vienna, was deported from Prague to Theresienstadt on 18 August 1944 and from there to Auschwitz on 29 September, where he perished.

Julius Frankl, aged fifty-nine in 1938, a businessman, was among those rejected applicants who managed to survive both Vienna and Dachau concentration camps against overwhelming odds. He lived underground in Vienna until his arrest on 11 May 1943, and was held in Dachau concentration camp from July 1943 until its liberation on 29 April 1945.

In the DÖW files, we have Julius Frankl's Gestapo photographs, showing him unshaven with a moustache and greying hair. A note says the former businessman, of no fixed abode, lived 'disguised as Aryan' in Vienna. He had evaded capture for almost five years, by living as an 'U-Boat' – someone who kept out of sight and changed addresses to evade the Nazi authorities. His Gestapo file said that when he was arrested he was living in a secret 'mixed relationship' (with a non-Jew, banned under Nazi law) and, fearing 'evacuation' (deportation), had lived a homeless existence and earned his living through illegal trading. He had received previous convictions for communist activity and deception, and was recommended for 'protective custody' (internment). It is not known what became of his family or the two unnamed workers he wanted to bring out.

Several people applied and were rejected, but escaped from Vienna only to be picked up by the Nazis in other occupied countries. Arthur Fischer, aged fifty-three, of Taubstummengassse 6, was arrested after the German invasion of France in May 1940 and taken to Drancy concentration camp on the outskirts of Paris. He was deported to Sobibor (Majdanek) on 4 March 1943 and perished there. His relatives appear to have survived the war.

Otto Neugebauer, aged fifty-six, of Salztorgasse 2, escaped to France but was also arrested and sent to the concentration camp at Drancy. He was deported to Auschwitz on 19 August 1942 and was killed there.

Edgar Kisch, aged fifty-one and Edith Kisch, aged forty-four, of Hinterese Zollamststrasse 9, escaped Vienna but were arrested sometime after May 1940 and taken to the concentration camp in Westerbork in Holland. From there they were deported to Sobibor on 25 May 1943 and murdered on arrival on 28 May. Their son Peter seems to have survived because there is no mention of him in the DÖW archives. He may have made it out on a Kindertransport from Vienna in later 1938 or early 1939.

Gustav Schreiber, aged fifty-two, of Mariahilfer Strasse 211, emigrated from Austria to France, but was arrested and taken to Drancy concentration camp. He was deported to Auschwitz on 12 August 1942 and perished there. His wife is mentioned but not named in his application to the Ministry of Commerce, but no other Schreiber is listed with a Mariahilfer Strasse address in the DÖW archive, so it is possible that she survived.

Stella Fuchs, aged forty-two, was deported from Praterstrasse 38 to Auschwitz on 7 July 1942 and perished there. It seems that Josef Rostholder, mentioned in Stella Fuchs' application to the Ministry of Commerce, survived the war.

Heinrich Kantor, aged sixty-five, and Fanny Kantor, aged fifty, of Kegelgasse 14, were deported to Lödz on 2 November 1941. Heinrich perished there on 7 July 1942, and Fanny was murdered in Chelmno in Poland on 7 September 1942.

Gisela Kompert, aged fifty-two, and Kamillo Kompert, aged fifty-nine, were deported from Pazmanitengasse 4, to Izbica on 15 May 1942 and perished there.

Ernst Mautner was deported from his last address at Tuchlauben 19 to Maly Trostinec on 27 May 1942 and murdered there on 1 June. It appears that his wife and son, who were not named in their application, both survived the war.

Adrienne Fekete, aged thirty, Hertha Fekete, aged twenty-seven, and Laura Fekete, aged sixty-nine, were deported together from Wiesingerstrasse 3 on 15 October 1941 to the Lödz ghetto and were killed there.

Dr Oskar Grauer, aged forty-four, his wife Berta, aged forty-six, and their son Maximilian, aged seventeen, were deported from Ditscheinergasse 3 to Kaunas in Lithuania on 23 November 1941 and killed there six days later.

The DÖW archive details the fate of the Grauers and the other 1,000 Viennese Jews deported on that transport. It left the Aspangbahnhof but never made it to Riga, Latvia, its original destination. Like a number of transports destined for Riga from Germany and Austria, it was for reasons that are still unclear diverted to Kaunas in Lithuania and handed over to Einsatzkommando (EK) 3, one of the Nazi special murder formations specifically tasked with murdering Jews, communists, intellectuals and other condemned groups in the occupied east. Part of Einsatzgruppe A, this formation had with the intense participation of local forces been involved in making Lithuania 'Judenfrei' (free of Jews) and had murdered 130,000 people since June 1941. Immediately after their arrival, the Vienna deportees were taken to Fort IX, part of the old Czarist fortress of Kaunas, which had become a place of regular massacres by Lithuanian volunteers under the command of members of EK 3, and shot. Of the 1,000 Viennese deportees not one is known to have survived.

Heinrich Idelovici, aged fifty-five, of Obermüllerstrasse 5, was deported from Vienna to Lödz on 28 October 1941, and later to Auschwitz; on 3 September 1944 he was deported to Stutthof, where he died on 8 October 1944. Babette Idelovici, then aged fifty-five, made the same journeys, with a fourth deportation from Stutthof to Flossenbürg on 29 November 1944, where she died on 15 March 1945. Marie Idelovici, aged forty-nine, accompanied Babette and died in Flossenbürg on an unknown date. All three lived at the same address in Vienna before their deportation. A Sigmund Idelovici, aged forty-nine, who had travelled to France, was deported from Drancy to Auschwitz on 30 June 1944, and murdered there. He may have been a relative. Charles Grüner, mentioned in the Idelovicis' application, is not listed in the DÖW files, so he probably survived the war.

Fritzi Kohn, aged thirty-three, Rudolf Kohn, aged fifty-nine, and Karl Kohn, aged eleven, of Marxergasse 10, were deported from Vienna to Wlodowa, a small town eleven kilometres from Sobibor extermination camp, on 27 April 1942. There is no DÖW record of the Dr Spitz or the Joseph Kohn mentioned in Fritzi Kohn's original letter, so it seems they were not deported with them and survived. Of the 1,000 Austrian Jews deported to Wlodawa, almost all from Vienna, only three survived.

Arthur Fried, aged thirty-five, of Ungargasse 59a, was deported to Nisko in Poland on 20 October 1939 and perished there.

Stefan and Stella Guttmann, both aged forty-nine, were deported together from Hollandstrasse 9 to Theresienstadt on 20 August 1942 and to Auschwitz on 23 January 1943, where they were killed. A son mentioned in their application is not named in the death list and appears to have survived the Holocaust.

Nelly and Simon Gaspar, aged forty-two and fifty-nine, were deported from Vienna to Poland on 15 February 1941. Their daughter Ruth survived, possibly by getting out on a Kindertransport, and emigrated to the US. The DÖW archive gives a rare description of the eviction process which was imposed on them and tens of thousands of Jews in Vienna. The family had lived in a council apartment in Ybbsstrasse 31 in Leopoldstadt. In late June 1938 the Vienna city authorities issued 2,000 eviction notices to Jewish renters of council apartments, and the Gaspars were ordered to quit their home by 31 July. This was extended to 31 August, but on 12 September the district court of Leopoldstadt approved their forcible removal and this was accomplished on 18 November 1938, one of the many evictions carried out quickly after Kristallnacht. According to the DÖW archive, the couple were among 2,003 Jewish men, women and children who left Vienna's Aspangbahnhof on 15 February and 26 February 1941 for Opole, a town south of Lublin with a large Jewish community. Then all trace of them ends. When the war broke out, 4,000 Jews lived there, making up 70 per cent of the population, a figure soon swelled by Jewish forced labourers from other parts of Poland.

By March 1941 around 8,000 Jews had been deported to the newly created ghetto of Opole. The new arrivals were placed partly with local Jews, and partly in mass quarters such as a synagogue and a newly erected barracks. In the ghetto the freedom of movement of the inhabitants was not restricted – since there were no barriers – but leaving Opole without official permission was forbidden on pain of severe punishment. The control of the ghetto was undertaken by the Sicherheitsdienst (the security section of the SS), police and, according to eyewitness statements, members of the German army. The ghetto inhabitants were in general restricted in their food supplies. From May 1941, 800 men capable of working were sent for forced labour to Deblin in Poland.

Appendix

The liquidation of the ghetto of Opole began in spring 1942. On 31 March 1942 a transport went to the extermination camp of Belzec, and in May and October 1942 deportations to Sobibor death camp followed. Of the 2,003 Viennese Jews deported, 28 survivors are known.

Wilhelm and Sofia Schieber, aged sixty-seven and fifty-nine, were deported together from Wipplingerstrasse 13 to Theresienstadt on 24 September 1942. Wilhelm died there on 4 December 1942. Sofia is not named in the DÖW list of victims, so may have survived the war.

Amalie Korn, aged forty-five, Paula Korn, aged forty-three, and Siegmund Korn, aged seventy-six, were deported together from Förstergasse 8 to Maly Trostinec on 6 May 1942. They were murdered there on 11 May 1942. Of the 8,700 Austrian Jews deported to Maly Trostinec, about 8,500 came from Vienna, and only 17 are known to have survived.

Irene Klein, aged forty-four, and her husband Johann, aged forty-six, described as homeless, were deported to Theresienstadt on 24 June 1943. They survived almost a year there until they were deported to Auschwitz on 18 May 1944, where they perished.

Friederike Klein, aged sixty-one, and her daughter Grete Klein, aged thirty-six, were deported from Porzellangasse 53, to Maly Trostinec on 17 August 1942 and were murdered on their arrival four days later.

Moritz Katz, aged fifty-five, his wife Therese, aged forty-one, and their son Bruno, aged fifteen, were deported from Grosse Mohrengasse 40 to Maly Trostinec on 31 August 1942 and killed there on 4 September.

Emil Löbl, aged forty-eight, and his daughter Ingeborg, aged fourteen, were deported from Haasgasse 8 to Riga, Latvia on 26 January 1942 and killed there.

Sidonie Wolkenstein, aged forty-eight, of Seegasse 3, was deported to Izbica on 5 June 1942 and perished there.

Josef Neubrunn, aged fifty-nine, and his wife Marianne, aged forty-four, were deported from Schwarzspanierstrasse 15, to Wlodawa on 27 April 1942 and perished there.

Bernhard Mosonyi, aged fifty-nine, of Stumpergasse 9, was deported from Budapest to Dachau on 18 November 1944 and died there six days later.

Arthur and Hermine Neumann, both aged fifty-one, were deported from Gregor-Mendel-Strasse 44 to Maly Trostinec on 5 October 1942 and murdered there four days later.

Louise and Ida Nussbaum, aged sixty-seven and forty-three respectively, of Porzellangasse 45, were deported to Theresienstadt on 1 October 1942 and then to Auschwitz on 9 October 1944. Both perished.

Olga Porges, aged fifty-nine, and Melanie Porges, aged sixty-four, of Wipplingerstrasse 12, were deported together to Kaunas, Lithuania on 23 November 1941 and murdered there on 29 November.

Arnold Rosenberger, aged forty-two, Jela Rosenberger, aged forty-five, and Max Rosenberger, aged eighty-one, of Rembrandtstrasse 22, were deported together to Lagow-Opatow, two small towns in the region of Kielce in Poland, on 12 March 1941, and perished there. They were among 997 Jewish men women and children on the train. The deportees were held in a ghetto at Opatow or taken to a forced-labour camp.

Between 20 and 22 October 1942, 6,000 ghetto inhabitants were deported to Treblinka and murdered, several hundred were shot in the ghetto, and 500–600 moved to a work camp at Sandomierz. Some Jews were kept alive to clean the ghetto and sort out the belongings of the dead. These people were later shot in the ghetto cemetery. Of the 997 Austrian Jews deported on 12 March 1941, only 11 were known to have survived.

Wilhelm Goldberger, aged fifty-seven, was deported from Löwengasse 2 to Izbica on 9 April 1942, and killed there. He was one of 4,000 Austrian Jewish men, women and children sent there. On 15 October 1942, 10,000 Jews were crowded together at Izbica railway station and transported to Belzec extermination camp, where they were murdered, while 500 were shot in Izbica. Otto Schulmann, who had applied with Wilhelm to open a pen and pencil factory in Northern Ireland, is not listed on the DÖW website, so appears to have survived the war.

Richard Rosenbaum was deported from Rembrandtstrasse 13 to Riga on 3 December 1941 with his wife, Grete. Both perished there.

Of the 20,000 Jewish men, women and children deported to Riga from the Third Reich, about 800 survived, 100 of them Austrian.

Bernhard Rosenbaum, aged sixty, of Ferdinandstrasse 19, was deported to Maly Trostinec near Minsk on 27 May 1942. He was murdered there on 1 June 1942. Hedwig Hausmann, aged sixty-eight, of Grundlgasse 1, was deported to Riga on 11 January 1942, and perished there. Adele Rosenbaum appears to have survived.

Marie Rosenberg, aged forty-eight, and her daughter Lilly, aged nineteen, of Gumpendorfer Strasse, were deported to Maly Trostinec on 6 May 1942. Both were murdered on 11 May 1942.

Szyfra Schneider, aged forty-six, was deported to Auschwitz from Rueppgasse 3 on 17 July 1942 and murdered there.

Seven members of one extended family were murdered after one couple were refused entry by the Ministry of Commerce in Belfast. Johanna Stein Brand, aged fifty-five, had tried to come to Northern Ireland to set up a business along with her husband Nikolaus Michael Stein, aged sixty-one. Johanna, listed as Ella Johanna Brand, of Lichtenauergasse 1, was deported to Theresienstadt on 14 July 1942 and to Auschwitz on 15 May 1944. Nikolaus, also living at Lichtenauergasse 1 was deported on a date unknown to Topovske Supe, Belgrade, and perished there. Chane Anna Brand, aged seventy-nine, of Lichtenauergasse 1, was deported to Theresienstadt on 14 July 1942, and died there on 9 December that year.

Four further members of the Stein family were deported together from Vienna to Theresienstadt on 24 September July 1942 and later perished. Johanna, aged sixty-five, Moses, aged seventy, and Selma, aged thirty-one, were all living at Blumauergasse 20 while Hans, aged seven, was living at Lichtenauergaasse 1. Johanna died in Theresienstadt on 29 October 1944, Moses on 8 August 1943, while Selma and Hans were deported to Auschwitz on 16 May 1944 and perished there.

Paul Stagel, aged twenty-nine, and Fritzi Stagel, aged twenty-six, were deported together from Sterngasse 12, to Theresienstadt on 9 October 1942. Fritzi was deported from there to Auschwitz on 6 October 1944, where she died. Her husband Paul, described as a businessman, is not on the DÖW victims list, so appears to have survived.

Hugo and Sara Schütz, aged sixty-seven and sixty-four, along with Robert Schütz, aged thirty-eight, were deported from Fleischmarkt 15 to Izbica on 12 May 1942. Hugo and Sara were murdered, probably at Belzec extermination camp. Robert Schütz died in Majdanek, also in Poland, on 23 September 1942.

Ernestine and Friederike Silber, aged sixty-six and fifty-nine, were deported from Maria Treugasse 3, to Riga on 6 February 1942 and perished there.

Josefine Spielmann, aged forty, her husband Benno, aged forty-four, and their son Saul, aged eleven, were deported from Fleischmarkt 22 to Theresienstadt on 1 October 1942. Josefine was deported to Auschwitz on 18 December 1943. She perished there. Benno was transported to Gross Rosen and then to Buchenwald on 11 February 1945. He died there on 22 February. Saul is not listed in the DÖW list and appears to have survived.

Max and Margarete Seidner, aged forty-one and thirty-six, were deported together to Sobibor on 14 June 1942. Margarete was killed in Sobibor, but Max was transported to Majdanek, where he was murdered on 8 August 1942. The train they were deported on, the 27th transport from Vienna, was the only one that went direct to Sobibor. Of the 1,000 Jews on the train, 950 were gassed immediately on arrival. The exact number of Austrian Jews killed in Sobibor is difficult to ascertain; the majority of the 4,000 deported to Izbica and the Viennese Jews already in the 'General Government' in spring 1941 were killed in Sobibor and Belzec. Almost all the 1,000 Jews transported from Vienna to Wlodawa were murdered in Sobibor. Of the 4,000 Jews deported from France to Sobibor, 130 were Austrian. From March 1942 until the camp closed in autumn 1943, an estimated 250,000 Jews were murdered in Sobibor.

Isak and Golde Seidmann, aged sixty-two and sixty-six, were deported from Glockengasse 10 to Theresienstadt, on 22 July 1942. Isak died there, and on 16 May 1944 Golde was deported to Auschwitz, where she was murdered.

Jakob and Jetti Sonnenfeld, aged seventy-two and seventy, were deported from Springerstrasse 28 to Theresienstadt on 28 July 1942. Jakob died there and Jetti was transported to Treblinka on 26 September 1942, where she perished.

Sali and Edith Schattner, aged twenty-five and twenty-seven, of Krummbaumgasse 10, were deported to Lödz on 28 October 1941 and perished there. Malke Schattner, aged sixty-five, of the same address, was deported from Vienna to Maly Trostinec on 31 August 1942 and was murdered on 5 September. Hermann Schattner, Sali's husband, aged thirty-seven, who had written their letter of application from their former home at Rembrandtstrasse 10, had also been rejected by the Ministry of Commerce, but appears to have survived.

Siegfried and Rosa Wiener, aged fifty-six and fifty-five, of Seegasse 6, were deported to Lödz on 2 November 1941 and perished there.

Marie Weiss, aged seventy-three, was deported from Malzgasse 11 to Theresienstadt on 14 July 1942 and died there on 26 September.

Wilhelm and Sally Band, aged sixty-three and fifty-nine, of Obere Donaustrasse 73, were deported to Riga on 6 February 1942 and perished there.

Gertrude Chat, aged fifty-six, and her husband Arthur, aged sixty-nine, of Stoss im Himmel 3, were deported together to Theresienstadt on 10 July 1942. Arthur died there on 29 December 1942, but Gertrude survived until 23 January 1943, when she was deported to Auschwitz, and killed. Edith Chat, aged twenty-four, of the same address and almost certainly their daughter, was deported to Sobibor on 14 June 1942 and murdered there.

A family called Holzer, one of the few to be recommended for admission by the Ministry of Commerce, did not make it to Northern Ireland, but managed to get out of Austria to Belgium, where they had relatives. They were captured by the Nazis. Cäcilie, aged thirty-seven, and Erika Holzer, aged eleven, were deported from Malines to Auschwitz on 19 April 1943, and Arthur, aged thirty-eight, was sent to Auschwitz on 31 July 1943. All three were murdered there.

Eight members of the Schorr family were deported together from Vienna to Theresienstadt on 1 October 1942 and only one survived. Dorothea Schorr, aged fifty, and David Schorr, aged fifty-nine, were transported to Auschwitz on 12 October 1944. Eduard Schorr, aged twenty-seven, was deported to Auschwitz on 1 October 1944, from Auschwitz to Buchenwald on 23 January 1945 and from there to Bergen Belsen on 8 March 1945. Jakob Schorr, aged forty-eight, and Rosa Schorr, aged forty-four, were deported to Auschwitz on 4 October 1944. All five lived at Haidgasse 1. Hugo Schorr, aged sixteen, was deported to Auschwitz on 28 September 1944 and died there, Anita Schorr, aged twelve, of Lazenhof 2, died in Theresientstadt on 4 January 1944. Margarete Schorr, aged twenty, was among the eight members of her family deported to Theresienstadt, but she is not listed in the DÖW victims list, and it appears that she survived the Holocaust.

Sigmund Singer, aged sixty-five, his wife Ida Singer, aged fifty-four, and daughter Marianne, aged twenty-five, then of Körnergasse 7, were deported to Maly Trostinec on 14 September 1942 and murdered there on 18 September.

Ignatz Weiss, aged eighty-one, and Mathilde Weiss, aged eighty-four, were deported from Seegasse 9 to Theresienstadt on 20 August 1942. Mathilde died there on 14 September 1942 and Ignatz on 11 January 1943.

Klara Fisch, aged thirty-five, and Markus Fisch, aged forty-three, formerly of Mariahilfer Strasse 99, were captured in Croatia and sent to death camps on 4 August 1941. Klara Fisch was transported from Daruvar/Laborgrad to Auschwitz and Markus Fisch was killed at Jasenovac, an extermination camp in Croatia notorious for the cruelty of its fascist Ustashe regime guards, where between 80,000 and 97,000 Serbs, Jews and Gypsies were murdered. Solly Spitalink, mentioned in the Fisches' application, appears to have survived.

Carola Günsberger and her husband Charles were separately murdered by the Nazis. Carola, aged forty-five, was deported from Springerstrasse 4 to Izbica on 12 May 1942, while Charles, aged forty-eight, with a last address at Hiessgasse 7, escaped to France but was deported from Drancy to Auschwitz on 31 August 1942 and killed there. The couple were named in a letter written by Mathilde Fischer, aged forty-six, of Castellezgasse 20 seeking to transfer her dress-making business to Northern Ireland and to train and employ local girls. She sought to bring out her husband Emil, aged sixty-one, and the Günsbergers. Mathilde said Charles, a manufacturer of underclothing, would be willing to start a manufacture of ladies' wear of all kinds. The Fischers appear to have survived.

Arthur Haas, aged fifty-three, and his wife, Beila Haas, aged fifty-four, were deported together from Böcklinstrasse 33 to Modliborzyce in Poland on 15 March 1941 and killed there. It seems their daughter, whose name or age was not given in their application, may have survived.

Berthold Kohn, a clothing manufacturer, had sought permits for himself and two assistants to set up a factory in Northern Ireland. These were Hans Kraus, of Ingenhausz 4, and Emil Eckstein, of Reisnerstrasse 16. They were not admitted, and no note was written on their application. Two Berthold Kohns from Vienna were killed in the Holocaust, one aged fifty-five, from Postgasse 16, deported to Izbica on 5 June 1942, the other, aged seventy, deported with Fanny Kohn, aged sixty-eight, from Czerningasse 4, on 19 October 1941 to Lödz. At some stage Berthold was transported to the death camp of Chelmno and died there on 11 September 1942. Fanny is not listed among the victim list on the DÖW website, so it is possible she survived. Since Berthold did not give his age on his application, it is not possible to say for certain which man wrote to Northern Ireland. But in his application he had said he owned a weaving company, Vienna Mechanical Weaving (Wiener Mechanische Weberei) and this might indicate that the older Berthold murdered at Chelmno might be the more likely applicant.

Berthold named two assistants, Emil Eckstein and Hans Kraus, in his PRONI application. Emil Eckstein, aged sixty, and Wilhelmine Eckstein, aged thirty-seven, were deported from Riemergasse 16 to Maly Trostinec on 26 May 1942, and were murdered there six days later. It is not certain what became of Hans Kraus, though a 32-year-old man of that name was deported from his native Prague to Theresienstadt on 23 July 1942 and from there to Auschwitz on 18 May 1944. His age profile fits the PRONI applicant. He did not survive.

Hermann Arnold, aged fifty-four, of Wallensteinstrasse 20, was deported to Buchenwald on 8 August 1939, and died there on 30 December.

Dr Walter Subak, aged sixty-five, Mathilde Subak, aged sixty-nine, and Emilie Subak, aged seventy-one, of Annagasse 6, were deported to Riga on 11 January 1942 and murdered there. Four relatives were also killed by the Nazis. Robert, aged sixty, and Nelly Subak, aged forty-six, were deported from their Novaragasse 40 home on 26 January 1942 to Riga, and Ernst, aged fifty-seven, and Marie, aged fifty, of Tandelmarktgasse 19, were deported to Izbica on 15 May 1942.

In addition to those applicants in the PRONI archives, of the 550 people who wrote directly to the BJRC, an unknown number were murdered in the Holocaust. One case gives a sense of the peril not just for individuals but for extended families who had the support of the BJRC but did not manage to emigrate. Fritz Fantl, fifty-three, the former manager of a large manufacturing company in Vienna, wrote to the BJRC in January 1939, hoping to use Northern Ireland as a temporary base until he secured entry to the United States. He had an affidavit offering financial support from sponsors in New York and Washington, but the US's strict quota system for German and Austrian nationals prevented direct entry. Leo Scopp, a member of the Belfast Hebrew Congregation, who owned a radio and electrical company, agreed to support Fantl during his Belfast stay, and confirmed that in writing to the Home Office. But Fantl could not escape from Vienna. He was deported from his home at Liechtensteinstrasse 23 to Lödz, along with his wife, Hilda, aged forty-three, on 15 October 1941. Fritz died there on 19 May 1942 and Hilda on 15 May 1943. Nine other people named Fantl, possibly relatives, were deported on the same transport and none survived. Fritz's twin brother, Otto, aged fifty-four, and his wife, Frieda, aged fifty-two, were also deported from Prague to Theresienstadt on 6 March 1943 and then to Auschwitz on 28 October 1944 and did not survive.

SELECT BIBLIOGRAPHY

This list comprises works that were especially useful in the writing of this book. In particular, several valuable essays relating to Northern Ireland are included in Gisela Holfter (ed.), *The Irish Context of Kristallnacht, Refugees and Helpers.* There is a comprehensive bibliography in Gisela Holfter, and Horst Dickel, *An Irish Sanctuary, German-Speaking Refugees in Ireland 1933–1945,* which deals in detail with southern Ireland. Louise London's *Whitehall and the Jews* explores the British response to the persecution of the Jews under the Nazis in often trenchant detail, and John Privilege's article 'The Northern Ireland Government, the New Industries Act, and Refugees from the Third Reich, 1934–1940' is an authoritative analysis of the Stormont response to the crisis.

Books

Bardon, J., *A History of Ulster* (Belfast: Blackstaff Press, 2001).

Barton, B., *Northern Ireland in the Second World War* (Belfast: Ulster Historical Foundation, 1995).

Bouverie, T., *Appeasing Hitler: Chamberlain, Churchill and the Road to War* (London: Bodley Head, 2019).

Cesarani, D., *Eichmann, His Life and Crimes* (London: William Heinemann, 2004).

Clare, G., *Last Waltz in Vienna* (London: Macmillan, 1981).

Clare, G., *Before the Wall, Berlin Days, 1946–1948* (New York: Dutton, 1990).

Doorly, M.R., *Hidden Memories* (Dublin: Blackwater Press, 1994).

Fachler, Y., 'Three Tragic Sea Voyages: St. Louis, Dunera, Struma', in *Balfour, Boycotts, Blood Libels, Black Books* (Davmor Press with the Jewish Historical Society of Ireland, 2017).

Fachler, Y., *The Vow: Rebuilding the Fachler Tribe after the Holocaust* (Victoria, British Columbia: Trafford, 2003).

Fink, M., *From Belfast to Belsen and Beyond* (Victoria: PenFolk Publishing, 2008).

Finnegan, A., *Reaching for the Fruit: Growing Up in Ulster* (Birmingham: Callender Press, 1992).

Fisk, R., *In Time of War* (Dublin: Gill Books, 1985).

Franklin, A., *Involuntary Guests* (Isle of Man: Lily Publications, 2017).

Friedlander, S., *Nazi Germany and the Jews 1933–1945* (London: Phoenix, 2009).

Gardiner, M., *Code Name 'Mary': Memoirs of an American Woman in the Austrian Underground* (London: Freud Museum, 2021).

Gedye, G.E.R., *Fallen Bastions: The Central European Tragedy* (London: Victor Gollancz, 1939).

Gilbert, M., *Kristallnacht: Prelude to Destruction* (London: HarperCollins, 2006).

Gillman, P. and L., *'Collar the Lot!': How Britain interned and expelled its wartime refugees* (London: Quartet Books, 1980).

Gross, E. and Gross, W., *A Kinder Life and the Star of David on my Luggage* (Belfast: Eva Gross and Wolff Gross, printed by Biddles Ltd, Guildford, 2003).

Gross, L., *The Last Jews in Berlin* (New York: Carrroll & Graf, 1999).

Grenville, A., *Jewish Refugees from Germany and Austria in Britain 1933–1970* (London: Mitchell, 2010).

Hagan, C., *Farewell to Dear Old Shrigley* (Downpatrick: Plus 2 Print, 2012), Kindle edition.

Hayes, M., *Black Puddings and Slim: A Downpatrick Boyhood* (Belfast: Blackstaff Press, 1996).

Hitler, A., *Hitler's Mein Kampf,* ed. D.C. Watt (London: Hutchinson Publishing, 1969).

Holfter, G., and Dickel, H., *An Irish Sanctuary: German-Speaking Refugees in Ireland 1933–1945* (Berlin: Walter de Gruyter GmbH, 2018).

Holfter, G. (ed.), *The Irish Context of Kristallnacht: Refugees and Helpers*, Irish-German Studies, Vol. 8 (Trier: WVT Wissenschaftlicher Verlag, 2014).

Johnson, D., 'The Interwar Economy in Ireland', *Studies in Irish Economic and Social History 4*, (Dundalk: Dundalgan Press, 1989).

Keogh, D., *Jews in Twentieth-Century Ireland. Refugees, Anti-Semitism and the Holocaust* (Cork: University College Press, 1998).

Kershaw, I., *Making Friends with Hitler: Lord Londonderry and Britain's Road to War* (London: Allen Lane, 2001).

Kluger, R., *Landscapes of Memory: A Holocaust Girlhood Remembered* (London: Bloomsbury Publishing, 2003).

Kohner, N., *My Father's Roses* (London: Hodder and Stoughton, 2008).

Leverton B., and Lowensohn, S. (eds), *I Came Alone: The Stories of the Kindertransports* (Lewes: The Book Guild, 1990).

Lewis, H., *A Time to Speak* (Belfast: Blackstaff Press, 1992).

London, L., *Whitehall and the Jews, 1933–1948* (Cambridge: Cambridge University Press, 2001).

Maass, W.B., *Assassination in Vienna* (New York: Charles Scribner's Sons, 1972).

Maier, R., *Ruth Maier's Diary: A Young Girl's Life Under Nazism*, ed. Jan Erik Vold (London: Harvill Secker, 2009).

MacMillan, M., *Peacemakers: Six Months that Changed the World* (London: John Murray, 2020).

McCavery, T., *Newtown: a history of Newtownards* (White Row Press, 2nd edition, 2013).

McKittrick, D., et al, *Lost Lives* (Edinburgh: Mainstream Publishing, 2000).

Nagorski, A., *Saving Freud: A Life in Vienna and an Escape to Freedom in London* (London: Icon Books, 2022).

Oliver, J.A., *Come Away with Me* (Ely, Cambridgeshire: Melrose Books, 2006).

O'Grada, C., *Jewish Ireland in the Age of Joyce: A Socio-economic History* (Princeton/Oxford: Princeton University Press, 2006).

Pauley, B.F., *From Prejudice to Persecution: A History of Austrian Anti-Semitism* (Chapel Hill: The University of North Carolina Press, 1992).

Phoenix, E., *Northern Nationalism: Nationalist Politics, Partition and the Catholic Minority in Northern Ireland, 1890–1940* (Belfast: Ulster Historical Foundation, 1994).

Pick, H., *A Journalist in Search of Her Life* (London: Weidenfeld & Nicolson, 2021).

Rabinovici, D., *Eichmann's Jews: the Jewish Administration of Holocaust Vienna, 1938–1945* (London: Polity, 2011).

Rivlin, R., *Shalom Ireland: A Social History of the Jews in Modern Ireland* (Dublin: Gill & Macmillan, 2003).

Rosenblatt, S., *The Compendium of Irish Jewry 1700–2024 with 84,378 individual entries. A biographical directory of 84,378 family names including births, marriages, burials, with inscriptions & Hebrew names, 1901 & 1911 census, school enrolments, occupation and address of Northern Ireland Jewry, school enrolments, alien registration 1914/22, ascendants and descendants* (London: self-published, 2024).

Rosenkranz, H., 'The Anschluss and the Tragedy of Austrian Jewry 1934–45' in J. Fraenkel (ed.), *The Jews of Austria* (London: Valentine, Mitchell Ltd, 1967).

Rosenkranz, H., *Verfolgung und Selbstbehauptung: Die Juden in Österreich 1938–1945* (Vienna: Herold, 1978).

Safrian, H., *Eichmann's Men* (New York: Cambridge University Press, [year]).

Sands, P., *East West Street: On the Origins of Genocide and Crimes against Humanity* (London: Weidenfeld & Nicolson, 2016).

Sekules, E., *Surviving the Nazis, Exile and Siberia* (London: Valentine Mitchell, 2000), pp. 1938–9.

Shachter, J., *Ingathering, Collected Papers, Essays and Addresses* (Jerusalem: Bazak Press, 1966).

Sherman, A.J., *Island Refuge: Britain and Refugees from the Third Reich, 1933–1939* (London: Frank Cass, 2nd edition, 1994).

Singer, P., *Pushing Time Away: My Grandfather and the Tragedy of Jewish Vienna* (London: Granta Books, 2004).

Sommer, M., Raggam-Belsch, M., Uhl, H., *Das Wiener Modell der Radikalisierung, Österreich und Die Shoah* (Wien: Haus der Geschichte Österreich, 2021).

Stangneth, B., *Eichman Before Jerusalem: The Unexamined Life of a Mass Murderer* (New York: Alfred A. Knopf, 2014).

Szanto, G., *Bog Tender* (Victoria, Canada: Brindle and Glass, 2013).

Taylor, M., *Faraway Home* (Dublin: The O'Brien Press, 2018).

Tobin, R., *The Minority Voice: Hubert Butler and Southern Irish Protestantism, 1900–1991* (Oxford: Oxford University Press, 2012).

Ungar-Klein, B., *Schattenexistenz: Jüdische U-Boote in Wien 1938–1945* (Vienna: Picus Verlag, 2019).

Wachsmann, N., *KL: A History of the Nazi Concentration Camps* (London: Little, Brown, 2015).

Weyr, T., *The Setting of the Pearl: Vienna under Hitler* (Oxford: Oxford University Press, 2005).

Unpublished Memoirs, Essays, Articles

Bartlett, I., 'Derry Jewish historical notes', unpublished.

Beattie, S., 'Ludwig Schenkel 1900–1988', *Due North* (Vol. 3. Issue 4, 2020/2021); 'Donegal through the Lens', *Donegal Annual*, (No. 65, Donegal Historical Society, Letterkenny, 2013).

Bentwich, N., 'Report on a visit to Vienna', 17 August 1939. Wiener Holocaust Library, London, MF Doc 27, Reference Number 27/10/53.

Calder, A., 'The Myth of 1940' (*London Review of Books*, Vol. 2, No. 20, 16 October 1980).

Crangle, Dr J., 'The Italian Fascist Party in Interwar Northern Ireland: Political Hub or Social Club?' (*Queen's Political Review*, 24 May 2016).

Goldberger, O., 'Memories and Reflections' (Toronto: Published by Michael Goldberger, 2020).

Goldstone, K., '"Benevolent Helpfulness?" Ireland and the International Reaction to Jewish Refugees, 1933–39' in Michael Kennedy and Joseph Morrison Skelly (eds), *Irish Foreign Policy, 1919–1966: From Independence to Internationalism* (Dublin: Four Courts Press, 2000).

Jaffé, S., 'History of the Community' in *The Jewish Community in Belfast* (Belfast: Wolfson Centre, 2014), pp. 13–19.

Kessler, G., 'Unpublished Memoir'.

Kohner, F., 'Unpublished Memoir'.

Linden Aveyard, Pamela, 'Gathered Lightpoints: A Reconstruction of the lives, work and journeys of Alice Berger Hammerschlag and Helen Lewis'. Talk, Linen Hall Library, Belfast, 21 February 2024.

Woodside, M., 'Diary MO5462', Tom Harrison Mass Observation Archive, University of Sussex.

Maier, B., 'The Farm at Millisle' (Belfast: *Irish Pages, Ireland in Crisis*, Vol. 6, No. 1).

McCoy, G., 'A Synagogue in Saintfield: The Experience of Gibraltarian Evacuees in the Land of Milk and Snow', *Saintfield Heritage,* Book Nine (Armagh: Saintfield Heritage Society, 2004)

Privilege, J., 'The Northern Ireland Government, the New Industries Act, and Refugees from the Third Reich, 1934–1940', *Holocaust and Genocide Studies,* Vol. 31, Issue 1, Spring 2017.

Singer, Rabbi David, *Judaism, A Brief Outline* (Belfast Hebrew Community, no date given).

Charlie Warmington. Presentation, 17 December 2018.

Archives, Newspaper Collections, Unpublished Theses

Public Record Office of Northern Ireland; Queen's University, Belfast; Belfast Central Library; Linen Hall Library, Belfast; Cardinal Tomás Ó Fiaich Memorial Library, Armagh; Derry Central Library; Trinity College Dublin; The National Archives, Kew; Wiener Holocaust Library, London; United States Holocaust Memorial Museum, Washington, USA; Documentationsarchiv des Österreichischen Widerstandes (Documentation Archive of the Austrian Resistance), Vienna; Österreichische Nationalbibliothek (Austrian National Library) Vienna; Wiener Stadt und Landesarchiv (Vienna City and Regional Archive); Amt der Niederösterreichischen Landesregierung, (Office of the Lower Austria State Government, St Pölten, Austria); Central Zionist Archives, Jerusalem.

Linden, P., 'Jewish identity and community in Belfast, 1920–1948', PhD thesis, Queen's University Belfast, 2016.

NOTES

Introduction

1. H. Rosenkranz, 'The Anschluss and the Tragedy of Austrian Jewry 1934–45' in J. Fraenkel (ed.), The Jews of Austria (London: Valentine, Mitchell Ltd, 1967), p. 486.

1 'Perish Judah!'

1. T. Bouverie, *Appeasing Hitler: Chamberlain, Churchill and the Road to War* (London: Bodley Head, 2019), p. 162.
2. Rosenkranz, 'The Anschluss', p. 480.
3. Ibid., pp. 480–1.
4. D. Rabinovici, *Eichmann's Jews: The Jewish Administration of Holocaust Vienna, 1938–1945* (London: Polity, 2011), p. 27.
5. Gisela Holfter and Horst Dickel, *An Irish Sanctuary: German-Speaking Refugees in Ireland 1933–1945* (Berlin: Walter de Gruyter GmbH, 2018), p. 44.
6. G. Clare, *Last Waltz in Vienna* (London: Macmillan, 1981), pp. 177–8.
7. Ibid., p. 178.
8. https://wienerholocaustlibrary.org
9. B.F. Pauley, *From Prejudice to Persecution: A History of Austrian Anti-Semitism* (Chapel Hill: The University of North Carolina Press, 1992), p. 284.
10. Ibid., p. 284.
11. Rosenkranz, 'The Anschluss', p. 483.
12. Rabinovici, *Eichmann's Jews,* p. 27.
13. Ibid., p. 33.

14. A. Hitler, *Hitler's Mein Kampf,* ed. D.C Watt (London: Hutchinson Publishing, 1969), p. 3.
15. L. Lauterbach, 'The Jewish Situation in Austria', Report to World Zionist Organisation, 29 April 1938, Central Zionist Archive, S5-653, 6.
16. *Belfast Telegraph*, 14 March 1938. Youth Aliyah was a Jewish organisation founded in Berlin in January 1933 which rescued 5,600 Jewish children from the Third Reich and brought them to kibbutzim and youth villages in Palestine.
17. D. Cesarani, *Eichmann, His Life and Crimes* (London: William Heinemann, 2004), pp. 19–20.
18. H. Safrian, *Eichmann's Men* (New York: Cambridge University Press), p 17.
19. Cesarani, *Eichmann*, pp. 24–5.
20. Rabinovici, *Eichmann's Jews*, p. 35.
21. Cesarani, *Eichmann*, p. 64.
22. Safrian, *Eichmann's Men*, p. 27.
23. Fraenkel, *The Jews of Austria*, p. 485.
24. Rabinovici, *Eichmann's Jews*, p. 35.
25. Ibid., p. 35.
26. Ibid., p. 35.
27. Safrian, *Eichmann's Men*, p. 29.
28. Ibid., p. 29.
29. Rabinovici, *Eichmann's Jews*, p. 64
30. Safrian, *Eichmann's Men*, p. 28.
31. Fraenkel, *The Anschluss*, p. 483.
32. *Belfast Telegraph*, 16 March 1938.
33. *Belfast Telegraph,* 16 March 1938.
34. *Belfast Telegraph*, 28 March 1938.
35. *Belfast Telegraph*, 28 March 1938.
36. H. Rosenkranz, *Verfolgung und Selbstbehauptung: Die Juden in Österreich 1938–1945* (München: Herold, 1978), p. 25. [Author's translation]
37. Clare, *Last Waltz in Vienna,* p. 191.

Notes

2 'Baby-coffins were coming out of every street'

1. J. Bardon, *A History of Ulster* (Belfast: Blackstaff Press, 2001), p. 529.
2. Ibid., p. 531.
3. J. Privilege, 'The Northern Ireland Government, the New Industries Act, and Refugees from the Third Reich, 1934–1940', *Holocaust and Genocide Studies,* Volume 31, Issue 1, Spring 2017, pp. 87–109.
4. Ibid., p. 98. W.D. Scott to Robert Gransden, 2 June 1938, PRONI, CAB 9/F/126/2.
5. L. London, *Whitehall and the Jews, 1933–1948* (Cambridge: Cambridge University Press, 2001), p. 59.
6. Ibid., p. 61.
7. Ibid., p. 61.
8. Ibid., p. 63.
9. Ibid., p. 67.
10. Ibid., p. 82.
11. Ibid., p. 89.
12. Ibid., p. 96.
13. Ibid., p. 104.
14. Ibid., p. 80.
15. Ibid., pp. 102–9.
16. Ibid., p. 134.
17. Ibid., p. 136.
18. Ibid., p. 131.

3 'A daily barbarism'

1. Safrian, *Eichmann's Men*, p. 30.
2. Hubert Butler, *The Children of Drancy* (Mullingar: Lilliput Press, 1988), p. 198.
3. Ibid., p. 201.
4. Ibid., p. 204.
5. Fraenkel, p. 487.
6. N. Wachsmann, *KL: A History of the Nazi Concentration Camps* (London: Little, Brown, 2015), p. 177.
7. Fraenkel, p. 488.

Notes

2 'Baby-coffins were coming out of every street'

1. J. Bardon, *A History of Ulster* (Belfast: Blackstaff Press, 2001), p. 529.
2. Ibid., p. 531.
3. J. Privilege, 'The Northern Ireland Government, the New Industries Act, and Refugees from the Third Reich, 1934–1940', *Holocaust and Genocide Studies,* Volume 31, Issue 1, Spring 2017, pp. 87–109.
4. Ibid., p. 98. W.D. Scott to Robert Gransden, 2 June 1938, PRONI, CAB 9/F/126/2.
5. L. London, *Whitehall and the Jews, 1933–1948* (Cambridge: Cambridge University Press, 2001), p. 59.
6. Ibid., p. 61.
7. Ibid., p. 61.
8. Ibid., p. 63.
9. Ibid., p. 67.
10. Ibid., p. 82.
11. Ibid., p. 89.
12. Ibid., p. 96.
13. Ibid., p. 104.
14. Ibid., p. 80.
15. Ibid., pp. 102–9.
16. Ibid., p. 134.
17. Ibid., p. 136.
18. Ibid., p. 131.

3 'A daily barbarism'

1. Safrian, *Eichmann's Men*, p. 30.
2. Hubert Butler, *The Children of Drancy* (Mullingar: Lilliput Press, 1988), p. 198.
3. Ibid., p. 201.
4. Ibid., p. 204.
5. Fraenkel, p. 487.
6. N. Wachsmann, *KL: A History of the Nazi Concentration Camps* (London: Little, Brown, 2015), p. 177.
7. Fraenkel, p. 488.

Notes

2 'Baby-coffins were coming out of every street'

1. J. Bardon, *A History of Ulster* (Belfast: Blackstaff Press, 2001), p. 529.
2. Ibid., p. 531.
3. J. Privilege, 'The Northern Ireland Government, the New Industries Act, and Refugees from the Third Reich, 1934–1940', *Holocaust and Genocide Studies,* Volume 31, Issue 1, Spring 2017, pp. 87–109.
4. Ibid., p. 98. W.D. Scott to Robert Gransden, 2 June 1938, PRONI, CAB 9/F/126/2.
5. L. London, *Whitehall and the Jews, 1933–1948* (Cambridge: Cambridge University Press, 2001), p. 59.
6. Ibid., p. 61.
7. Ibid., p. 61.
8. Ibid., p. 63.
9. Ibid., p. 67.
10. Ibid., p. 82.
11. Ibid., p. 89.
12. Ibid., p. 96.
13. Ibid., p. 104.
14. Ibid., p. 80.
15. Ibid., pp. 102–9.
16. Ibid., p. 134.
17. Ibid., p. 136.
18. Ibid., p. 131.

3 'A daily barbarism'

1. Safrian, *Eichmann's Men*, p. 30.
2. Hubert Butler, *The Children of Drancy* (Mullingar: Lilliput Press, 1988), p. 198.
3. Ibid., p. 201.
4. Ibid., p. 204.
5. Fraenkel, p. 487.
6. N. Wachsmann, *KL: A History of the Nazi Concentration Camps* (London: Little, Brown, 2015), p. 177.
7. Fraenkel, p. 488.

Notes

2 'Baby-coffins were coming out of every street'

1. J. Bardon, *A History of Ulster* (Belfast: Blackstaff Press, 2001), p. 529.
2. Ibid., p. 531.
3. J. Privilege, 'The Northern Ireland Government, the New Industries Act, and Refugees from the Third Reich, 1934–1940', *Holocaust and Genocide Studies,* Volume 31, Issue 1, Spring 2017, pp. 87–109.
4. Ibid., p. 98. W.D. Scott to Robert Gransden, 2 June 1938, PRONI, CAB 9/F/126/2.
5. L. London, *Whitehall and the Jews, 1933–1948* (Cambridge: Cambridge University Press, 2001), p. 59.
6. Ibid., p. 61.
7. Ibid., p. 61.
8. Ibid., p. 63.
9. Ibid., p. 67.
10. Ibid., p. 82.
11. Ibid., p. 89.
12. Ibid., p. 96.
13. Ibid., p. 104.
14. Ibid., p. 80.
15. Ibid., pp. 102–9.
16. Ibid., p. 134.
17. Ibid., p. 136.
18. Ibid., p. 131.

3 'A daily barbarism'

1. Safrian, *Eichmann's Men*, p. 30.
2. Hubert Butler, *The Children of Drancy* (Mullingar: Lilliput Press, 1988), p. 198.
3. Ibid., p. 201.
4. Ibid., p. 204.
5. Fraenkel, p. 487.
6. N. Wachsmann, *KL: A History of the Nazi Concentration Camps* (London: Little, Brown, 2015), p. 177.
7. Fraenkel, p. 488.

8. Rabinovici, *Eichmann's Jews*, p. 45.
9. Rosenkranz, *Verfolgung*, p. 41.
10. Ibid., p. 41.
11. Fraenkel, p. 487.
12. Ibid., p. 494.
13. Pauley, *From Prejudice to Persecution*, p. 285.
14. Ibid., p. 285.
15. Fraenkel, p. 493.
16. Ibid., p. 493.
17. Ibid., p. 490.
18. Ibid., p. 494.
19. Hubert Butler, *The Invader Wore Slippers* (London: Notting Hill Editions, 2012), p. 257.
20. Ibid., p. 258.
21. Ibid., p. 259.
22. Safrian, *Eichmann's Men*, p. 34.

4 'The makings of a real Ulsterman'

1. COM/17/3/13 363.
2. *Zionistische Rundschau*, 26 August 1938; see Rosenkranz, *Verfolgung*, p. 103.
3. https://discovery.nationalarchives.gov.uk/details/r/C4186286, File HO 144/13836.
4. Letter from Hedwig Neufeld mentioning 'Mr. A. Neumann's action', COM 17/3/3B 1–79.
5. Privilege, p. 99, and Ulster Development Council memorandum 21 November 1938, PRONI, COM/20/2/18.
6. *Northern Whig*, 9 August 1938.
7. www.belfastjewishheritage.org; '150 Years of Belfast's Jewish Community', https://www.bbc.co.uk/news/uk-northern-ireland-31003098.
8. Steven Jaffe, 'History of the Community' in *The Jewish Community in Belfast* (Belfast: Wolfson Centre, 2014), pp.13–19.
9. Privilege, pp. 88–9; James Loughlin, 'Northern Ireland and British Fascism in the Inter-War Years', *Irish Historical Studies*, November 1995, Volume 29, No. 116, pp. 537–52.

10. Letters from Sidney Salomon, Secretary to the Board of Deputies of British Jews, to Shachter, Central Zionist Archives (CZA), Jerusalem, A350-10-7, A350-10-19, A350-10-37.
11. Pamela Linden, 'Jewish identity and community in Belfast, 1920–1948', PhD thesis, Queen's University, Belfast, 2016, p. 201.
12. Linden, p. 201; report of refugee names, addresses, case details, undated (CZA, SPA350/82/2).

5 'Please help a despaired family'

1. Email from Dr John Privilege, 31 December 2021.
2. PRONI file, COM 17/3/8.
3. COM/17/3/3 B 1-79.
4. COM/17/3/24.
5. COM/17/3/3 B 1-79.
6. COM/17/3/3 B 1-79.
7. COM/17/3/3 B 1-79.
8. COM/17/3/3 B 1-79.
9. COM/17/3/6.
10. COM/17/3/7.
11. COM 17/3/12.
12. COM 17/3/31.
13. COM/17/3/17.
14. COM/17/3/17.
15. COM/17/3/24.
16. COM/17/3/12.
17. COM/17/3/22.
18. COM/17/3/24.
19. COM/17/3/24.
20. COM/17/3/17.
21. COM/17/3/20.
22. COM/17/3/4.
23. COM 17/3/5.
24. COM/17/3/19.
25. COM/17/3/13.
26. COM/17/3/20.
27. COM/17/3/23.

28. COM/17/3/28 (COM 17/3/1/s).
29. COM 17/3/35.
30. COM/17/3/40.
31. COM/17/3/42.
32. COM 17/3/44.
33. COM/17/3/48.
34. COM/17/3/49.
35. COM/17/3/23.
36. COM/17/3/49.
37. COM/17/3/13.
38. COM/17/3/13.

6 'A good deed for humanity'

1. G. Douglas, 'Norah Douglas and the Belfast Committee for German Refugees' in Gisela Holfter (ed.), *The Irish Context of Kristallnacht: Refugees and Helpers*, Irish-German Studies, Vol. 8 (Trier: WVT Wissenschafltlicher Verlag Trier, 2014), pp.89–101.
2. https://www.newulsterbiography.co.uk/
3. Margaret G. Fink, *From Belfast to Belsen and Beyond* (Victoria: PenFolk Publishing, 2008), p. xii.
4. Ibid., p. 32.
5. Ibid., p. 33.
6. Ibid., p. 33.
7. Agnes Finnegan, *Reaching for the Fruit: Growing Up in Ulster* (Birmingham: Callender Press, 1992), p. 95.
8. Ibid., p. 94.
9. Ibid., p. 95.
10. Ibid., p. 96.
11. Ibid., p. 96.
12. Ibid., p.103.
13. Ibid., p. 103.
14. Ibid., p.104.
15. Ibid., p. 106.
16. Ibid., p. 106.
17. Ibid., p. 107.

18. Interview with Owen Finnegan, 24 October 2017.
19. Ibid.

7 'Mr Neumann's scheme'

1. COM/17/1. Minutes of Advisory Committee Meetings.
2. COM/17/3.30.
3. HA/8/68.
4. HA/8/68.
5. HA/8/67.

8 'A big settling of accounts with the Jews'

1. Rabinovici, *Eichmann's Jews*, p. 58.
2. *Belfast Telegraph* 4 May, 1938; *Belfast News Letter*, 11 November 1938; *Irish News*, 20 June 1938; also Privilege, p. 89; G.E.R. Gedye, *Fallen Bastions: The Central European Tragedy* (London: Victor Gollancz Ltd, 1939), pp. 300–13; also see Gisela Holfter (ed.), *The Irish Context of Kristallnacht*, p. 17.
3. Privilege, p. 89 and p. 104.
4. https://wienerholocaustlibrary.org/
5. Ibid.
6. Rosenkranz, 'The Anschluss', p. 502.
7. S. Friedlander, *Nazi Germany and the Jews 1933–1945* (London: Phoenix, 2009), p. 120.
8. Cesarani, *Eichmann*, p. 73.
9. Ibid., p. 73.
10. Ibid., p. 74.
11. Otto Goldberger, unpublished memoir, 'Memories and Reflections', given to author by Melvyn Goldberger.
12. Ibid.
13. Ibid.
14. Ibid.
15. Ibid.
16. Ibid.
17. Ibid.
18. G. Szanto, *Bog Tender* (Victoria, Canada: Brindle and Glass, 2013), p. 136.

19. Ibid., p. 136.
20. Ibid., p.138.
21. Interview, Elly Szanto, USC Shoah Foundation archive, April 1996; audio testimony supplied by Ms Gloria Apfel, her daughter, transcribed by the author 25 October 2019.

9 'I implore you for the quickest help'

1. Rabinovici, *Eichmann's Jews*, p. 63.
2. COM/17/3/28 (COM 17/3/1/s).
3. COM/17/3/28 (COM 17/3/1/s).
4. COM/17/3/28 (COM 17/3/1/s).
5. COM/17/3/49.
6. COM/17/3/49.
7. COM/17/3/49.
8. COM/17/3/49.
9. COM/17/3/49.
10. COM/17/3/8 B.
11. COM/17/3/8 B.
12. COM/17/3/12.
13. COM 17/3/17.
14. COM/17/3/18.
15. COM/17/3/19.
16. COM/17/3/20.
17. COM/17/3/20.
18. COM/17/3/23.
19. COM/17/3/23.
20. COM/17/3/5.
21. COM/17/3/6.
22. COM/17/3/24.
23. COM/17/3/8 B.
24. COM/17/3/17.
25. COM/17/3/7.
26. COM/17/3/24.
27. COM/17/3/24.
28. COM/17/3/24.
29. COM/17/3/2.

30. COM17/3/2.
31. COM/17/3/19.
32. COM/17/3/4.
33. COM/17/3/24.
34. COM/17/3/24.
35. COM/17/3/5.
36. COM/17/3/6.
37. COM/17/3/5.
38. COM/17/3/6.
39. COM/17/3/3 B1-79.
40. COM/17/3/7 A
41. COM/17/3/1.
42. COM/17/3/12.
43. COM/17/3/20.
44. COM/17/3/17.
45. COM/17/3/13.
46. COM/17/3/15.
47. COM/17/3/49.
48. COM/17/3/24.
49. COM/17/3/24.
50. COM/17/3/24.
51. COM/17/3/28.
52. COM/17/3/28.
53. COM/17/3/24.
54. COM/17/3/17.

10 'Like wounded animals, licking their wounds'

1. https://www.hmd.org.uk/
2. Interview with Walter Kammerling, 10 June 2018.
3. Ibid.
4. Ibid.
5. Ibid.
6. Gertrude Kessler, unpublished memoir, supplied by her son Charlie Warmington.
7. Ibid.
8. Ibid.

9. Ibid.
10. Ibid.
11. Ibid.
12. Ibid.
13. Letter supplied to the author by Charlie Warmington.
14. Gertrude Kessler, unpublished memoir.

11 'Be strong and courageous'

1. Privilege, p. 93.
2. Pamela Linden Aveyard, 'Gathered Lightpoints: A Reconstruction of the lives, work and journeys of Alice Berger Hammerschlag and Helen Lewis', Talk, Linen Hall Library, Belfast, 21 February 2024.
3. Franz Kohner, unpublished memoir.
4. Ibid.
5. Ibid.
6. N. Kohner, *My Father's Roses* (London: Hodder and Stoughton, 2008), pp. 227–8.
7. Ibid., p. 228.
8. Franz Kohner, unpublished memoir.
9. Ibid., p. 240.
10. Ibid. For details of the Farm see Marilyn Taylor, 'Millisle, County Down – Haven from Nazi Terror', *History Ireland*, 18th–19th-Century History, 20th-century/Contemporary History, Features, Issue 4 (Winter 2001), Volume 9, World War I; and https://wartimeni.com.
11. Gisela Holfter and Horst Dickel, *An Irish Sanctuary: German-Speaking Refugees in Ireland 1933–1945* (Berlin: Walter de Gruyter GmbH, 2018), pp. 361–2.
12. Interview with Ruth Kohner, 8 March 2017; and unpublished memoirs, Copy 2/4 by Franz Kohner lent to the author by Billy Kohner.
13. Interview with Ruth Kohner, March 2017.

12 'I will show you the worst place'

1. Chris Hagan, *Farewell to Dear Old Shrigley* (Downpatrick: Plus 2 Print, 2012), Kindle edition; and Facebook page, *Old Shrigley*, post 31, October 2016.

2. Privilege, p.104; and Hagan, *Farewell to Dear Old Shrigley.*
3. Hagan, *Farewell to Dear Old Shrigley.*
4. Ibid.
5. Ibid.
6. Privilege, p. 102.
7. Hagan, *Farewell to Dear Old Shrigley.*
8. Ibid.
9. Ibid.
10. Ibid.
11. Interview with Vivienne Vermes, 18 February 2021; and *The Down Recorder*, 'Saved from the Holocaust to Managing in Shrigley', 24 January 2018.
12. Interview with Vivienne Vermes, 18 February 2021.
13. *January 1940: The Narrow Gate,* https://youtu.be/EM1zur8Jm48?si=co1U6UUucRIKgjUa.
14. Interview with Vivienne Vermes 18 February 2021; email from Dr Ursula Schwarz re Berndorf, 22 February 2021; email from Dr Stefan Eminger, Amt der NÖ Landesregierung, St Polten, Austria, 2 March 2021.
15. *January 1940: The Narrow Gate.*
16. Ibid.
17. Hagan, *Farewell to Dear Old Shrigley.*
18. Interview with Maurice Hayes, 12 October 2017.
19. Ibid.
20. Ibid.
21. Maurice Hayes, *Black Puddings and Slim: A Downpatrick Boyhood* (Belfast: Blackstaff Press, 1996). The sergeant may have been Sergeant G. McCullough at Killyleagh.
22. Email to author from Shirley Lennon.
23. Interview with Maurice Hayes.
24. Ballykinlar History Hut, Facebook.
25. Ibid.
26. Interview with Maurice Hayes.
27. Ibid.

13 'Help us to save our parents'

1. *Londonderry Sentinel*, 11 March 1958.
2. Finnegan, p. 99.
3. *Londonderry Sentinel*, 31 December 1938.
4. John Whyte, 'How much discrimination was there under the Unionist regime, 1921–1968?' in Tom Gallagher and James O'Connell (eds), *Contemporary Irish Studies* (Manchester: Manchester University Press, 1983).
5. https://jewishgen.org/
6. Sarah E. Karesh and Michael M. Hurwitz (eds), *Encyclopedia of Judaism* (New York, Facts on File Inc., 2005), p. 10.
7. Ian Bartlett, Derry Jewish historical notes, supplied to the author.
8. Sean Beattie, 'An Austrian Jewish Refugee in Clonmany', *Due North* (Vol. 3, Issue 4, 20 February 2021). Thanks to Ian Bartlett, Derry, for informing me about this article.
9. Ian Bartlett, Derry notes.
10. *Northern Whig*, 8 November 1938.
11. PRON I COM/17/1, Advisory Committee Meeting 2 November 1938.
12. Privilege, pp. 101–2.
13. PRONI COM40/2/1292, Advisory Committee meeting, 7 December 1938.
14. Brüder Deutsch to the Ministry of Commerce, 3 September 1938; and D. Kelly to Brüder Deutsch, 8 September 1938, PRONI COM/63/1/56, and Privilege, p. 102.
15. PRONI HA/8/69, Jewish Community, Londonderry.
16. Ibid.
17. Ibid.
18. Barton, pp. 100–1.
19. Barton, pp. 50–1.
20. Edith Sekules, *Surviving the Nazis, Exile and Siberia* (London, Valentine Mitchell, 2000), pp. 138–9.
21. Seán Beattie, 'How the North West Welcomed Jewish Refugees in the 1940s', *Due North* (Downpatrick), Vol. 3, Issue 4, 20/02/2021); email to author from Eva Arnott, Paul Schenkel's daughter, 9 May 2021.

22. Interview with Owen Finnegan, 15 August 2018.
23. Beattie, *How the North West Welcomed Jewish Refugees in the 1940s.*
24. Ibid.
25. Ibid.; and interview with David Bigger, 3 November 2017.
26. Obituary, *Jewish Chronicle*, 20 August 1971.
27. PRONI HA/8/69, Jewish Community, Londonderry.
28. Skriebeleit, Jörg, (2009), 'Leitmeritz', in Geoffrey P. Megargee (ed.). *Early Camps, Youth Camps, and Concentration Camps and Subcamps under the SS-Business Administration Main Office (WVHA).* Encyclopedia of Camps and Ghettos, 1933–1945. Vol. 1. Translated by Stephen Pallavicini (Bloomington: United States Holocaust Memorial Museum), pp. 626–8.
29. PRONI HA8/69, MS464/1939/1940/1945 in letter dated 23 Dec. 1938, listing applications for admission to NI (Londonderry), and www.DÖW.at
30. Email to author from Dr Sidney Katzen, 25 February 2021.

14 Where is Mr Neumann?

1. Privilege, pp. 91–9.
2. Ibid., p. 108, footnote 84: a memo on 24 April 1939 from H.E. Jones at the Ministry of Commerce to J.E. Makin at the Ministry of Finance gave details of the money Stormont had paid to help new industries. COM/20/2/18.
3. Ibid.
4. W.L. Robinson, Ulster Development Council memorandum to the Ministry of Commerce, 15 May 1939, PRONI, COM /20/2/18; and Privilege, p. 99.
5. Central Zionist Archive, Jerusalem (CZA, SPA350/79/29-31).
6. W.L. Robinson, Ulster Development Council memorandum to the Ministry of Commerce, 15 May 1939, PRONI, COM /20/2/18; and Privilege, p. 99.
7. Interview with Vivienne Magee, 22 May 2018.
8. Ibid.

15 'A multiplication of catastrophes'

1. London, *Whitehall*, p. 132.
2. Ibid., p. 132.
3. Ibid., p. 133.
4. Ibid., pp. 135–6.
5. N. Bentwich, 'Report on a visit to Vienna', 17 August 1939. Wiener Holocaust Library, London, MF Doc 27, Reference Number 27/10/53.
6. Ibid.
7. Ibid.
8. Ibid.
9. London, *Whitehall*, p. 141.

16 'There were German soldiers everywhere'

1. Interview with George Bloch, 25 October 2017, and notes supplied to the author by Nicholas Bloch, 8 April 2024.
2. Interview with Paul Sochor, 28 August 2019.
3. Ibid.
4. Interview with Eric Langhammer, 18 March 2018.
5. Ibid.
6. https://en.wikipedia.org/wiki/Alf_Dubs,_Baron_Dubs
7. Interview with Alf Dubs, 13 June 2018.
8. *Belfast News Letter*, 1 October 1939.

17 'Collar the lot!'

1. PRONI, CAB 9/CD/2/2, Gransden to Markbreiter, 2 September 1939.
2. Linden, p. 219; *Jewish Chronicle*, 24 November 1939.
3. London, *Whitehall*, p. 170.
4. https://www.burytimes.co.uk/news/16309866.hidden-history-horror-brutality-injustice-warth-mills-wwii-prison-camp/
5. Julius Neumann to Rabbi Shachter, 15 January 1940, CZA, SPA350/125/5.
6. Julius Neumann to Rabbi Shachter, 21 February 1940, CZA, SPA350/125/3.

7. Julius Neumann to Rabbi Shachter, 5 March 1940, CZA, SPA350/125/7.
8. Julius Neumann to Rabbi Shachter, 10 March 1940, CZA, SPA350/125/8.
9. Undated letter, CZA, SPA350/125/4.
10. Linden, p. 221.
11. Margaret G. Fink, *From Belfast to Belsen and Beyond* (Victoria: Penfolk Publishing, 2008), p. 34.
12. Ibid., p. 35.
13. Otto Goldberger memoir.
14. Holfter and Dickel, *An Irish Sanctuary,* p. 362.
15. https://www.DÖW.at/
16. https://www.lisburnmuseum.com/
17. Fink, p. 36.
18. Holfter, *The Irish Context of Kristallnacht,* p. 97.
19. Ibid., p. 36.
20. Ibid., p. 97.
21. Fink, p. 37.
22. Otto Goldberger memoir.
23. Linden, p. 223; H. Campbell to Shachter, 15 July 1940 (CZA/SDA350/125/50).
24. Fink, p. 41.
25. PRONI, HA8/69, AND MS 473/C.S. 37/86/52 and interview with Mrs Vivienne Magee, 22 May 2018.
26. PRONI MS 499, C.S. 37/86/57.
27. Peter and Leni Gillman, *'Collar the Lot!': How Britain interned and expelled its wartime refugees* (London: Quartet Books, 1980), pp. 104–5.
28. Diary of Moya Woodside, MO5462, Tom Harrison Mass Observation Archive, University of Sussex.
29. Ibid.
30. Ibid.
31. Ibid.
32. Ibid.
33. A. Franklin, *Involuntary Guests* (Isle of Man: Lily Publications, 2017), p. 49.

18 'With you in spirit'

1. https://www.DÖW.at/
2. Safrian, *Eichmann's Men*, p. 61.
3. Rabinovici, *Eichmann's Jews*, p. 96.
4. Thomas Weyr, *The Setting of the Pearl: Vienna under Hitler* (New York: Oxford University Press, 2005), p. 156. The ruling left-wing Social Democrats built more than 60,000 apartments for the less well-off in Vienna between 1925 and 1934.
5. Rabinovici, *Eichmann's Jews*, p. 98.
6. Ibid., p. 98.
7. Weyr, *The Setting*, p. 164.
8. Ibid., p. 165.
9. Ibid., p. 165.
10. Ernst Weiniger statement, supplied to the author by David and Siobhan Weiniger, Belfast.
11. Ibid.
12. Ibid.
13. Ibid.
14. Email to author from Dr Ursula Schwarz, DÖW, 23 January 2020.
15. Ibid.
16. Interview with Walter Kammerling, 10 June 2018.
17. Interview with Herta Kammerling, 10 June 2018.
18. Ibid.
19. Ibid.
20. Ibid.
21. Interview with Walter Kammerling.

19 'A mighty hiss, a cry – and all was over'

1. Angus Calder, 'The Myth of 1940', *London Review of Books*, Vol. 2, No. 20, 16 October 1980.
2. Peter and Leni Gillman, *'Collar the Lot!'*, p. 191.
3. Ibid., p. 191.
4. Robert Fisk, *In Time of War: Ireland, Ulster and the Price of Neutrality 1939–45* (Dublin: Gill Books, 1985), p. 151.
5. Peter and Leni Gillman, *'Collar the Lot!'*, p.192.

6. Email to author from Dr Jack Crangle, Department of History, Maynooth University, 5 March 2024.
7. Fisk, *In Time of War*, p. 379; and Dr Jack Crangle, 'The Italian Fascist Party in Interwar Northern Ireland: Political Hub or Social Club?', *Queen's Political Review*, 24 May 2016.
8. Peter and Leni Gillman, '*Collar the Lot!*', p.194.
9. Estimates of the nationalities of the dead vary, though the most accurate figure for the Italians is 446 listed on a memorial at Termoncarragh cemetery, Belmullet, Co. Mayo. The Gillmans' overall estimate, published in 1980, is still the most reliable.
10. https://uboat.net/
11. Fisk, *In Time of War*, p. 155.
12. Yanky Fachler, 'Three Tragic Sea Voyages: St. Louis, Dunera, Struma', in *Balfour, Boycotts, Blood Libels, Black Books* (Davmor Press with the Jewish Historical Society of Ireland, 2017).
13. Peter and Leni Gillman, '*Collar the Lot!*', p. 246.
14. Ibid., p. 247.
15. Calder, 'The Myth of 1940'.
16. Peter and Leni Gillman, '*Collar the Lot!*', p. 256.

20 'The one place where we had safety'

1. G. McCoy, 'A Synagogue in Saintfield: The Experience of Gibraltarian Evacuees in the Land of Milk – and Snow', in *Saintfield Heritage*, Book Nine (Armagh: Saintfield Heritage Society, 2004), pp. 81–90.
2. *Belfast Telegraph*, 19 July 1944.
3. Barton, p. 44, and McCoy, 'A Synagogue in Saintfield', p. 1.
4. McCoy, p. 3.
5. Ibid., p. 3.
6. Ibid., p. 4.
7. *Belfast Telegraph*, 31 July 1944.
8. McCoy, 'A Synagogue in Saintfield', p. 3.
9. Ibid., p. 4.
10. *The Times,* 18 December 1944.
11. *The Down Recorder*, 25 November 1944.
12. *The Irish News*, 29 July 2013.

13. *The Down Recorder,* 2 September 1944.
14. McCoy, 'A Synagogue in Saintfield', p. 6.
15. *Belfast Telegraph,* 19 March 1946.
16. *Belfast Telegraph,* 12 March 1947.
17. *Down Recorder,* 5 June 1948.
18. McCoy, 'A Synagogue in Saintfield', p. 5.
19. *The Down Recorder,* 9 July 1971.

21 Back to Vienna

1. Interview with Walter Kammerling.
2. Ibid.
3. Ibid.
4. Interview with Herta Kammerling.
5. Ibid.
6. Interview with Walter Kammerling.
7. https://www.DÖW.at/
8. Interview with Walter Kammerling, and https://www. DÖW.at
9. Letter lent to author by Charlie Warmington.
10. Email, Dr Ursula Schwarz, DÖW, 8 January 2020.
11. Interview with Charlie Warmington, 20 February 2018.
12. Ibid.
13. Ibid.
14. Ibid.
15. Ibid.
16. Presentation by Charlie Warmington, 17 December 2018, supplied to the author.
17. Interview with Charlie Warmington, 20 February 2018.
18. Interview and text supplied by Franziska Meinhardt, July 2019.
19. https://www.DÖW.at/
20. PRONI, HA8/76, HA8/77 and Interview with Mrs Vivienne Magee, 22 May 2018.

22 'There's cream in the bottle'

1. Interview with George Bloch, 25 October 2017.
2. Ibid.

3. Ibid.
4. Ibid.
5. Ibid.
6. Notes supplied to the author by Nicholas Bloch, 8 April 2024.
7. N. Kohner, *My Father's Roses*, p. 260.
8. Ibid., p. 263.
9. Ibid., pp. 264–5.
10. Interview with Ruth Kohner, 8 March 2017.
11. Interview with Billy Kohner, 27 February 2018.
12. Ibid.
13. D. McKittrick et al., *Lost Lives* (Edinburgh: Mainstream Publishing, 2000), p. 31.
14. H. Lewis, *A Time to Speak* (Belfast: Blackstaff Press, 1992), pp 6–10.
15. Interview with Ruth Kohner, 8 March 2017.
16. Ibid.
17. Interview with Billy Kohner, 27 February 2018.
18. Ibid.
19. Ibid.
20. Ibid.
21. Ibid.
22. Interview with Richard Weiniger, son of Walter, 9 April 2019.
23. Ibid.
24. Ibid.
25. Ibid.
26. Ibid.
27. Interview with Paul Sochor, 28 August 2019.
28. www.belfastjewishheritage.org
29. Ibid.
30. Interview with Michael Black, 11 February 2020.
31. Ibid.
32. Ibid.

23 'So lucky you were born Jewish'

1. Interview with Ronnie Appleton, 22 August 2018.
2. Interview with Shoshana Appleton, 22 August 2018.
3. Ibid.

4. Ibid.
5. Ibid.
6. Ibid.
7. Ibid.
8. Interview with Ronnie Appleton, 22 August 2018.
9. Email, Michael Black, 27 February 2024. Figures from 2021 Northern Ireland Census.
10. Interview with Ronnie Appleton, 22 August 2018.
11. Rosenkranz, 'The Anschluss', in Fraenkel (ed.), *The Jews of Austria*, p. 521.
12. Ibid., p. 526.

24 Pilgrimage of memory

1. Interview with Charlie Warmington, 20 February 2018.
2. Ibid.
3. Speech, Charlie Warmington, Vienna, 25 June 2019.
4. Ibid.

Appendix
1. Email from Austrian State Archives to author, 22 March 2024.
2. Ibid.

INDEX

Index

299

Index

Index

Index

Index